GUTS AND GENIUS

GUTS AND GENIUS

The Story of Three Unlikely Coaches
Who Came to Dominate the NFL
in the '80s

BOB GLAUBER

GRAND CENTRAL
PUBLISHING

NEW YORK   BOSTON

Grand Central Publishing
Hachette Book Group
1290 Avenue of the Americas, New York, NY 10104
grandcentralpublishing.com
twitter.com/grandcentralpub

First Edition: November 2018

Grand Central Publishing is a division of Hachette Book Group, Inc. The Grand Central Publishing name and logo is a trademark of Hachette Book Group, Inc.

The publisher is not responsible for websites (or their content) that are not owned by the publisher.

The Hachette Speakers Bureau provides a wide range of authors for speaking events. To find out more, go to www.hachettespeakersbureau.com or call (866) 376-6591.

Library of Congress Cataloging-in-Publication Data

Names: Glauber, Bob, author.
Title: Guts and genius : the story of three unlikely coaches who came to dominate the NFL in the '80s / Bob Glauber.
Description: First edition. | New York : Grand Central Publishing, [2018]
Identifiers: LCCN 2018021719| ISBN 9781538760413 (hardcover) | ISBN 9781549194801 (audio download) | ISBN 9781538763889 (ebook)
Subjects: LCSH: Football coaches—United States—Biography. | Football—United States—History—20th century. | Walsh, Bill, 1931-2007. | Gibbs, Joe, 1940- | Parcells, Bill, 1941- | National Football League—History—20th century.
Classification: LCC GV939.B79 .G53 2018 | DDC 796.3320922 [B] —dc23
LC record available at https://lccn.loc.gov/2018021719

ISBNs: 978-1-5387-6041-3 (hardcover), 978-1-5387-6388-9 (ebook)

Printed in the United States of America

LSC-C

10 9 8 7 6 5 4 3 2 1

For Jutta, Andi & Emily. The Quad Squad—est. June 22, 1985.

CONTENTS

Introduction   I

Walsh: Rock Bottom After Being Passed Over   9

Gibbs: An Unlikely Apprenticeship   33

Parcells: The Jersey Guy Who Nearly Blew
    It from the Start   44

Walsh: Fighting Back from the Brink   57

Gibbs: Nearly Fired Before He'd Even Won a Game   75

Walsh: From Doubt and Desperation to Vindication   90

Gibbs: Going Against Every Fiber of His Being   118

Parcells: Fighting Back While Risking It All   142

Walsh: A Fall from Grace   162

Parcells: Frozen Out One Year, On Top the Next   179

Gibbs: The Hunch That Made All the Difference   208

Walsh: The Pressure from Within and the Impossible
    Expectations from Outside   221

Parcells: When No One Else Believed... Except Him   247

Gibbs: Raising a Third Trophy   270

Gibbs: Something Had to Give   278

Three Unlikely Coaches, Three Hall of Fame
    Careers, and a Lasting Impact   283

Acknowledgments   293

Index   297

About the Author   307

"Bill Walsh was the biggest, purest reason for my success. The thing that made us successful was that I understood what his offense was about, and I didn't feel like I had to throw a touchdown all the time."

—Joe Montana

"From a human being standpoint, nobody can deal with people better than Joe Gibbs. He knew every player on his team, what they were capable of athletically and what their mind-set was. He knew the buttons to push on every player."

—Doug Williams

"Bill Parcells is the best thing that ever happened in my life. Bill made us who we were. If it wasn't for Bill, I'd have been leading a different life."

—Phil Simms

GUTS AND GENIUS

INTRODUCTION

Bill Walsh walked up to the front door of the greenish-gray split-level home on Silverwood Drive and fell into the arms of his best friend.

Mike White could see the anguish in Walsh's face. Had expected it, actually. As he held Walsh, he knew how utterly defeated his friend had felt after suffering such a crushing blow to his career. A blow Walsh was convinced had meant the end of his decades-long dream of becoming an NFL head coach.

In January 1976, Walsh had thought he'd get the chance after Paul Brown had announced his retirement from coaching. But when Brown turned not to Walsh, but to Bill "Tiger" Johnson, there was anguish. There was anger. There was doubt.

By the time he'd made his way to White's home in Lafayette, California, Walsh was devastated. He needed an escape, a place to gather himself and figure out what he'd do next.

White—Walsh's longtime confidant with whom he could share his innermost thoughts and fears—took in his friend.

No questions asked.

"He was just this beat-up person when he showed up," Mike White remembers of the lowest moment of Walsh's career. "He just had to find solace somewhere so he could get his thinking together and react to what had just happened."

Despite Brown having placed his complete faith in Walsh to run what would eventually come to be known as the renowned West Coast offense, the seventy-one-year-old head coach and Cincinnati Bengals owner passed over his forty-four-year-old assistant and instead selected Johnson, his offensive line coach, who offered a more tradi-tional approach to coaching. History would ultimately bear out how utterly misguided that decision was, but at the time Brown was con-vinced Johnson would be the better leader and that Walsh's expertise in running the offense would give the Bengals a more reliable staff.

Walsh was inconsolable.

"Paul Brown once told me the reason he didn't make Bill the head coach was because he felt Bill was too high and too low, that he couldn't handle the lows of coaching to create enough consistent highs, that a loss would just wipe him out emotionally and he wouldn't be able to function the next week," said former Philadelphia Eagles and St. Louis Rams coach Dick Vermeil, another of Walsh's closest friends.

And there was some truth to that.

"Bill would go through tremendous mood swings, and the mood swings are a sign of insecurity," Vermeil said. "I had it myself. Bill was always insecure. He had to prove to himself that he was as good as he thought he was."

Walsh's mood as he walked into White's home was as disconsolate as his friend had ever seen. Walsh had flown to California alone, leav-ing behind his wife, Geri—who was pregnant with the couple's third child, Elizabeth—and sons Steve and Craig. He needed a safe space, and he turned to his longtime friend White, whom he had first met in 1960 when the two were assistant coaches at the University of Califor-nia, Berkeley.

"I remember getting this phone call from Bill, and it was like some-one had just died," Marilyn White said. "He said, 'Marilyn, it feels like you're the only ones I can call.' It was sad, because Bill was very happy in Cincinnati. They had roots there, and they planned on being there for a long time."

"He just needed to take a deep breath," Mike White said.

So they converted an all-purpose room in the basement to create a makeshift bedroom for Walsh, and they spent the next few days together, trying to process what had just happened and figure out where Walsh could go from there.

Walsh didn't know where he would turn next. The one thing he did know was that he could never go back to Cincinnati.

Dave Butz came off the practice field and was headed toward the Washington Redskins locker room when Joe Gibbs walked over to him for a private chat.

This was early in the 1981 season, when Gibbs was a rookie NFL head coach still in search of his first win and Butz, a thirty-one-year-old veteran defensive tackle and a holdover from former coach George Allen's "Over-the-Hill Gang," was uncertain about the direction of the team. The losing streak would eventually grow to five straight games to start the year, and Gibbs was tormented over his team's slow start.

Gibbs was concerned that team owner Jack Kent Cooke, a notoriously demanding personality, was growing impatient to the point of making a change. Cooke had taken a chance on Gibbs, formerly an obscure forty-year-old offensive coordinator from the San Diego Chargers who'd run Don Coryell's wide-open passing offense, known as "Air Coryell."

Yes, Gibbs feared he'd become the first coach in NFL history to be fired without ever winning a game.

Gibbs had installed Coryell's offense when he got to the Redskins, figuring he could out-scheme his rivals in the NFC East, a division known for its reliance on the running game as the central focus on offense, and imposing size and power on defense. The Dallas Cowboys and Philadelphia Eagles were the class of the division at the time, with Tom Landry in his late prime as the Cowboys' coach and Dick Vermeil coming off the Eagles' first Super Bowl appearance the previous January. The New York Giants were beginning to emerge from the worst period in franchise history under disciplinarian coach Ray Perkins. And the St. Louis Cardinals had a dynamic young running back named Ottis Anderson.

Gibbs's first four games were against divisional opponents, and he lost every single one of them: 26–10 to the Cowboys, 17–7 to the Giants, 40–30 to the Cardinals, and 36–13 to the Eagles. It was no better in his fifth game, as Bill Walsh's San Francisco 49ers, in the early stages of their first Super Bowl championship run, beat the Redskins, 30–17, at RFK Stadium.

Concerned that some of his most important veteran players like Butz might check out and lose faith in the first-year coach, Gibbs offered words of reassurance.

"We had lost a whole bunch of games, and Gibbs came out to me and said, 'Dave, we are so close. I don't want you to give up and get demoralized. We are so close to doing great things. I want you to keep trying. We are on the edge of doing great things.'"

Butz nodded and thanked Gibbs for the encouragement, unsure whether Gibbs truly knew what he was talking about, or whether the losing would continue and Gibbs's time in Washington would indeed be short-lived.

Butz didn't know it at the time, nor did any of Gibbs's other players, but the coach was about to go against every conviction and every principle he'd ever learned—not knowing if it would work, but convinced he had no other alternative.

The consensus was unanimous: Bill Parcells had to go.

The Giants were staggering to a 3-12-1 finish in Parcells's first year as the Giants' head coach, and memories of the darkest years of the franchise were haunting the Mara family. Team president Wellington Mara had presided over the lost years of 1964–1978, when the Giants had gone from a consistent championship-contending team to a franchise besmirched by failure. Rock bottom had come on November 19, 1978, when the Giants were seemingly headed toward victory over the Eagles at Giants Stadium and simply had to run out the clock in the final seconds against an Eagles team with no time-outs remaining.

But rather than having quarterback Joe Pisarcik do the sensible thing and take a knee, offensive coordinator Bob Gibson inexplicably called for a handoff to Larry Csonka. The ball caromed off Csonka's right hip and was scooped up by Eagles defensive back Herman Edwards, who returned it for a 26-yard touchdown to give Philadelphia a 19–17 win. Gibson was fired the next day, and during the Giants' next home game, a small plane flew over the Meadowlands carrying a banner: 15 YEARS OF LOUSY FOOTBALL—WE'VE HAD ENOUGH.

The fallout from a play referred to by Giants fans simply as "The

Fumble" eventually led to the hiring in 1979 of George Young as general manager, a compromise choice that was acceptable to Wellington and his nephew Tim. The two were not on speaking terms but had agreed to Commissioner Pete Rozelle's recommendation of Young, then a personnel assistant with the Miami Dolphins. Ray Perkins was Young's choice to become head coach in 1979, but when Perkins left in 1982 to coach at the University of Alabama, Young appointed Parcells, a promising defensive coordinator under Perkins.

But by December of Parcells's first year on the job, it became clear to all three of the Giants' decision makers that a change had to be made.

"Parcells gets hired in 1983, and really the only basis upon which he was hired was that he had some head coaching experience, which wasn't a heck of a lot," said John Mara, Wellington's oldest son and now the team's president and co-owner. "We come to the end of that season, and the jury is very much out on Bill at that point."

It was an excruciating season in every possible way, and not simply because of the final record.

Parcells had misjudged his quarterback situation, anointing Scott Brunner over former first-round pick Phil Simms. More than two dozen players wound up on injured reserve. After getting off to a 2-2 start, the Giants lost ten of their next twelve games.

Parcells's personal loss that season was incalculable. His mother, Ida, had died in December. His father, Charles, had died two months later. His running backs coach, Bob Ledbetter, suffered a stroke in late September and died less than three weeks later.

"Both my parents died. My backfield coach died. Hey, it was tough, but that's still no excuse," Parcells said, looking back on the most difficult year of his life. "Listen, they'd seen enough. Everyone was on board with it."

The decision had been made: The Giants would look for a new coach.

Howard Schnellenberger was their man.

Parcells was as good as gone.

There could not have been a more unlikely set of circumstances binding together three coaches who would eventually grow to dominate the NFL, preside over what might have been the greatest era of football the league has ever seen, and transform their own legacies into Hall of Fame careers.

Walsh, Gibbs, and Parcells went about building championship teams in vastly different ways, some of it involving the sheer genius of play calling, and some of it brute strength and the kind of mental and physical perseverance required to reach the pinnacle of success in the toughest league in professional sports. And while they all overcame uncertain beginnings, they grew into masterful tacticians and universally respected leaders.

They came of age during a time in the NFL when their coaching profession was dominated by Hall of Famers Tom Landry, Don Shula, Chuck Noll, and John Madden, a daunting list of coaching geniuses in their own right. But Walsh, Gibbs, and Parcells would eventually become the pillars for the next generation of coaching greats, and their influence over the league was unmistakable, as these three men built teams that dominated the era.

Walsh would go on to win three Super Bowl titles and leave behind a team that won another a year after he retired. Gibbs won three titles in a ten-year span, and Parcells won the Vince Lombardi Trophy twice. In the eleven Super Bowls from 1981 to 1991, teams built by Walsh, Gibbs, and Parcells played in ten of them and won nine championships.

Along the way, they coached many of the greatest teams and the greatest players in NFL history, and coached in many of the greatest games ever. They also had rivalries among themselves, with some surprising results. While Walsh and Gibbs were unquestioned offensive geniuses whose systems were at the heart of their greatness, it was Parcells who mostly got the better of his two rivals in big-game situations.

They drove their teams hard, and they drove themselves hard, eventually to the point where they all had to step away because the game had consumed them. Often motivated by fear and insecurity—two characteristics they all went to great lengths to hide—they brought out the best in themselves and in all the people whose lives they touched.

Beneath the fear and insecurity, a rare combination of guts and genius fueled their ascension and gave rise to what many consider the greatest era in the history of professional sports, the impact of which continues to resonate in today's game. Consider this: Since 1981, a combined thirty Super Bowl championships have been won either by Walsh, Gibbs, Parcells, or coaches who either worked directly under them or were part of their coaching trees. That's an astonishing thirty of the thirty-seven championships since Walsh won his first title.

This is the story of their lives and their careers, and the indelible imprints they left on America's game.

WALSH

ROCK BOTTOM AFTER BEING PASSED OVER

Considering he never thought this day would come, Walsh needed only a few minutes with Ed DeBartolo Jr. to convince the 49ers owner he was the right choice to help the team emerge from years of losing and dysfunction.

DeBartolo had chosen the iconic Fairmont Hotel in San Francisco as his meeting place, and he knew right away that Walsh—who only three years earlier had been devastated at being passed over by Brown and was convinced his chance to be an NFL head coach had come and gone—would be his guy.

"We met in just a regular bedroom, not a suite," DeBartolo said. "I don't think we were much longer than fifteen or twenty minutes when I knew I wanted to hire him."

DeBartolo was just thirty-two years old at the time, and he had started running the 49ers two years earlier, after his father, a wealthy developer from Youngstown, Ohio, had purchased the team for $17 million. At the time of the purchase, the 49ers were considered one of the NFL's weaker franchises, with the Oakland Raiders captivating the Bay Area market during the halcyon days of maverick owner Al Davis and future Hall of Fame coach John Madden.

DeBartolo was at a crucial time in his career as a young owner, having initially failed to put the 49ers on a winning trajectory. In 1976, the year before his family purchased the team, the 49ers were 8-6 under Monte Clark—a decent final record, yes, but one that came after a 6-1 start. The 49ers missed the playoffs, and Clark was fired by general manager Joe Thomas, whose later personnel moves would prove disastrous.

Before the 1977 season, Thomas hired Ken Meyer as his coach, but the 49ers promptly lost their first five games before finishing 5-9. Meyer was fired after just one season. Thomas replaced him with Pete McCulley, releasing quarterback Jim Plunkett—who became a backup and eventually a Super Bowl winner for the Raiders—and then pulled off a blockbuster trade. Thomas gave up five draft picks for Buffalo Bills running back O. J. Simpson, despite the fact that Simpson was thirty-one years old and was coming off one of his worst seasons, in which he didn't score a touchdown and had suffered a knee injury.

Simpson was born and raised in San Francisco, and thrilled to be back home.

"Obviously, I'm ecstatic," Simpson said at an introductory news conference. "I was a 49er fan when I was a kid and I've never stopped being a 49er fan. I had some good years in Buffalo, but hopefully I can get here what I couldn't get there, and that is a championship."

It turned out to be a cataclysmic failure, with Simpson gaining just 593 yards and scoring one touchdown, and the 49ers going 2-14, their worst finish in franchise history. McCulley was fired after going 1-8, and Fred O'Connor went 1-6 as his replacement. As if the woeful record wasn't enough, the 49ers would be without a first-round pick—which turned out to be the first overall choice—in 1979 because Thomas had traded it to the Bills as part of the Simpson deal. Thomas had also traded away second- and third-round picks in 1978, and second- and fourth-round picks in 1980. All that for a player who gained just 1,053 yards and scored four touchdowns in his last two dismal years in the NFL.

In their meeting at the Fairmont, that spectacularly beautiful hotel at the top of Nob Hill with sweeping views of San Francisco, DeBartolo almost instantly had a gut feeling that Walsh would be the one to bring the franchise out of its darkest days. That feeling had actually begun to emerge when DeBartolo watched the Bluebonnet Bowl a few days earlier. Walsh was now the head coach at Stanford, where he had eventually landed after his difficult breakup with the Bengals, and he led the Cardinal to a stunning comeback win over Georgia.

"I remember being back in Youngstown on a cold New Year's Eve watching Bill in the Bluebonnet Bowl," DeBartolo recalled. "They were getting knocked around pretty good, but he ended up coming back and winning that game.

"That win was very impressive," DeBartolo said of the comeback. "The way his team came back says a lot. This man just struck me as someone who was different. Following his career at Stanford, knowing what happened to him in Cincinnati, when Paul Brown gave the [head coaching] job to Tiger Johnson. That was a bad situation for him. But I really wanted to meet with him and talk to him, because there was just something about him."

The two men spoke about more than football that day.

"We talked about the way he operates, his philosophy," DeBartolo said. "We talked about my family, his family, his wife Geri and their kids, my wife Candy and our kids. We even talked about his mom. We talked about his long-range plans."

Walsh then told DeBartolo his vision of what the two could do together.

"He said, 'I know you've had some coaches in here, but if I'm lucky enough to get this job, I plan on being your coach and us having a lot of success together.'"

DeBartolo had found his man.

"We ended our meeting with me standing up and saying, 'I would really love to have you coach this football team,'" DeBartolo said. "He said, 'Well, you have yourself a coach.'"

Walsh was delighted after the meeting, his dream of becoming an NFL head coach finally realized after so many years, so many different jobs, and all that self-doubt and all that anger over having been passed over. At forty-seven years old, Walsh's time had arrived. He could look back on his career and his life that at times seemed quixotic in its grand aspirations, that sometimes seemed hopeless, but that always—always—had at its core a single-minded focus and purpose to do whatever it took to get to this point.

Walsh learned early in life that his greatest asset was self-reliance, even when it meant going his own way in the face of difficult circumstances. Born in Los Angeles in 1931, Walsh grew up in a blue-collar household. His father, William, made ends meet as a body-and-fender repairman. The family moved frequently, spending time in southern California and Oregon, and Bill was mostly a loner who found it difficult to make and keep friends because of the frequent moves. Over one three-year period, he attended three different high schools.

"I had never had the same teacher twice in my whole academic career, and all that adjusting had kept me from being much of a student," Walsh told author David Harris for his 2008 book *The Genius: How Bill Walsh Reinvented Football and Created an NFL Dynasty.* "Having to be the new kid always destroyed me."

"My dad resented his dad because he moved him around," said Walsh's son Craig. "He grew up in an era of a lot of drinking, and there wasn't a lot of sharing of emotions between my grandfather and my father. They had a different relationship. They were never very close. There'd be a lot of drinking and screaming and yelling at his mom. It was a blue-collar world. There wasn't a lot of hand-holding."

One incident in particular had a profound influence on Walsh. When he was around twelve years old and living in Los Angeles, his mother, Ruth, got him a pet duck.

"It was a little baby duckling that my father raised," Craig Walsh said. "The duck would wait for my dad to come home from school, and the duck would come over, and my dad would embrace the duck, feed the duck."

The duck grew over a period of time, and Walsh delighted in tending to it.

One day he came home around dinnertime, and the duck was gone.

He looked around the yard and couldn't find it, and finally went inside and asked what had happened to the duck.

His parents didn't answer.

Walsh then smelled what his mother was cooking for dinner.

"My grandfather had killed it and was going to eat it," Craig said.

It was a devastating moment.

"I think right then and there, everything just formed solid for him," Craig said. "He didn't want to be part of this group. He was close to his mother, but his dad was out of business. He couldn't stand him. He realized right then that it was going to be up to him. He wasn't going to get any guidance from his parents. He was going to get what he wanted through hard work."

Sports had become Walsh's way of fitting in when the family had begun moving around, and he took to football and later boxing. Though only an average running back and defensive end at Hayward High School in the East Bay, about twenty-five minutes south of Oakland, he longed to play for a big-time program at either UC Berkeley or Stanford. There were no offers, though, and Walsh wound up playing quarterback for two years at the College of San Mateo, a junior college, and transferred to San Jose State as a junior, where he played receiver for two years.

Walsh also took a keen interest in boxing, winning the school's 190-pound intramural championship as a junior and eventually boxing in some amateur bouts. At the beginning of his senior season, he met freshman Geri Nardini and fell in love almost immediately. It was Nardini's first day of school.

"He invited me to a boxing match, and I said 'I don't even know where I am. I'm here with my roommate,'" Geri said of her first meeting with Walsh. They married shortly after Walsh's graduation and just before he enlisted in the Army for a two-year stint at Fort Ord in Monterey.

Walsh was promoted from private to corporal shortly before his enlistment was up, and he also continued boxing. Geri gave birth to their first child, Steve, while Walsh was still in the service.

While Walsh was still uncertain about his career path, something disturbing happened at Fort Ord. During the period of basic training, one of Walsh's platoon mates committed suicide. It would have a lasting impact on Walsh and change his way of thinking about how to be an effective leader.

"I think my dad's takeaway was that you can only push someone so far before they act out," said Craig Walsh. His father had shared this story with him shortly before Craig graduated from UC Davis, when he was considering whether to go into the military. "It really turned him off to that type of leadership, where you see the drill instructor in everyone's face. That was one of the life lessons that changed him. He decided that this was not the kind of coach he wanted to be."

Walsh briefly considered a career as a professional boxer, but he decided it wasn't a practical way of supporting his family and chose coaching instead. His first job was as a high school football coach at Washington Union High in Fremont, California, where he also coached the swim team, taught physical education classes, and drove the team bus. He inherited a football team that had lost twenty-six of its last twenty-seven games, but Walsh had won the league championship within two years.

And now, nearly a quarter century later, he was about to live out his dream with the 49ers.

After an odyssey that included more than half a dozen stops at places as disparate as UC Berkeley, the Raiders, Stanford, Cincinnati, and even a semipro team called the San Jose Apaches—a team that went out of business a year after Walsh coached there—this was his chance.

"Bill always wanted to be a pro head coach so bad," said John Madden, who, like Walsh, grew up in the Bay Area and served his coaching apprenticeship on the West Coast. "He wanted it so bad that he took the San Jose Apaches job. It took him a long time to get there [to become an NFL head coach] and if you look at his trail, it wasn't an easy trail. He thought it would happen a lot earlier."

Madden thought he'd have a chance to work on the same staff as Walsh in 1967, when Madden got the job as the Raiders' linebackers coach after a three-year run as the San Diego State defensive coordinator under Don Coryell. Walsh had been the Raiders' running backs coach under John Rauch in 1966, and it was one of the most miserable experiences of his life. Not because of Rauch, but because of Al Davis, who expected all his coaches to put in brutally long hours.

Not only that, but the constant second-guessing from Davis, who had just given up his role as coach but remained a micromanager of every aspect of the football operation, grated on Walsh that entire year.

"We were living in Palo Alto on Maplewood Avenue, and Bill bought a dog for me and the kids to protect us," Geri recalled. "That was his way of saying, 'I'm not going to be around much.'"

He wasn't. And when he did get home, Geri could feel his frustration.

"The coaches would finish their game plan, and Al [Davis] would say, 'I don't like it,'" Geri Walsh said. "So getting home at one or two in the morning was a bit much."

His next stop was no better, though. Walsh was so desperate to coach his own team and call his own shots that he took a job as head coach and general manager of the San Jose Apaches in the Continental Football League. It was a ragtag semipro team of former high school and middling college players, an operation so rudimentary that Walsh would have to ask if he could use a classroom at his alma mater, San Jose State, to do film work with his players.

"The Apaches were a very low-grade operation," said Bob LaMonte, a prominent agent for NFL coaches who played at Santa Clara University when Walsh coached the Apaches. "It was just a bunch of tough, older guys and a makeshift team. We scrimmaged them just for fun when we started fall camp, and Walsh was the coach. This was obviously before he made it big, but even this seemed like it was beneath him."

"It was a dark part of his life," Geri Walsh said.

Geri remembered once going to an Apaches game in Vancouver, and the spotter for the radio broadcast didn't show, so the announcer asked if she'd help out.

"The guy that was supposed to be the spotter for the defensive players wasn't there," she said. "So I was pointing out the defensive players for the announcer. He said, 'When I point to a number, you give me a name.' It was a real ham-and-egg operation. I guess the best thing about it for Bill is he got a little experience."

But Walsh himself almost never spoke about his time with the Apaches, as if he was embarrassed he had taken the job.

"Is there anywhere he ever talks about that?" Madden said of Walsh's aversion to even admitting he coached a semipro team. "You just don't hear much about that. I did think he was crazy for taking that job. I was hired in 1967 by the Raiders as a linebackers coach, and Bill Walsh had been the backfield coach in 1966. So in the spring, before the '67 season, I'm moving in, and I got Bill's desk. He was moving out to coach the San Jose Apaches. I couldn't believe it. He was leaving pro football to coach semipro. I thought, 'You shouldn't be doing that,' but he wanted to be a head coach."

A year after coaching the Apaches, Walsh's career took off when he joined the Bengals and got the chance to work under the legendary Paul Brown.

This was the Bengals' first year of operation as an AFL expansion franchise, and Brown, who had been one of the NFL's most revolutionary coaches during his days leading the team that was named after him—the Cleveland Browns—to their greatest heights, was the perfect choice to build a new team.

Brown was a legendary figure from his days as a dominant high school coach at Massillon Washington High in Massillon, Ohio—not far from Canton, where Brown would have his bust on permanent display as one of the sport's all-time greats. Brown coached the Browns to four All-America Football Conference championships before his team joined the NFL in 1950, and the coach won NFL titles in 1950, 1954, and 1955. But his time in Cleveland would eventually come to an end not long after Brooklyn-born television and advertising executive Art Modell took control of the team in 1961. With Modell wanting to take an active role in the day-to-day operations of the team, and with Brown shutting the owner out of most key decisions, it didn't take long for the two strong-willed men to clash. Modell fired Brown after the 1962 season and replaced him with Blanton Collier, one of Brown's offensive assistants. The Browns would wind up winning the 1964 NFL championship, albeit with many of the players Paul Brown had brought in. But they haven't won a title since, and Modell would go on to become the most reviled man in Cleveland when he moved the team to Baltimore after the 1995 season. Before he did so, he fired another innovative head coach, Bill Belichick, who is now considered by many among the best coaches—if not *the* best—in NFL history.

Paul Brown never forgave Modell. But he wanted to continue coaching and got the chance when he cofounded the Bengals in 1968. One of his first hires was Walsh, who had been recommended to Brown after he'd called around looking to flesh out his staff. Cincinnati was the perfect landing spot for the thirty-six-year-old Walsh, and Brown was the perfect coach for whom to work. Brown was sixty years old at the time, and with nearly a lifetime of coaching behind him, he was ready to delegate more responsibility. Walsh was an eager accomplice and Brown a willing mentor.

It was a deeply fulfilling time in Walsh's life, and he thought he'd found a permanent home in the NFL, a place where he might one day inherit Brown's team when the time was right. Cincinnati was a terrific place to raise a family—he and Geri already had two sons, and Elizabeth was born there.

"We were very happy there, and would have been happy to stay," Geri said. "Bill loved it in Cincinnati."

Walsh continued to be immersed in football, almost to the exclusion of everything else.

"Bill was always distracted, always thinking about football," Geri said.

She'd even poke fun at him for being so focused on his job.

"How would you like to have horse's head for dinner tonight?" Geri once asked her husband.

"Great," Bill said.

"Okay, you'll get the biggest piece of it, too."

Walsh then snapped out of his trance and realized what his wife had told him.

"Oh, Jesus, Geri," he said.

"'Oh Jesus, Geri.' I thought that was my name for a long time," she later recalled.

"Bill would hug me, and I could feel him drawing the plays on my shoulder," she said. "After he was done, I'd ask, 'Did they score a touchdown?' He was always distracted. You could see it on his face. I would say, 'You're gone again.'"

Then again . . .

"We did have Elizabeth in Cincinnati, so he wasn't too distracted," Geri said. "I have to add that in there. He never forgot about that."

Walsh's arrangement with Brown seemed ideal. While Brown was clearly the dominant personality of the organization, he liked Walsh's offensive philosophy and imaginative play calling, which Brown came to rely on more and more during their nine seasons together. To this point, there was no West Coast–style offense featuring a quick passing game, because Walsh hadn't come up with it yet. In fact, Brown preferred a big-armed quarterback who could get the ball down the field, and the owner-coach thought he had found the Bengals' savior in 1969, when he drafted University of Cincinnati star Greg Cook with the fifth overall pick.

"Bill thought Cook was going to be a superstar," said Ernie Accorsi, a longtime NFL general manager of the Baltimore Colts, Cleveland Browns, and New York Giants. Or perhaps more than just a superstar; as Walsh reflected back on his career during an interview for NFL Films, he said Cook "could very well have been remembered as the greatest quarterback of all time."

Accorsi said Walsh told him he felt personally responsible for what happened next.

Midway through the second quarter of the Bengals' third game of the season, Cook was sacked by Kansas City Chiefs linebacker Jim Lynch, who landed on Cook's right shoulder. Cook later said he felt a pop, and while he somehow came back to finish out the season after missing three of the next four games, the damage was done. Cook had suffered a rotator cuff injury, and he played in only one more game for the Bengals after undergoing surgery.

"Walsh said, 'I blame myself for calling the play that got him hurt,'" Accorsi said. "He said, 'If I don't make that call, he doesn't get hurt.'"

Little did Walsh know that Cook's injury would lead to the start of one of the greatest offensive transformations in NFL history, whose impact is still felt today.

Cook's surgery revealed the injury was even worse than just a torn rotator cuff; he had also suffered a detached bicep. He underwent three procedures, none of which sufficiently repaired the damage. Desperate for help at quarterback the next season, the Bengals signed former Chicago Bears backup Virgil Carter. Unlike Cook, Carter's greatest asset wasn't arm strength.

"If you tied a string on Virgil, it would have a radius of about thirty yards where he was effective, if that," Paul Brown's son, Mike, now the Bengals owner, told the *Cincinnati Enquirer.* "Beyond that, it was just a hope shot."

Walsh knew he had a problem with Carter.

In a league that coveted arm strength in quarterbacks, Walsh understood his play-calling ability would be constrained, and he could no longer stretch the field because of Carter's limited arm strength. So he improvised, and soon came up with the first halting steps of what would one day be called the West Coast offense—even though its roots were actually in Cincinnati.

"In studying films of Virgil and watching him in practice, I determined that while he didn't have much of an arm, he was composed under pressure and could read defenses and was nimble physically and quick mentally," Walsh wrote in his book *The Score Takes Care of Itself*, which was written in collaboration with author Steve Jamison and Walsh's son Craig, who worked as a ball boy in Cincinnati during his father's days as a Bengals assistant. "Carter was very intelligent...Additionally, he was able to throw short passes pretty well. But dependable long strikes? No, that wasn't him.

"Virgil's skills weren't considered premium assets for an NFL starting quarterback, but that's all there was. Consequently, I began creating plays that tried to make the most of Virgil's 'limited' abilities—first one play, then another and another."

Walsh would come up with a series of quick throws with short dropbacks by Carter, who could use timing patterns by his receivers and throw to open areas that Walsh was able to configure based on defensive alignments and the route-running ability of his own wideouts, running backs, and tight ends. He also used multiple formations for the same play, basically using sleight of hand to fool defenses into thinking something else was coming.

"While each individual receiver's running route was not complicated—simple, by position—*collectively* it was complex and made almost dizzying to the defense by the fact that over the years I eventually began 'hiding' the same play cosmetically by altering our formation at the line of scrimmage," Walsh wrote.

If you read Walsh's description of Carter and insert Joe Montana, you'll see a remarkable resemblance, at least in terms of their strongest attributes. Carter turned out to be a mostly forgotten player in NFL history; his biggest impact on the game was simply being the quarterback on whom Walsh formulated what would become the NFL's dominant offense in the years and decades to come.

But Carter wasn't the answer for the Bengals right away. Despite Carter's being traded to the Bengals after two seasons with the Bears, the starter heading into the 1970 season was another quarterback who would figure prominently in Walsh's life—and ultimately the direction of the 49ers and Bengals: Sam Wyche.

Wyche was in his third season with the Bengals, having barely made the team as a free agent out of Furman University in 1968. He was a multitalented athlete who also excelled in baseball, but was passed over in the draft and wound up as a long shot to make the Bengals. Looking back on it now, Wyche believes he made the team partly as the result of saving Walsh from being hit by a football.

Both were new to the team, Wyche as a player and Walsh as an assistant coach after his miserable year running the Apaches.

"I was having a pretty good day in practice, although not a great day," Wyche said. "Bill was turned away and a ball is coming at him. I was trying to protect him, and then as the ball's coming, I realize it's going to miss him. But I look down, caught the ball with one hand, and we just made eye contact." Walsh looked at him as if to say, *How the hell did you just do that?*

Wyche ended up making the team and quickly grew close to Walsh.

"Bill and I connected immediately," Wyche said. "We were only about five years apart in age, and we just bonded. He had a room on the bottom floor of the dorm where the players and coaches stayed at Wilmington College, where we had training camp. Paul Brown allowed no air-conditioning and allowed one fan per room, so you kind of survived together."

Wyche became Brown's starter at the beginning of the 1970 season, but after Wyche went 1-2 and completed less than 45 percent of his passes, Brown switched to Carter. With Walsh doing most of the play calling and tailoring his game plan to Carter's strengths—which were limited because of his lack of arm strength—the Bengals wound up going 9-5 and becoming the first expansion team in NFL history to get to the playoffs within three years. Brown had been selected as the AFC's Coach of the Year the previous season, and winning the AFC Central with the likes of Carter was considered one of his finest coaching jobs in a career filled with championship seasons.

But Walsh had deserved much of the credit, because Brown had delegated much of his decision-making on offense to his underappreciated assistant.

"Paul Brown, for all of his gifts, was not inclined to give credit for the new ideas I was bringing to his team," Walsh wrote in *The Score Takes Care of Itself.* "For a period of time, many on the outside assumed he was the one putting pencil to paper as architect of an emerging paradigm for offensive football in the NFL. He did not go out of his way to dissuade them."

Walsh said Brown had come up with a system of shuttling in plays to the huddle that made it look as if Brown was the one making the calls. In reality, Walsh had communicated the play to an assistant coach on the sidelines, and Brown was then told what the play was. Brown would tell a player, who would then run to the huddle to tell the quarterback. "Obviously, this was an impediment to swift communication and hurt us from time to time. Brown was willing to pay that price to convey the impression that he was running the whole show."

Craig Walsh could sense the tension between his father and Brown, and recalled a time when the two got into a heated exchange during training camp. "I had to be thirteen years old at the time, and my father and Paul got into it on the practice field," Craig Walsh said. "They were screaming at each other. My dad was someone who, when he saw a chance to take control, he'd take control, and sure enough, Paul backed him off, got in Bill's face in front of the team."

It was an awkward moment after practice when Craig and Brown were alone in the locker room. "He said, 'Hey, you saw that between your father and I, and you understand that's coaching.'"

But Brown told the younger Walsh something else that day. "What I want to tell you is that your dad will be a great coach someday. He has what it takes to be a premier coach in this league," Craig recalled Brown telling him. "He just needs to understand that there are boundaries."

Another prominent assistant on Brown's staff was offensive line coach Bill "Tiger" Johnson. Johnson had been a center for the 49ers during the days of the "Million Dollar Backfield," which featured fullbacks John Henry Johnson and Joe Perry, halfback Hugh McElhenny, and quarterback Y. A. Tittle, all of whom went on to be inducted into the Hall of Fame. Johnson and Walsh had joined Brown in 1968, and both were indispensable lieutenants for him. But Brown viewed Johnson as a more conventional coach—a tough-guy former player who wasn't afraid to impose his will with some old-school discipline.

But Johnson was also a gifted tactician and teacher of blocking technique and, like Walsh, showed an imagination for offensive ingenuity. In one particular game, when Bob Trumpy was a Bengals tight end, he was assigned to line up to the left of the formation on a passing play. Trumpy, who would go on to a long and colorful career as an NBC television broadcaster, realized he was supposed to line up to the right side, and just before the snap he ran to that side. After the play ended in an incomplete pass, Trumpy came to the sidelines and apologized to his coaches for lining up on the wrong side.

But as he studied tape of the play the next day, Johnson noticed that there was confusion on the defensive side, and several players weren't sure where to go to account for Trumpy. Johnson ran the play back several times, and realized that the Bengals could gain an advantage if they *purposely* moved the tight end before the play. Walsh had his own aha moment, too, and realized that Johnson was absolutely right.

Thus was born a tactic that is used multiple times by every team in today's NFL: putting a player in motion before the snap.

That kind of imaginative thinking went over very well with Brown. Eventually, he named Johnson as the Bengals' next head coach.

Walsh was shattered.

At age forty-four, having been passed over for a job he assumed he'd get, Walsh felt that Brown had turned his back on him, had failed to become his advocate. He thought there was nothing more he could have done to earn Brown's trust, and being spurned for the head coaching job simply felt unfair. Once Walsh found out that Brown had tried to actually keep him from getting another job by not telling him about teams that had expressed an interest in hiring him, Walsh resolved that if he ever did become a head coach, he would actively help others wherever he could.

That promise to support those who worked with him—and for him—turned out to be a watershed moment in NFL history. Walsh would transform his promise into what would ultimately become the biggest and most successful coaching tree in professional football, a tree that continues to add branches and Super Bowl championships like no other coaching genealogy in the history of sports.

As he tucked himself away inside Mike and Marilyn White's home, Walsh contacted a number of associates, both to lament his situation and to plot his next move.

"We had a split-level house, and this all-purpose room downstairs that we used as a guest room," Marilyn White said. "Bill was mostly on the telephone, and I got the feeling he was just trying to figure out what he was going to do next, whether he was going to stay in Cincinnati or not, or whether he would go somewhere else."

Walsh looked into the New York Jets' vacant head coaching job, but he was not considered a serious candidate. The Jets ended up choosing North Carolina State coach Lou Holtz over Johnny Majors, Darryl Rogers, and Marv Levy. Holtz wound up going 3-10, resigned with one game left in the season, and never coached in the NFL again. "God did not put Lou Holtz on this earth to coach in the pros," Holtz said after leaving the Jets.

What now for Walsh? The only certainty was he had to leave Brown's team.

As it turned out, Chargers head coach Tommy Prothro needed an offensive coordinator to replace John David Crow after a 2-12 season in 1975, and it didn't take long for the veteran head coach, who was trying to keep his own job after a dismal season, to offer Walsh the position.

It was a perfect landing spot. Walsh joined forces with quarterback Dan Fouts, who at the time was on the verge of being released if he didn't improve his play. That's right—long before Fouts turned into a Hall of Fame quarterback, his struggles were so pronounced that he feared he might have to play elsewhere.

Fouts was a third-round pick out of Oregon in 1973, and though blessed with a strong arm, toughness, and an exceptionally high football IQ, he had not played well in his first three seasons, throwing just 16 touchdown passes and 36 interceptions from 1973 to 1975.

"So this was my fourth year when Walsh came to us, and things hadn't been going very well," Fouts said. "I was right on the brink of being cut."

Fouts met with Walsh early in the off-season, and the two spent hours together. Walsh taught Fouts things he'd had no idea about when the two dissected the quarterback's game.

"It was huge for me, because he was the first great offensive coordinator I had, the first technician, and the first that broke down my entire game and rebuilt it," Fouts said. "From the physical side, to the drops, to the footwork."

It was a dramatically improved season for Fouts, who had 14 touchdowns and 15 interceptions, and the Chargers went from 2-12 to 6-8. Before the final game of the season against the Raiders in Oakland, Walsh pulled Fouts aside.

"He came up to me and said, 'I took the Stanford job,'" Fouts recalled.

The quarterback was despondent.

"I did not have a good game," Fouts lamented. "I said [afterward], 'Thanks a lot.'"

The Chargers were crushed, 24–0, and Fouts was awful, throwing for just 82 yards and two interceptions. Fouts had privately hoped the Chargers would replace Prothro with Walsh, but it was too late. The Chargers did fire Prothro midway through the next season, replacing him with Don Coryell, who went on to have a terrific career in San Diego and produced some of the team's greatest offensive seasons with Fouts.

"I was so pissed Bill didn't get the head coaching job," Fouts said. "He carried himself like a head coach. He was in his forties, but he looked older, because he had white hair. He was great, and I'm so lucky to have had him. I'm not a Hall of Fame quarterback without Bill Walsh."

Fouts need not have worried, though. After Walsh left, the Chargers' next offensive coordinator: Joe Gibbs.

Stanford proved to be a perfect place for Walsh to spend the next two years before moving on to the 49ers. He'd been the Cardinal's defensive backs coach from 1963 to 1965 under John Ralston and would also work with his great friends Vermeil and White. Walsh, a deeply intellectual man who thrived in a college atmosphere, loved being back on campus.

He guided the Cardinal to bowl games in back-to-back seasons, winning the Sun Bowl over Louisiana State University in 1977 and then staging the dramatic comeback win over Georgia the next year in the Bluebonnet Bowl.

Along the way, Walsh also thought he'd found the quarterback he'd take with him to San Francisco.

Steve Dils had everything Walsh valued in a quarterback. At six-one, 190, he had good size and mobility. His arm was strong enough to run Walsh's offense. And his intellect was up to Walsh's specifications.

Walsh was so convinced that Dils should be his first quarterback with the 49ers that he pulled him aside at a wedding the two had attended a few weeks before the draft. Another former Stanford quarterback, Guy Benjamin, was getting married.

"Bill asked if I had an agent," said Dils, now a successful real estate executive in Atlanta. "I said I didn't, but he said, 'Don't worry. We're going to take care of you. We're going to draft you.'"

Walsh, who had eventually been given the role of general manager by DeBartolo after the two had been rejected by several candidates, had settled on Dils as his guy. There was interest in Morehead State's strong-armed quarterback, Phil Simms, who would eventually be George Young's first-round pick with the Giants, and Joe Montana had been briefly considered. But Walsh had a strong enough conviction on Dils to tell him the job would be his, just a matter of days before the draft. Walsh didn't have a first-round pick as a result of the botched O. J. Simpson trade, but there was no need to worry about not being in position to select Dils, who was pegged as a third- or fourth-round choice.

It was his old quarterback in Cincinnati, Sam Wyche, who set the wheels in motion on the decision that would eventually transform the 49ers into one of the greatest teams of all time and Walsh into one of the league's greatest coaches ever.

Wyche had been hired by Walsh to be his first offensive coordinator with the 49ers, and as part of the predraft evaluation process, Wyche was dispatched to Los Angeles to work out a highly coveted prospect the 49ers were interested in: UCLA's James Owens, a multidimensional player who could be used as a receiver, running back, and kick returner. Wyche needed someone to throw passes to Owens, and had heard that Montana was in Manhattan Beach at the time. The three met at a nearby field.

"We're at this park across from a hotel, and Sam is working a lot on my footwork," Montana said. "Feet, feet, feet. I'm like, 'I thought this was over with.' But there was a lot to teach. The thing about Sam that was good is that he understood the position, and he also understood I didn't have a cannon for an arm. I'm the first to admit it. But how many balls go over fifty-five yards anyway? The accuracy and the touch passing was important."

As the workout progressed, Wyche found himself concentrating more on Montana than Owens, who was being targeted as the team's second-round pick. By the time the workout was over, Wyche was convinced Montana, not Dils, should be considered as the team's next quarterback.

"Everyone in the organization knew that Bill had a strong feeling on Dils," Wyche recalled. "I was a rookie coach and I didn't know anything about protocol, but I told Bill, 'You need to work this guy [Montana] out. I think he's pretty good, and there's also something special about him. It's the intangibles that you see with winning players.'"

Walsh was willing to find out for himself, and accompanied Wyche back to Los Angeles a few days later to work out Owens and Montana once more. After the workout, Wyche wanted to know what Walsh thought.

"So we're flying back on the shuttle plane to San Francisco, and I'm sitting across the aisle from Bill," Wyche said. "He leans his head over and says, 'Sam, when we get in, tell them we'll take Owens in the second round and Montana in the third.'"

Wyche immediately grew concerned when he heard Walsh say he'd wait until the third round on Montana.

"I said to Bill, 'I'd sure hate to lose Montana,'" recalled Wyche. He urged Walsh to consider the Notre Dame quarterback with the second-round pick and not the third. "Bill said, 'Don't worry. We'll get him in the third. He's not high on the list for other teams.'"

Sure enough, on draft day, the 49ers took Owens in the second round and drafted Montana in the third—number 82 overall. As it turned out, Wyche's fears were not without merit. Wyche recalled a conversation he had with then Green Bay Packers coach Bart Starr, who had also been the team's general manager at the time; Starr confided that the Packers were giving serious consideration to drafting Montana with their own third-round pick. Green Bay wound up taking Maryland defensive tackle Charles Johnson.

"Bart said to me one day after that draft, 'You know, we were arguing over Montana and another player [Johnson] and we took the other player and left Joe on the board, and shortly thereafter, you guys take him,'" Wyche said. "'Otherwise, [Montana] would have been the next in a line of great Green Bay quarterbacks.'"

It was a fateful decision indeed; the Packers would go on to produce just one winning season until 1992, when former Walsh assistant Mike Holmgren took over as head coach and eventually brought the Packers their first Super Bowl title since Starr's legendary days with Vince Lombardi.

It was not an easy transition in San Francisco.

Walsh had inherited a 2-14 team that was broken in so many ways. There weren't enough good players. They had no first-round pick. Dysfunction seeped through every aspect of the organization.

Fortunately for Walsh, his trusted longtime friend was on the coaching staff he inherited, and Mike White turned out to be a valuable source of information in helping to pull the team out of its years-long morass.

White would also play a role in making sure Walsh didn't succumb to his own self-doubt and retire as a coach after just four seasons.

"When Bill got to the 49ers, it was bad, really bad," White said. "It was one of the most chaotic situations in the history of football."

The roster was a mess. Quarterback Steve DeBerg was coming off a season in which he had just 8 touchdown passes and 22 interceptions. Simpson had just one rushing touchdown and was clearly at the end. White couldn't believe some of the stuff that went on. Like this: McCulley, who had spent most of his career as an assistant coach with teams that played on the East Coast, actually had the team stay on East Coast time. So when he told his coaches he wanted them in at 7 a.m. each morning, he meant 7 a.m. Eastern—or 4 a.m. Pacific. White actually moved to a motel near the team's practice facility so he wouldn't have to drive over the Bay Bridge to work. "It was unbelievable," White said. "Can you believe a guy would do something like that?"

Defensive coordinator Dan Radakovich walked off the field before a preseason game in 1978 because secondary coach Jimmy Carr had ignored his calls from the press box and McCulley refused to step in.

"We're coming out for pregame warmups, and we're like, 'Where's Rad?'" White said. "He was sitting up in the stands with his wife."

White ran down all the problems, many of which Walsh had already known about, and remembers a conversation shortly after Walsh became the coach.

"He looked me in the eye and said, 'Here's what we've got to do,'" White said. "We've got to change the whole attitude and effort of this football team, either by addition or subtraction. You've got to help me. No matter how good a player is, if he's a negative influence, he needs to go.' Bill operated from what I call the locker room out. He felt that the locker room and the locker room leaders were either a benefit to the system, or they were negative and created an atmosphere that was dysfunctional. Those few leaders could take them in a positive direction, or they could destroy them. Bill used restraint and found players that would soldier up in the locker room, that would follow the real leaders, and then we'd lop off those that were negative."

Randy Cross was understandably skeptical when he sat down for Bill Walsh's first team meeting at training camp in 1979 at Santa Clara University. Cross, a versatile offensive lineman who could play guard or center, was the 49ers' second-round pick out of UCLA in 1976. By the time Walsh arrived, the twenty-five-year-old Cross had already been through four head coaches.

"He was a college guy, and sure, he had the history with the Raiders and Chargers and Bengals, and he was the guy that should have had the Cincinnati job," Cross said, remembering the meeting as if it were last month. "Then he goes to Stanford and he wins there. But at that point, we were so worn out from the losing. I don't know what Eddie DeBartolo's actual train of thought was with Bill, because he didn't run it by us. Personally, I just wanted to win. I didn't care who the hell the person was. If that coach was going to win, I'm all for it."

Walsh looked around the room, making eye contact with every player as he laid out his vision for the team and what he expected from the players. This was the beginning of what Walsh would call his "Standard of Performance," a detailed plan for every single member of the organization, from the owner, to the general manager, to the coach, to the players...even to the secretarial staff.

Yes, Walsh would actually instruct the team's receptionist on how to answer the telephone.

Several minutes into the meeting, Walsh stopped talking for a moment to get his players' full attention.

"He said, 'I can see some of the skepticism out there,'" Cross said. "'It's like, I'm just another one of these guys, and I'll outlast him. I'll just play somewhere else. The team was 2-14 last year, so I'll just find another team.'"

Then Walsh delivered a rhetorical question that hit home with everyone in the room.

"If you can't play for me," he told the team, "then who the hell are you going to play for?"

"It was a sobering moment," Cross said. "It made his point of reference even better. It hit home with guys."

Walsh knew he had one of the worst rosters in the NFL, and he knew it would be a difficult transition. He also knew he had to find some players from that team who would be able to adapt their skills to the coach's expectations, even if the overall team had performed so poorly in the years before his arrival.

"Whenever a coach gets released and another staff comes in, the reason the coach before got released was because he didn't have enough players," said former 49ers' front-office executive John McVay, who became Walsh's most trusted personnel lieutenant throughout his run with the team. "When Bill got here, I made a pledge to him and to Eddie DeBartolo: 'I guarantee you I will get every good football player I can get my hands on and get him in here.'"

McVay's partnership with Walsh turned out to be one of the most important elements of the Niners' dynasty. Yet it was an unlikely alliance, at least in the beginning. Walsh's initial agreement with DeBartolo was that the two would settle on a general manager to run the personnel side, but one by one, the candidates turned them down.

Accorsi and Young were of particular interest to Walsh, and they interviewed with him at the Doral Hotel in Miami a few days before the Steelers beat the Cowboys, 35–31, in Super Bowl XIII. Accorsi was the Colts' assistant general manager at the time, and he was considered a promising young talent in league circles. Young, the bespectacled former history teacher turned Colts offensive line coach, had been a successful personnel executive under Don Shula with the Dolphins.

Accorsi was blown away by Walsh during his interview.

"I must have met with him for eight hours, and it was enlightening," said Accorsi, who went on to become GM of the Colts, Browns, and Giants. "Just so much knowledge about the game and about people. When I walked out of that meeting, George was next, and I told him, 'This guy's a friggin' genius. He's got ideas I never even thought about.'"

But Accorsi didn't want to leave Baltimore.

"I loved the Colts," he said. "My body and soul was with the Colts. I was only thirty-seven, my kids were nine, seven, and five, I was still married. I didn't want them growing up on the West Coast. I knew I didn't want to live out there. My family, including my mother, was all in the east."

Accorsi remained with the Colts and was eventually given the general manager's job.

Young was on the verge of getting his own GM gig, and despite discussing the 49ers vacancy, he turned Walsh down, too.

"There's only one job I want," Young told Walsh. "That's the Giants job, and I've got a shot at that."

DeBartolo then suggested to Walsh that they scrap the idea of hiring a general manager and give Walsh the title instead. Walsh accepted, but he still needed someone to oversee the personnel department. DeBartolo, who grew up in Youngstown, Ohio, and went to Notre Dame, had known McVay from his days as the head coach at

Dayton, and the two had kept in touch over the years. McVay eventually went on to become head coach of the Giants but was fired after the 1978 season, just weeks after the game that had come to symbolize the Giants' futility of the previous fifteen seasons.

"The Fumble" had claimed McVay.

He wasn't sure what would become of the rest of his career, or whether there would even be a place for him in the NFL. But his relationship with DeBartolo and a meeting with Walsh just months before The Fumble would eventually lead to his new path.

"When I was with the Giants before the 1978 season, we invited Bill to come to New York and have a clinic for our offensive coaches," McVay said. "We sort of became pals after that. He was with us for three days, and after each session, we'd go out to dinner and have a glass of wine, and we got to be pretty good friends. So when the 1978 season was over, I called Eddie to congratulate him on hiring Bill. Eddie said, 'What are you going to do?' I said I didn't know. He said, 'Why don't you come with us?'"

McVay didn't hesitate.

"I was on the next plane to San Francisco," he said.

McVay and Walsh knew how barren the 49ers' 1979 roster was, and quickly set out to find players whose skill set would translate to Walsh's complicated scheme on offense and a tough-minded group on defense. Among the potential holdovers were guys like Cross, wide receiver Freddie Solomon, kicker Ray Wersching, guard/tackle John Ayers, cornerback Dwight Hicks, tackle Keith Fahnhorst, and middle linebacker Dan Bunz. DeBerg was a veteran quarterback who could at least be functional while Montana developed. (Remember, it was rare in that era that quarterbacks—even highly drafted ones—saw the field immediately. Unlike today's NFL, where quarterback development is at warp speed, with rookies often starting from Day 1, it was common practice for young passers in the 1970s and 1980s to sit back and watch before getting into the lineup.)

Walsh knew other veteran players had to go, either now or in short order. At the top of that list was Simpson, who was clearly at the end and the symbol of how far the team had fallen. Aside from the fact he couldn't play any longer, the 49ers still had to pay for Thomas's disastrous trade by losing out on the number 1 overall pick in 1979 (which turned out to be linebacker Tom Cousineau of Ohio State, who went to the Bills).

But much like he did in Cincinnati, when he had lost the strong-armed Cook to injury and turned to Carter as his quarterback, Walsh improvised early on and saw a scrappy young running back as an early solution. Paul Hofer, an eleventh-round pick out of Mississippi in 1976, was a special teams ace who was buried on the depth chart at running back.

He started to get work on offense in 1978, and when Simpson had further knee problems in 1979, Walsh used him in a role that would eventually form the prototype for the great all-purpose back Roger Craig. An undersized runner at 190 pounds, Hofer's grit and determination made him a fan favorite—WORKING MAN'S BACK, read one *San Francisco Chronicle* headline—and Walsh put him in a position where he could maximize his talents. He rushed for 615 yards and 7 touchdowns, and caught 58 passes for 662 yards and two scores during Walsh's 2-14 season in 1979—impressive numbers when you consider just how bereft of talent this offense had been.

"If you want to talk about an all-around, all-purpose running back, I don't think there are any better [than Hofer]," Walsh told reporters before the 1980 season. "Who's been more productive? And he blocks."

Unfortunately for Hofer, he would not be a part of the 49ers' championship years. He suffered a season-ending knee injury in 1980 and reinjured the knee in the next-to-last game of the 1981 regular season; less than two months later, the 49ers won their first Super Bowl.

Another player who didn't fit into Walsh's plans when he took over: veteran linebacker Al Cowlings—whose name would eventually be linked to Simpson for a far different reason than football.

Any way you looked at it, Walsh had his work cut out. Inheriting a 2-14 team with a minimally talented roster and now working for a franchise that was considered so poor Walsh couldn't even find a general manager willing to take a shot, this would be as big a rebuilding job as any in the NFL.

Maybe in NFL history.

GIBBS

AN UNLIKELY APPRENTICESHIP

Back in 1964, John Madden loved having Joe Gibbs on his staff at San Diego State, and the two men couldn't have been closer.

Madden was the defensive coordinator for head coach Don Coryell, whose passing concepts were in the initial stages of what would become transformative changes in football at every level, and that to this day are a central part—maybe *the* central part—of the game.

Gibbs, meanwhile, had been the Aztecs' quarterback under Coryell, and he realized he wanted to become a coach after his playing days were over.

"I wound up in San Diego State and I got to be about a junior or senior out there and used to kid my mother because I was trying to make up my mind," he said. "Do I want to be a neurosurgeon, a physicist, or a football coach? I said, 'What the heck. I'll be a football coach.'"

It was an obvious choice, and Gibbs—a C student most of his life—knew he'd never be a neurosurgeon or physicist.

So he went to Coryell and asked if he could be a graduate assistant for the Aztecs, and Coryell found a spot for him. It would be on defense, where Madden, Coryell's newly hired coordinator, could use some help.

"I was the new defensive coordinator, and I needed another guy, so Don hired [Gibbs], and he was my assistant," Madden said. "We worked pretty good together. I worked with the linemen and linebackers, and if I was working with the defensive line, Joe would take the linebackers, and if I were working with the linebackers, he took the defensive line."

The two enjoyed playing racquetball and handball after practice, and the games were sometimes heated.

"Those games got to be pretty doggone competitive," Madden said.

The relationship soon changed.

And, as Madden would suggest, so did football history.

"It's the spring, and they were gonna have an alumni game, where Joe was going to coach the alumni," said Madden, who handled the San Diego State players' team. "So I told Joe, 'Give me your plays.' I didn't mean he had to give me any secrets, just tell me what you're going to use, so I know how to get the guys to line up."

Madden was stunned at Gibbs's reply.

"He goes, 'No,'" Madden said. "I said, 'What do you mean, no?' Joe says, 'I'm not going to give them to you.' I said, 'Look, if you don't give me these plays, you're never going to work for me for the rest of your life.'"

Gibbs still wouldn't tell Madden the plays.

"We killed them in the game, and after that Joe went to Don and told him, 'I don't know if I'm going to be back.' Coryell said, 'What do you mean?'"

Gibbs explained the situation, and Coryell came up with a suitable alternative: Gibbs would become the Aztecs' offensive line coach.

"And that's how Joe Gibbs became an offensive coach," Madden says now, chuckling at the memory.

Don Coryell had a profound impact on Gibbs, starting with their work as player and coach, but more so when they coached together.

Coryell's own career had gone through a major metamorphosis, born out of necessity once he got to San Diego State in 1961. Coryell, a former U.S. Army paratrooper during World War II, played defensive back at the University of Washington from 1949 to 1951. His first coaching job was at Farrington High School in Hawaii, and he ran a traditional run-based offense that revolved around the I formation.

Coryell became expert in running plays out of the I formation, and he relied on that style of offense as a head coach at Farrington, the University of British Columbia, Wenatchee Valley College, Fort Ord, and Whittier, and then as an assistant under legendary University of Southern California coach John McKay.

After a year under McKay, Coryell got the head coaching job at San Diego State—a solid landing spot, no doubt, but one that left him at a significant disadvantage when it came to recruiting.

"We could only recruit a limited number of runners and linemen against schools like USC and UCLA," Coryell told the *San Diego Union-Tribune*. "And there were a lot of kids in southern California passing and catching the ball. There seemed to be a deeper supply of quarterbacks and receivers, and the passing game was also open to some new ideas. Finally, we decided it's crazy that we can win games by throwing the ball without the best personnel. So we threw the hell out of the ball and won some games."

The offense known as Air Coryell had been born.

Gibbs was one of those quarterbacks Coryell recruited several years after the Gibbs family made an unanticipated move to the West Coast.

Gibbs was born in 1940 in Mocksville, North Carolina, a small town in the northwestern part of the state where Daniel Boone once lived. Gibbs's father, J.C., was a deputy sheriff—spending much of his time chasing moonshiners—and his mother, Winnie, worked for the phone company. By 1954, J.C. had decided to move the family to southern California.

"My dad was a deputy sheriff, a highway patrolman, a rough-and-tough guy who everybody in town loved," Joe Gibbs said. "He always took care of our family, and I had a mama that was sweet as all get-out. My dad went mainly for a job, because it was hard to make a living. I had an uncle who moved to southern California, so we went out there."

It was at Santa Fe Springs High School that Joe Gibbs fell in love with football. He went out for the team as a freshman, and went on to become a terrific quarterback, although not a good enough player to be considered by any major college programs. Because the coach couldn't compete against the bigger schools in the area, Coryell relied on players like Gibbs, who played two years at Cerritos Junior College before joining Coryell at San Diego State.

After playing two seasons under Coryell, Gibbs asked if he could work for him as a graduate assistant, and Coryell paired Gibbs with Madden.

"One of my biggest jobs was to go to the local Jack in the Box for hamburgers," Gibbs said. "And if I didn't come back with the right sauce, I'd be in trouble. I was the 'gofer' for the coaches. Most importantly, I hung with Madden—he taught classes on Wednesdays—and I used to drive him up to the school two and a half hours each way. He'd sit in the back seat, reading the paper, smoking, and eating peanuts. I'd wait and drive him back."

Gibbs's apprenticeship under Madden didn't last long, though, thanks to the young coach's unwillingness to tell Madden the plays he would run in the alumni game.

"Coryell told me, 'You coach the alumni against us,'" Gibbs recalled. "I said, 'These are all my buddies. Do you want us to just not try and win?' He says, 'No, try and beat us.' I said okay. So we worked for two, three weeks getting ready for that game, and Madden walked up to me four days before the game [to get the plays]. I said, 'I'm not giving you the plays.' He said, 'I want all those plays.' I said, 'Coach Coryell said for us to try and win the game.'"

While Madden said his team crushed Gibbs's squad, Gibbs remembered the score as "something like 14–7."

"He walks up to me afterward, and I'm finishing getting through the tunnel and he was like, 'You're done.' I went to Coryell the next morning and said, 'John fired me.' I'm a graduate assistant and I wasn't making anything, so Coryell looks at me and he says, 'Shoot, fella, c'mon and work with us.'"

After three seasons as Coryell's offensive line coach, Gibbs joined Bill Peterson's staff at Florida State to coach the Seminoles' offensive line. After two seasons, he joined John McKay's staff at USC after Coryell had suggested to McKay that Gibbs would be a terrific addition.

Gibbs made an immediate impression on his fellow Trojans coaches, including Al Saunders, who was a graduate assistant on McKay's staff at USC in 1969–70, when Gibbs was the offensive line coach. Saunders said he was impressed by how meticulous Gibbs had been with his preparation and teaching methods.

"Joe was the offensive line coach at USC, and I was working with the tight ends," said Saunders, who succeeded Coryell as the Chargers' head coach (1986–88) and eventually became the Redskins' offensive coordinator when Gibbs returned to the team in 2004. "He did not change one bit from the time he was at USC to the time he was head coach of the Redskins. He's a phenomenal teacher. The essence of coaching is teaching, and the ability to convey information and have people respond and react to your direction in a positive way. I always marvel at how detailed and precise Joe was as a teacher. That really made an impression on me as a young coach."

Saunders also saw something else in Gibbs: his adoration of the offensive line. Years before "the Hogs" would come to define Gibbs's offenses with the Redskins, the coach came to believe that the fundamental effectiveness of any offense rested with the five men up front.

"Joe's true love of football was offensive line play and the running game," Saunders said. "Joe was all about being physical. He wanted a physical, tough, relentless football team, and that usually travels well. It starts with the offensive line. He had a passion for the run game."

Saunders looks back and realizes something else about Gibbs and his offensive-line-coaching brethren.

"Of any position on the coaching staff, I think the offensive line coaches are the best teachers," he said. "Typically, they are very detailed. They have to have a great ability to meld the talents of different people."

After two seasons at USC, Gibbs, who had now been married to his high school sweetheart, Pat, continued his nomadic journey, first at Arkansas as the Razorbacks' running backs coach in 1971–72, then with the Cardinals as the running backs coach under Coryell from 1973 to 1977, and then with the Tampa Bay Buccaneers under McKay in his first job as an offensive coordinator. It was a long-awaited step up for Gibbs, although it didn't last long. Even though the Bucs had shown major improvement with a 4-4 start under rookie quarterback Doug Williams, whom Gibbs had scouted extensively before the Bucs made him a first-round pick, McKay told Gibbs he would not continue as the play-caller in 1979.

Stunned at the impending demotion, Gibbs rejoined Coryell once more in San Diego, where Coryell had been hired as the Chargers' head coach. For the next two years, albeit in relative obscurity, Gibbs called the plays for the Chargers and continued to hope he'd get a chance to become an NFL head coach.

After George Allen's coaching tenure had come to an end in 1977 and the famed Over-the-Hill Gang of veteran players had run its course without a Super Bowl championship, the team's majority owner and president, Edward Bennett Williams, named Jack Pardee as the Redskins' new head coach.

It was a popular decision to bring in Pardee, who had just coached the Bears to a wild card playoff berth ahead of the Redskins. Pardee, who played for Bear Bryant at Texas A&M as part of a group popularly known as the Junction Boys, had been an All-Pro linebacker under Allen and also had been one of his assistants.

But a far less heralded hiring in 1978 would signal the eventual transformation of the franchise and would ultimately lead to Gibbs's hiring.

With Allen no longer calling all the personnel shots—many of which stripped the Redskins of valuable draft picks in exchange for veteran players who were simply not delivering the same kind of results early in Allen's tenure—Williams needed a general manager.

He eventually settled on a choice between Al LoCasale, a trusted personnel assistant with Al Davis's Raiders, and a little-known personnel man who had only weeks earlier resigned from the Dolphins in a dispute with team owner Joe Robbie.

Bobby Beathard, a former college quarterback who had once tried out for and been cut by the Redskins, was an intriguing prospect, especially with Williams signaling a shift in strategy by making Pardee cede the personnel authority once enjoyed by Allen.

Dolphins coach Don Shula gave his blessing to Beathard and told Williams he'd be a fine hire.

"I gave him my strongest recommendation," Shula told the *Washington Post* when Beathard was hired a month after Pardee was named coach. "Bobby's an excellent man. He knows what's going on around the league, and he'll be a great asset to the Redskins."

Beathard was an unconventional sort who didn't quite fit the stereotype of a prototypical personnel man, and his outside-the-box thinking reflected his unusual personal and athletic background. He was born in Zanesville, Ohio, about an hour's drive east of Columbus.

But he didn't stay long. Bob and Dorothy Beathard moved the family to El Segundo, California, when Bobby was just four. While football was popular in Beathard's native Ohio, he was more interested in water sports in his early days in California.

"The biggest thing in town was swimming, so when we were all little, everybody in that town learned to swim," he said. "It was water polo and swimming, and we'd play football in the sand dunes."

Football was just starting to come into prominence when Beathard was a child, and his father took him to see the Los Angeles Dons of the All-America Football Conference, a league that lasted just four years, but was dominated each year by the Cleveland Browns and their coach/founder, Paul Brown.

But his childhood was not without problems, and Beathard's poor performance in school ultimately steered him on a path toward football. His grades had slipped so badly by the ninth grade, and he was so unwilling to apply himself, that he was ordered by his parents to go to military school.

"Ridgewood Military Academy in the San Fernando Valley," Beathard said.

He quickly got the message and became a more diligent student, but there was one problem: The school had no swimming team.

"That's when I decided to play football," Beathard said.

Beathard played quarterback at El Camino Junior College, and happened to take a ride up with a friend to drop him off at California Polytechnic State University in San Luis Obispo.

"The coaches asked me what I was going to do, and I said I was going to go into the military," Beathard said. "The coach said, 'Why don't you play here?' I called my mom and dad, asked them to bring my clothes up, and stayed. Practiced every day the next spring, and played there the next three years."

His roommate for two years: an offensive and defensive lineman named John Madden.

"When John and I were playing together, we lost only two or three games," Beathard said.

Beathard later found his calling as a scout, joining the Chiefs as a part-timer in 1963 and then in a full-time role in 1966. Beathard moved on to the Atlanta Falcons from 1968 to 1971, and in 1972 was named the Dolphins' director of player personnel. The Dolphins would produce the only perfect season in NFL history his first year, and they successfully defended their Super Bowl championship the following season.

Beathard's early time with the Redskins wasn't smooth, though. While he was convinced the team needed to move away from Allen's practice of relying on veterans, Pardee wasn't on board with the philosophy.

It was also around this time that there was a power shift among the Redskins ownership. With Williams's influence waning, Jack Kent Cooke was beginning to assert himself. Beathard increasingly chafed against Pardee's preference to go with older players, and Cooke eventually sided with Beathard. By the end of the 1980 season, it was apparent that Cooke was ready to make a change, and he decided Pardee was the one who had to go.

Beathard would be the lead voice in the search for the Redskins' next coach, and Cooke was willing to roll the dice with his general manager. It was a somewhat bold move by Cooke, but certainly not out of character for the Canadian-born owner, who had already enjoyed success in both business and sports and whose eccentric personality would soon become a major part of the Redskins' culture.

Cooke first got into sports in 1951 as the owner of the Toronto Maple Leafs minor-league baseball team. Like Bill Veeck, another baseball owner who became famous for his quirky game-day promotions to draw fans, Cooke came up with his own publicity stunts with the Maple Leafs. But Cooke also developed an eye for talent and, more important, leadership.

Cooke had spent several days observing the Maple Leafs' practices, and he noticed one player in particular: George "Sparky" Anderson. The second baseman was only twenty-six years old at the time, and he had finally made it to the major leagues the previous year with the Philadelphia Phillies. But his stay was short-lived; a year later,

Anderson was sent back to the minors and played for Cooke's Maple Leafs.

Cooke thought so highly of Anderson that he offered him the manager's job in 1964, which Anderson accepted. It would be the start of a brilliant career for Anderson, who would go on to become a Hall of Fame manager after leading the Cincinnati Reds to two World Series titles and the Detroit Tigers to another.

Cooke's appetite for sports soon took him to the United States, and a year after selling the Maple Leafs, he purchased the Los Angeles Lakers and soon transformed them into a perennial contender and eventual champion. Under Cooke's tenure, the Lakers reached seven NBA finals and won the 1972 championship. Those were halcyon days for the Lakers and professional basketball, and some of the sport's greatest players—including center Wilt Chamberlain and guard Jerry West—made the Lakers one of the hottest tickets in pro sports.

Cooke's association with the Redskins began in 1961, when he bought a 25 percent interest in the team and was a far less auspicious figure than he was during his run as the Lakers owner. Even after he became the Redskins' majority owner in 1974, he delegated management duties to minority owner Williams, who served as team president.

But by the late 1970s, as Pardee's run was coming to an end, Cooke injected himself into the day-to-day operations and eventually decided that he—and not Williams—would be best suited to dictate the direction of the team.

"Williams ran the team as president, but as soon as Cooke sold the Lakers and went through his divorce, that's when he basically took over," said Len Shapiro, a former Redskins beat writer and NFL columnist for the *Washington Post* who covered the team during Pardee's tenure as coach. Shapiro referenced Cooke's divorce from his first wife, Barbara Jean Carnegie, a $42 million settlement that was the largest of its kind in history. "Williams was a terrific guy, but he didn't like Cooke very much. Pardee was a straight shooter, no bullshit about him, a guy who survived cancer. But Cooke wanted to put his imprint on the team."

Using his unique and sometimes unconventional powers of observation, Cooke gravitated toward Beathard, a maverick in his own right who was willing to take chances on players that other scouts and general managers considered too risky.

It was now on Beathard to find a new coach and transform the Redskins into a more vibrant football operation. It would be a monumental decision for Beathard, who was not a popular figure among many fans because of his willingness to part ways with so many veteran players—even if those players had outlived their usefulness.

"A lot of fans hated him," recalled Beathard's wife, Christine. "I can remember early on, we would go from Mr. Williams's owners' box and go over a little catwalk [at RFK Stadium] to get some food at halftime."

According to Christine, some fans were yelling: "Hey, Bobby! Hey, Beathard!"

Security told Bobby, "Mr. Beathard, keep walking."

Christine said, "No, they want to say hi to him."

Bobby finally stopped and looked at them, and they yelled, "Fuck you! Get out of town!"

"I almost started crying," Christine recalled later. "We'd only been married six months before. It was such a shock to me."

Clearly, a lot was riding on the embattled general manager's decision.

His search took only a matter of days, because Beathard already had Gibbs in mind. But he needed to make sure his hunch was the right one, that Gibbs was ready to make the transition from an offensive coordinator to running the entire team.

After all, Gibbs had never been a head coach before.

At any level.

Fouts himself wasn't quite sure how Gibbs would do running his own show, although he was impressed enough by what he'd learned from his offensive coordinator. He also knew that if Gibbs did get the job, his players and coaches would have to deal with a man whose personality wasn't always flexible.

"I think the one trait that the great coaches have is stubbornness," said Fouts, who played under Gibbs in 1979–80 and had two of his best NFL seasons, throwing for a combined 8,797 yards and 54 touchdown passes. "You can call it stick-to-itiveness, whatever. It would drive me crazy sometimes. In the same situations, he would call the exact same plays, and sometimes, when it didn't work, I'd say to him,

'Jesus Christ, is that all you got up there [in the coaches' booth]?' He'd say, 'Now, Dan...' I eventually realized that if I just did my job and read it all the way through, it would be successful."

Beathard relied heavily on the recommendation of a trusted friend, Chargers receivers coach Ernie Zampese, a fine offensive mind in his own right whose use of Coryell's deep passing system would eventually help Troy Aikman win his third Super Bowl title with the Cowboys.

"I'd known Ernie for quite a while, and when I wanted to know anything about Joe, I'd go to him and find out," Beathard said. "I knew what kind of guy Joe was, but I didn't really know his philosophy. So I found out a lot from Ernie. I wanted to know that at this stage of his career, was Joe ready to move up? Ernie said he was definitely ready. So if Ernie felt that way, I knew that was good. I had so much confidence in Ernie, so that became a pretty easy decision."

After seventeen years as an assistant coach—nine in college and eight in the NFL—Gibbs's time had arrived.

PARCELLS

THE JERSEY GUY WHO NEARLY
BLEW IT FROM THE START

George Young wanted to make this as seamless a transition as possible, so he acted quickly once he realized Ray Perkins was about to become head coach at his alma mater, Alabama.

Young, the Giants' general manager who had joined the team in 1979, had hired Perkins as his first coach. He was aware of Perkins's imminent departure once Alabama had requested permission to speak with him late in the strike-shortened 1982 season. This was the dream job for Perkins, who had led the Giants to the playoffs in 1981—the team's first postseason appearance since 1963—because he had played under Bear Bryant at Alabama and was now being chosen to succeed the legendary coach.

Bryant had decided to step down after a sixth-place finish in the Southeastern Conference in 1982, a season that included shocking losses to LSU and the University of Tennessee and a season-ending loss to rival Auburn. Bryant had built a legacy as the greatest coach in college football history, and for Perkins to be held in such high regard that he would be the first in line to succeed Bryant...well, this was a no-brainer.

(Bryant, incidentally, was asked what he planned to do in retirement and replied, "Probably croak within a week." Unfortunately, that turned out to be very close to the truth; on January 25, 1983, just a month after making that remark, Bryant died of a massive heart attack.)

By the time Perkins was first contacted by Alabama officials, Young knew he needed to have a backup plan.

"[Young] told me that he wanted to announce it the same day that Ray Perkins made his announcement, so there wouldn't be weeks of speculation as to who was going to be the next coach," Giants co-owner Tim Mara told *New York Times* columnist Dave Anderson. So with three games to go in the regular season and the Giants still in the playoff mix at 3-3, the Giants knew that Bill Parcells would be their next coach.

It seemed like the perfect fit; Young was familiar with Parcells's work as Perkins's defensive coordinator, which included his fine work with Lawrence Taylor, Young's first-round pick in 1981.

"Continuity is important, but you want to get the best guy," Young told Anderson. "If he contributes to the continuity, fine, but you want to get the best guy. You don't get the continuity guy first; you get the best guy first."

Young always abided by the philosophy of hiring someone you know.

"I learned a long time ago to evaluate the people around me for future reference," Young said. "But picking a coach is like wives. You only get one pick. You can't take two or three, unless you're in Arabia."

Young was concerned another team would hire away Parcells if he didn't make a move quickly. He remembered the Steelers hiring away Colts assistant Chuck Noll in 1969, and watching as Noll presided over the Steelers' dynasty in the 1970s. Remember, too, that the Giants had also lost two promising assistant coaches who went on to Hall of Fame careers. Before Vince Lombardi and Tom Landry became household names as head coaches of the Packers and Cowboys, they were both Giants assistants under Jim Lee Howell.

"Bill Parcells was first on my list, and it was a short list," Young said.

Parcells, who was very popular among his players, rejoiced in the opportunity in front of him. He was about to become the head coach of the team he rooted for as a child growing up in Oradell, New Jersey—just a few miles up the road from Giants Stadium.

"Coaching the New York Giants for Bill Parcells is what Alabama is for Ray Perkins," Parcells said upon learning he'd get his own dream job.

At forty-one years old and with the best job in the world about to begin, Parcells could never have imagined it would all go so hopelessly wrong, and that within less than a year, the people who had so enthusiastically endorsed him for the job would want him fired.

———

Parcells's journey to the Giants began in earnest—albeit unbeknownst to him at the time—on the gymnasium floor at River Dell High School in the suburban Bergen County, New Jersey, community of Oradell.

Charles "Chubby" Parcells and his wife, Ida, had moved the family from nearby Hasbrouck Heights—about five miles north of where Giants Stadium would be built—when Bill was a high school sophomore. And actually, he wasn't Bill at the time. Born Duane Charles Parcells, he never liked his first name, and when he was frequently mistaken for another student named Bill at River Dell, he took the name as his own.

Parcells played football, basketball, and baseball at River Dell, and loved all three sports. But it was his basketball coach, Mickey Corcoran, who saw something in the young Parcells that prompted him to take him under his wing. Corcoran was one of the county's top coaches, a basketball junkie who had the good fortune of playing for none other than Vince Lombardi at St. Cecilia High School in Englewood, New Jersey.

Corcoran first got a glimpse of Parcells in the summer of 1956 during a summer basketball camp. The coach had already heard of the six-foot-two kid with the big mouth and intense, competitive personality, and Corcoran wanted to know what he would have for the upcoming season. He liked what he saw: a fiery player who showed the kind of relentlessness that would go a long way on the court. But he also saw a cockiness that might become an issue. Parcells's father warned Corcoran a few days into the summer camp.

"Chubby showed up unexpectedly and took me aside and said: 'Sometimes Duane needs a boot in the ass. Feel free to take care of business,'" Corcoran told *Daily News* columnist Bill Madden during a 2013 interview, shortly before Parcells's Hall of Fame induction. (Corcoran died in 2015 at age ninety-three.) "At the same time, Bill was checking me out to see what I was doing. It wasn't until the football season was over and Bill came over to basketball that we started really getting to know each other."

Parcells played tight end, linebacker, and offensive tackle for Tom Cahill during the fall, and Cahill also saw that temper flare—often to the coach's dismay. Parcells's intensity would eventually work to his benefit when he and Cahill were reunited many years later at Army, where Cahill went on to become the head coach. At River Dell, Cahill didn't much care for it.

But where Cahill saw annoyance, Corcoran saw opportunity.

Remembering the advice Chubby Parcells had given him over the summer, Corcoran didn't hesitate to challenge the younger Parcells. If Parcells acted out—which he did—Corcoran stood his ground. Parcells would sometimes grow so frustrated if he didn't make the proper play or felt a teammate wasn't doing enough that he'd kick the basketball in disgust. On more than one occasion, Corcoran threw him out of practice.

"I threw him out of the gym two, three times that first year for not controlling his emotions," Corcoran said. "But he always came back the next day because I knew he'd come back. He was too much of a competitor."

There was one game in Parcells's first year with Corcoran that left an indelible impression, and it proved to be a turning point not only for Parcells as a player but for him as an eventual coach.

It was a junior varsity game in Parcells's sophomore season, and River Dell was ahead by seventeen points in the second half when Parcells got a technical foul. Corcoran immediately benched him. The lead eventually dwindled to nine points, then six, then it was gone. Corcoran's team lost by one point.

Parcells was furious that his coach didn't give ground. In the end, though, it transformed his attitude.

"If I'd have put him back we probably would have won the game," Corcoran said, "but I would've lost Parcells."

Parcells was a different player after that. He listened to his coach and did as asked. Always. Corcoran didn't take away the rage at losing that Parcells had always had, but he did direct his fury at finding ways to win.

Corcoran taught Parcells what it was to be a coach. Parcells studied Corcoran and how he adapted his teams to play a given opponent. He watched him mold other players the way he did Parcells. And Parcells took those lessons he learned in high school with him the rest of his life—first as a young athlete, then as a young coach, then as a champion.

More than half a century after first meeting Corcoran, Parcells sits in the living room of his two-bedroom apartment in downtown Saratoga Springs and smiles at the memory of his old basketball coach.

"Mickey always said there's ways to win all these games," Parcells said. "Your job is to figure it out. He was always emphasizing what your job is as a coach. The job is to give your players a good design. It doesn't have to be superior, but it has to be good and it has to be sound, and then you've got to get them to play it. That's your job. That's all you've got to do as a coach. Give 'em a good design and get 'em to play it."

Parcells also learned from Corcoran how to judge players, especially ones who had exceptional talent but questionable motivation.

"Mickey would say, if they're not self-starters, you're going to have a hard time getting them to play," Parcells said. "We used to call those guys Louisville Sluggers. You've got to hit 'em with a bat to get 'em going. Don't waste your time with those guys."

He never forgot the message, and he rarely wasted his time coaching players whose heart didn't match their talent. It would be of incalculable help throughout his career.

Parcells was a good enough all-around athlete at River Dell that he received several football scholarship offers, including from Auburn and Clemson. But because his father had stressed schoolwork to his son, Parcells eventually gravitated toward colleges with more of an academic emphasis. That included Ivy League schools, but he eventually settled on Colgate University in Hamilton, New York, where he got a football scholarship.

During his freshman year, Parcells received a contract offer from the Philadelphia Phillies, but Chubby Parcells strongly advised against it. Parcells decided to focus on football and transferred the following year to the Municipal University of Wichita (now called Wichita State), where he played linebacker and got a degree in physical education.

He was a seventh-round pick of the Detroit Lions in 1964, but Detroit was well stocked at linebacker, and Parcells had little chance to make a team that already had established players at his position like Joe Schmidt, Wayne Walker, Carl Brettschneider, and Ernie Clark. He was released before ever playing a regular-season game.

"I think I've always been a good self-evaluator in terms of what my chances were," Parcells said years later. "I think probably if I went back and did it over, I had a much better chance as a baseball prospect on the pro level than I did as a football prospect. I was kind of in-between size for the position I would [end] up playing. I wasn't overly big, and certainly not overly fast. I was just kind of an in-between guy who played almost every position in football at one time or another. I think I was versatile in that regard at a lower level. But when you had to get down and do something specific consistently well, I just didn't have enough ability."

But Parcells knew he wanted to stay in sports, and that his best path would be coaching. His apprenticeship with Corcoran taught him that much, and his sheer love of sports was all the motivation he'd require.

He quickly got a job as the linebackers coach at Hastings College, a small liberal arts school about 150 miles outside Omaha, Nebraska. The coach there was Dean Pryor, a former assistant at Wichita who had found a spot on his staff for the former linebacker.

"You know, you learn an awful lot of things," Parcells said of that one season at Hastings. "You had to do things that you don't consider—like, we had to wash the players' uniforms after practice. But [Pryor] taught me and he preached to me something that I carried with me my entire coaching career. And that is that the players deserve a chance to win. And you have an obligatory responsibility to try to give it to them. That means you as a coaching staff, you as an individual coach, have a responsibility to try to give these players who are putting themselves at risk and in harm's way, to have a chance to achieve success.

"And that goes for universities and professional teams as well. I know I preached that to every organization and to every coaching staff I ever had," he said. "These guys deserve a chance to win, and we've got to give it to them."

His salary was just $1,750 that year, and Parcells, who had been married since 1962 to his wife, Judy, and now had a daughter, lived in a one-bedroom apartment attached to a dentist's office for $62.50 a month.

He spent only a year working for Pryor before returning to Wichita to become the team's linebackers coach, but he learned an extremely valuable lesson from the coach. There was a game in which the opposing team ran a bootleg for a touchdown, prompting Parcells to light into his safety for not reacting to the play properly. Pryor told him to back off, but Parcells complained that he had drilled the team on this very play throughout the week. Pryor looked at him and said, "Well, you didn't work on it enough, because they scored."

Parcells returned to Wichita after a year and then began a period of his coaching life in which he hopscotched across the country as a college assistant, taking him to Army, Florida State, Vanderbilt, Texas Tech, Air Force, and finally to the Giants as Perkins's defensive coordinator in 1979.

It was a whirlwind fifteen-year journey—not unlike that of many coaches aspiring to advance and get in position to have their shot at a dream job running an NFL team. Along the way, he worked for coaches who continued to help him develop his voice as a leader and refine his vision of football from a tactical perspective.

One of his most memorable stops was at Army, where the head coach happened to be Parcells's high school football coach, Tom Cahill.

Unlike Corcoran, who had adored having Parcells on his team at River Dell and imparted lessons Parcells would take with him the rest of his life, Cahill wasn't a huge fan of Parcells. Where Corcoran saw potential in Parcells's volatile personality, Cahill saw a pain in the ass. Parcells was certainly a talented enough player, but Cahill didn't go for his cocky demeanor. So when Corcoran reached out to Cahill on Parcells's behalf to hire him at Army, there was initial reluctance.

But Corcoran convinced Cahill that Parcells would be an asset to his staff and that, if anything, his demanding style would be accepted by players who had voluntarily decided to attend a school where discipline was not only tolerated, but was an essential part of everyday life. Parcells started out as Cahill's linebackers coach and did such a thorough job that he was the team's defensive coordinator in 1968–69.

It was at Army where Parcells began what turned out to be a lifelong kinship with another coach who would go on to national prominence.

Bobby Knight was Army's basketball coach from 1965 to 1971 before going on to an illustrious—and controversial—career at Indiana, where he won three national championships.

Parcells and Knight quickly gravitated toward each other at Army and found they had a mutual interest in basketball and football, as well as baseball.

"Bill and I became really good friends, because we kind of looked at the world together," Knight said. "He was in football, and I was in basketball, and I think both of us really worked at trying to see how we could get the game—him with football and me with basketball—played in such a way that our teams would win. The thing that impressed me most about Bill early on was that he didn't just adopt what so-and-so did or what so-and-so had said about football. He looked at ways to devise how to play the game.

"He was always looking for a better way to play, yet he never got in over his head by trying to do things that so many coaches do when they don't have the personnel to do it. That's how you become a failure. With Parcells, it was totally different. He worked at what he thought was the best way to play. And above all, it was defense."

And there was the central connection, the commonality of their approach: defense. Knight abided by the unshakable belief that defense was the biggest priority for his teams, a deeply held conviction that was ultimately the centerpiece of his championship legacy at Indiana. And Parcells was all about defense, too, not only in football, but in basketball and baseball as well.

"A lot of people coach, but not many go at it in a defensive way," Knight said. "Everybody wants to score points. I don't care whether it's football or basketball or whatever it is. But the teams that win are the teams that keep you from scoring points. That's where Bill exceeded everyone. Defensive players aren't given the glory, but they do win games for you."

Parcells often attended Knight's practices at Army, and he even did some scouting on his off time.

"I worked for him in his camps coaching, and I scouted for him a few times," Parcells said. "I'd go see Fordham and St. John's, Seton Hall, schools like that. I liked basketball. I'd been around basketball guys my whole life, and I was interested in the systems teams ran. [Knight] would tell me what to look for, and I could kind of hold my own as a scout. I tried to be conscientious.

"Sometimes, I didn't understand what some teams were doing, why this or that was going on, and [Knight] would tell me why it was going on. Here's the origination of that, things like that."

"Bill sat on the bench with me a lot and we talked about basketball and we talked about football," Knight said. "I think that we both benefited from the way we both thought about things. I think the most important thing was, figure out whatever you're doing, passing or tackling, or whatever—in basketball it would be about rebounding. Just figure out what is the best way to do things. You don't have to do what's been done for thirty years. If you can figure out something better, quicker, easier to maneuver, that's why you're able to win."

They also shared a kindred spirit in their competitiveness, something that led to both men demanding more from their players than most—and at times angering those players. Knight wound up doing it to excess during his run at Indiana, and his frequent fits of temper ultimately led to his ouster in 2000. Parcells was quick to yell at his players, but he rarely went over the line.

"I always wanted to win," Knight said. "I remember the first Little League baseball game I ever played in, I walked out the door and I remember my mom saying, 'Now, you remember one thing. Somebody has to lose.' I walked to where she couldn't hear me and I said, 'That may be right, but it doesn't have to be me.'"

For Parcells, winning was everything, and he came up with a phrase that defined that mind-set: "There's no medals for trying."

Parcells stayed at Army until 1969, serving as Cahill's defensive coordinator his last two seasons there. He coached the linebackers at Florida State from 1970 to 1972 and then held the same position at Vanderbilt (1973–74) and Texas Tech (1975–77), then was the head coach at Air Force in 1978 before joining the Giants the following year.

Parcells not only had to serve as a position coach in college, but he also had recruiting responsibilities. He used every bit of his personality to convince players to come to wherever he was coaching. There's one guy he'll never forget.

"Brenard Wilson is a kid from Daytona [Beach], Florida, and I'm coaching at Vanderbilt," Parcells said. "Before that, I had been at Florida State, so I knew a lot of the coaches in that area. Wilson's high school coach was Phil Richart [a former quarterback at Louisville], and we played against each other in college when I was at Wichita. So I go over to the school [Father Lopez Catholic] when I was at Florida State, and Phil says, 'You know [Brenard] is a pretty good player, but he's going to the Ivy League.' So then I go to Vanderbilt, and I call Phil and ask if Brenard would be interested in Vanderbilt. He says, 'You probably need to go back down there to talk to him.'"

Parcells made the trip to Daytona Beach and met with Wilson.

"Brenard, I'm Bill Parcells from Vanderbilt, and I want to talk to you about coming to play football," Parcells told him.

"Coach, I'm going to Wake Forest to play basketball. The only way I'm not going to Wake Forest is if I get enough financial aid from an Ivy League school."

"Well, I saw you play basketball, and you don't go to your left very good. And when you do, you pull up and shoot your jump shot every time," Parcells said. "So I'll tell you what I'll do. I'll meet you after school at the park, and we'll play. If you win, you'll go to Wake Forest. If I win, you come to Vanderbilt."

"You got a park around here?" Parcells asked Wilson.

"You got tennis shoes?" Wilson said.

"Yeah, I got them in the car."

The two played in sweltering ninety-degree heat, and Wilson beat Parcells in the first game, 10–9. Parcells won the second game, 10–7. Wilson won the third and deciding game, 12–10 (the victor had to win by two).

Parcells then took Wilson aside.

"Son, you're six-one-and-a-half. The chances of you having a future in basketball are not as good as your chances of playing football."

Wilson decided to play at Vanderbilt, where he became an All-SEC free safety, and eventually signed as a free agent with the Eagles. Wilson enjoyed a nine-year NFL career. When they met once before a Giants-Eagles game, Parcells spoke to Wilson during warmups and said—loud enough for many of Wilson's teammates to hear—that Parcells was a big reason Wilson was in the NFL.

"If it wasn't for me, this guy would be playing for the 76ers, and Andrew Toney or Maurice Cheeks would be sitting on the bench," Parcells quipped. "Oh, yeah. He thought he was great. He doesn't have to play for you guys. He can go right over and play for the 76ers."

It was that type of humor, mixed with straight talk, that made Parcells a mostly endearing figure to those he was around, and something that ultimately carried him to the top of his profession. That and a relentlessness he'd always had in sports—from the time he grew up in north Jersey and then throughout his coaching career and all the iterations of that meandering journey as a college and NFL assistant, then through four runs as an NFL head coach and two as a front-office executive.

After two years at Vanderbilt and then another three at Texas Tech, Parcells finally got the break he wanted. He was named head coach at Air Force in 1978. It also helped that his family—he and Judy now had three daughters, Suzanne, Dallas, and Jill—loved the Colorado Springs area.

Parcells led the Falcons to back-to-back wins to start the season—beating University of Texas at El Paso and then Boston College on the road. But he won just one more game the rest of the year, finishing 3-8.

Wanderlust had kicked in again; Parcells wasn't a fan of the recruiting process, even though he had previously reveled in trying to convince young players to play wherever he was coaching at the time. But as a head coach, there were far more responsibilities for recruiting. So after just a year, he took an offer to be the Giants' defensive coordinator under Perkins.

But his first NFL job didn't last long. Judy felt she had finally found a place to spend time raising her young family, and after all the moves her husband had made, she pushed back at moving to the New York area. So Parcells resigned from the Giants and went back to Colorado, finding work with a land development company.

During the year away from football, he was so miserable that Judy ultimately relented and urged him to get back into coaching.

Next stop: the New England Patriots, where Parcells was hired as linebackers coach under Ron Erhardt.

Parcells was back in his element, coaching players and busting chops—and getting the most out of those players with that rare blend of knowledge and charisma he'd developed over time. He had a genuine appreciation for them, and they for him. Which was how they would eventually come to give him the nickname he carries with him to this day: Tuna.

"So they had this thing in New England where they were trying to get me to sign up for a free turkey and pie around Thanksgiving," Parcells said. "So I don't sign up. And the players, they're asking me, 'Coach, sign up for your turkey.' A lot of the guys' names are on the board. They tell you where to go to get the turkey, and then they film you and there's no turkey. There's no nothin'. It's just a vacant lot."

Parcells was beginning to realize this might be a practical joke. And even if it wasn't, he didn't want to go out of his way just to get a free turkey and pie. As the players kept pushing him to go, he knew this was a ruse.

"So they finally say to me, 'You gonna get your turkey?' So I say, 'Who do you think I am, Charlie the Tuna?' By that time I'm on to it, I know something's up. So I say that to 'em, and they started calling me Charlie the Tuna."

Charlie the Tuna, of course, is the mascot for StarKist-brand tuna. A picture of him appeared on cans of the tuna, and the players got such a kick out of the nickname that they created what Parcells called the "Charlie the Tuna decal."

Parcells had a system of rewarding players for making good plays during games, so they'd tape CHARLIE THE TUNA labels to their helmets, much the way college players affix stars to their helmets. Parcells didn't realize what they were doing until he noticed the picture on linebacker Steve Nelson's helmet.

"I didn't know what it was about," Parcells said. "So basically, the teacher's pet would get the tuna. Whoever I'd compliment the most would put a tuna fish on his helmet for the week. We ended up having a tuna banquet, Styrofoam cups, tuna fish, just having fun."

Perkins liked what he saw of Parcells and hired him back with the Giants in 1981 as defensive coordinator, and it was there that a partnership with a rookie linebacker named Lawrence Taylor would soon take root.

Taylor was the second overall pick in the 1981 draft, a gifted pass rusher out of North Carolina whose talents fit perfectly with Parcells's defensive concepts. At North Carolina, Taylor was nicknamed "Godzilla" because of the recklessness he showed both on and off the field.

"We'd always juke him about how he wasn't getting respect at this bar downtown," his roommate at the University of North Carolina, Steve Streater, once recalled. "So one night, Lawrence walked into the bar and busted up everything—chairs, glasses, everything. That's what he thought it took to gain respect."

"Reckless" was the word North Carolina assistant Bobby Cale used to describe Taylor. "As a freshman playing on special teams, he'd jump a good six or seven feet in the air to block a punt, then land on the back of his neck," Cale said. "He was reckless, just reckless."

Parcells viewed Taylor as the perfect weapon for his defense, which, unlike traditional defenses at the time, used four linebackers and three down linemen.

"I mean, the guy was a special player from the start," Parcells said. "He'd do everything I asked, and he'd do it at a very high level. It was pretty clear right away that we could do some things with him, and that we could start to disrupt things in a way that would be very beneficial."

The two were kindred spirits in many ways. Like Parcells, Taylor was a linebacker. Like Parcells, Taylor loved baseball and was a catcher in high school. Like Parcells, Taylor was as competitive an athlete as you'll ever find. And like Parcells, Taylor had a mouth on him and wasn't afraid to use it.

"We hit it off right away," Taylor said. "Some guys you want to play for, and some guys you don't want to play for, but Bill was one of those guys you wanted to play for. We had a relationship where, when I went out there, I wanted to do well, not just for myself, but I wanted to do well for Bill Parcells, too."

As it turned out, they would do well for each other and create one of the most successful coach-player bonds, which would be at the heart of Hall of Fame careers for both.

WALSH

FIGHTING BACK FROM THE BRINK

Bill Walsh was in his usual seat on the charter flight home from Miami—first class, first row, with an empty seat next to him.

"He'd always have a seat with nobody in it next to him on the plane, so whoever he wished to talk to or wanted to say something to would have a place to sit down and visit with him, which was the case this time," John McVay said.

The 49ers were flying home after a 17–13 loss to the Dolphins on a steamy afternoon at the Orange Bowl, and Walsh was morose. This was his eighth straight loss after a 3-0 start, and self-doubt had consumed him. That the misgivings Paul Brown had expressed about Walsh's ability to be a successful NFL head coach were true. After finishing a mind-numbingly difficult 2-14 season in 1979, and after losing to Don Shula, one of the league's iconic coaches, Walsh thought his career was about to be over.

He started to cry.

Within moments, he was sobbing.

McVay and a few other coaches noticed, and they quickly surrounded him so the players wouldn't see. They tried not to act as if something was wrong, pretending to be engaged in casual conversation.

"Everything I had dreamed of professionally for a quarter of a century was in jeopardy just eighteen months after being realized," Walsh wrote in his book *The Score Takes Care of Itself.*

He worried that DeBartolo would soon lose patience and fire him. He even decided briefly to turn in his resignation the next morning.

It had been a torturous rebuilding process for the 49ers team Walsh had inherited. With no first-round pick in Year 1 and a roster filled mostly with holdovers from ill-fated general manager Joe Thomas's failed drafts, Walsh's first two years were as difficult a transition as any imaginable.

His conflicting emotions made it all the more challenging. On the one hand, he truly believed his strategic approach to the game was fundamentally sound, even if it wasn't in line with traditional thinking—particularly on offense, where he believed to his core that his system revolving around the short passing game and rhythmic play calling could not only work but could dominate.

Yet the results were simply not there, fueling the insecurities that gnawed at him. The question that inevitably surfaced when things didn't go his way: Was he good enough?

With his face in his hands and tears in his eyes, Walsh was convinced the answer to that question was no.

But then something happened, something that allowed him to rediscover his resolve and fight through his self-doubt. "There was something else going on inside me, a 'voice' from down deeper than the emotions, something stirring that I had learned over many years in football and, before that, growing up; namely, I must stand and fight again, stand and fight or it was all over," he wrote.

By the time the flight landed early the next morning at San Francisco International Airport, Walsh had gathered himself. There would be no letter of resignation, only a greater sense of purpose after he had let his emotions pour out. What happened over the next three weeks only reconfirmed his belief that he could make this work, that he really did have what it took and that his decades of preparation for this moment would not be in vain.

Walsh won his next three games—including what turned out to be a transformative game at home against the New Orleans Saints—and became more convinced he could succeed.

"That Saints game is probably where we, as a team, really bought into the whole idea of don't ever look at the clock, which is something Bill always told us," Randy Cross said. "Just keep grinding. Just get the ball and score. You might punt, but next time, score. Don't even worry about anything having to do with the scoreboard. Teams don't understand how important that is. You always had this feeling in your back pocket. You could be down sixteen points with five or six minutes [to go] but then you think, 'We'll get the ball back three more times, defense will get it back, and we'll close the drive and we'll win.'"

Walsh was livid at halftime as his team, trailing 35–7 to the 0-13 Saints, left the field to go to the locker room in the corner of the end zone at Candlestick Park. Several fans had pelted the players with paper cups and other debris. But Walsh didn't scream at his players, nor did he try to embarrass them and thus coax an improved second-half performance. Instead, he appealed to their sense of self-worth— as players, as competitors, as men.

"Some of you may think we have already lost this game," he told them. "You might be right. We may lose this afternoon, and if we do, I can live with it. However, if we go down, you must decide how you want it to happen. How do you want to go down? Nobody would blame you for coasting the rest of this game, for throwing in the towel. And in fact, when you come back here in sixty minutes, only you will know if you did. Only you will know if you let New Orleans continue this assault or if you stood your ground and fought back. Frankly, I care a lot more about how we lose than if we lose. Gentlemen, in the second half, you're going to find out something important. You're about to find out who you are. And you may not like what you find."

There was silence after Walsh spoke. Before leaving the locker room, he asked one simple question of his players.

"Who are you?"

The team delivered its collective answer in stunning fashion.

This was when Joe Montana began to show the kind of late-game magic for which he became famous.

Down by 28 points after Archie Manning had lit up the 49ers' defense for 324 yards and 3 touchdown passes in the first half, Montana began the comeback with an 88-yard drive that included a

48-yard pass to Dwight Clark, an obscure tenth-round pick in 1979 who had been discovered almost accidentally by Walsh.

Before his first draft, Walsh had personally gone to scout several top quarterback prospects, even though he didn't have a first-round pick. One of them was Steve Fuller of Clemson.

"Bill used to do a lot of scouting on his own," McVay said. "He went to look at Fuller and asked, 'Can you get somebody [to catch passes]?' Here comes Dwight running out with a bag of footballs in it, so the quarterback was throwing balls, Dwight was catching them, and Bill kept warming up to him."

Clark was a lanky, six-foot-four, 212-pound receiver who didn't have particularly good speed but whose hands were terrific. Even so, he was mostly an afterthought in Clemson's offense. In three seasons with the Tigers, he had just 33 catches for 571 yards and 3 touchdowns.

Still, Walsh was so impressed by what he'd seen during Fuller's workout that he took a flier on Clark in the tenth round. After a modest rookie season in which he had 18 catches for 232 yards and no touchdowns, Clark became the 49ers' leading receiver in 1980, finishing the year with 82 catches for 991 yards and 8 touchdowns.

More than a year before he would make the most famous catch in 49ers' history and help transform a once-moribund franchise into an NFL dynasty, it was another Montana-to-Clark that sparked the remarkable second-half comeback against the Saints.

Montana hit Clark over the middle on a crossing route, and Clark ran past Saints defensive back Dave Waymer for a 71-yard touchdown to make it 35–21. Montana then hit Freddie Solomon for a 14-yard touchdown pass, and Lenvil Elliott ran for a 7-yard score before Ray Wersching won it, 38–35, with a 36-yard field goal in overtime.

"It was a great teaching moment for Bill," Montana said. "He said, 'Look, we're going to go back to our fundamentals. Let's just get out of here going in the right direction for next week.' We ended up winning the dang game, and he proved to us that we didn't always have to do something different or something special. We could win just by outexecuting people with the simple things that we learned from Day 1."

Montana himself had still not convinced doubters about his ability to thrive in the NFL, even after having beaten the Saints with the kind of comeback ability for which he would eventually take his place as one of the best NFL quarterbacks ever.

Montana pulled off what may go down as the greatest comeback in college football history, leading Notre Dame to a 35–34 win over Houston in the 1979 Cotton Bowl. This was legendary stuff, with Montana fighting off the flu and making a remarkable second-half comeback. Montana had become so ill during the course of the game that he couldn't even come out for the start of the second half because his body temperature had fallen to ninety-six degrees. The team's medical staff had him covered in blankets, and Montana was fed chicken bouillon to try to get his core temperature back up.

Montana didn't return to the field until midway through the fourth quarter, when Notre Dame trailed 34–12. But he led the Fighting Irish to a memorable comeback, scoring twenty-three points in the final minutes and finishing it off with a touchdown pass to Kris Haines with no time remaining on the clock. Kicker Joe Unis's second extra-point attempt—Notre Dame was penalized on the first—completed a comeback no one thought possible on that frigid afternoon in Dallas.

NFL scouts took a more skeptical view of Montana's heroics. Yes, they were impressed by what Montana had done; how could they not be? But the combination of his slight build—he was six foot two and barely two hundred pounds—and what was considered a weak arm was enough to scare off teams looking to draft him high.

In fact, Walsh was one of the skeptics.

Despite having created what would eventually become the most widely used offensive system in football—a system that continues to thrive in today's NFL—Walsh knew that, given his druthers, he'd rather have a quarterback built more like Greg Cook than Virgil Carter. Of course, it was the strong-armed Cook's injury in Cincinnati that led Walsh to create a scheme that revolved around a more precise short-passing game. But while the coach still liked the idea of that system, he also much preferred to have a big-armed passer to carry it out, providing versatility to throw it deep.

In fact, Walsh much preferred a passer who more closely resembled Cook: Phil Simms of Morehead State in Kentucky.

Walsh personally scouted Simms and seemed almost obsessed

with the idea of drafting him. But Walsh also knew he'd have to get lucky to be in position, because he didn't have a first-round pick. Had the 49ers owned that first overall choice, there's a good chance it would have been used on Simms.

"He came to Morehead and worked me out a couple of times," Simms said. "I'm like, 'He's going to get his first NFL job and I'm going to get my first NFL job, and he's spending time at Morehead State working me out?' It was great. We had two great workouts, watched film, and he's asking me questions the whole time."

Simms was intrigued by how Walsh looked at quarterbacks, and especially with the drills he asked him to perform during the workouts.

"The workouts were so physically great, and he was so different from every other coach talking to me about what to do," Simms said. "Everybody wanted to see me fire bullets and throw bombs, but he came in and was the exact opposite. He was like, 'Be more graceful' and 'Throw it softer. Make it prettier. Just try to be prettier when you do it.' I laughed at that, but it was great. I thought to myself, 'This is beautiful. This is so *easy* for me.' Then I watch Montana, and he's doing everything Bill Walsh taught me. I'm like, damn. And they always had somebody open for him."

Simms was convinced Walsh was going to somehow get him in the draft, whether that meant trading up for him into the first round or taking him with the first pick of the second round in the unlikely event Simms wasn't taken in the first round.

"I know he would have taken me," Simms said. "He personally told me that. He was calling me constantly. He'd ask, 'Who you working out for? Who's doing this or that?'"

Then again, Simms wasn't the only quarterback Walsh told that he'd select. Walsh said the same thing to Steve Dils, whom he'd coached at Stanford.

In the end—and thanks in no small part to Sam Wyche—Walsh ended up with Montana, which turned out to be the best thing for both.

But it took time for everything to come together, and the rebuilding process, though methodical and well thought-out, was painful nonetheless. It was delayed even further by Walsh's belief that he needed to be patient with Montana as he adapted to the pro game.

So rather than put Montana in at the start, Walsh instead named Steve DeBerg as his initial starter. And while the record was poor—the 49ers wound up going 2-14, just as they had the year before Walsh got there—DeBerg was a much-improved passer, which was a direct reflection of Walsh's influence.

He actually led the NFL in passing attempts (578) and completions (347) while throwing for 3,652 yards (which turned out to be his career high). But Walsh couldn't prevent DeBerg from throwing interceptions; he had 21, while throwing 17 touchdown passes.

Even so, Walsh wanted it known publicly that progress was being made with his offense. So he would frequently turn to Brian Billick, a former college tight end hired by Walsh to work in the team's public relations office.

"I dreaded Monday mornings, because Bill would come in and he'd go, 'Okay, Brian, when was the last time a quarterback threw for three hundred yards and lost?'" said Billick, who went on to become a prominent NFL offensive coordinator and later a Super Bowl–winning coach with the 2000 Baltimore Ravens. "Now, this is the 1970s, so it's not like you can just look this stuff up. I'd have to go call Elias [Sports Bureau] to get the answer, or else look through newspaper clippings."

When Walsh would speak to reporters, he'd somehow work in a reference to whatever stat Billick had provided.

"I'd give Bill this list, and in his news conference, he would turn someone's question into a chance to refer to that stat," Billick said. "And he'd do it like he was just thinking of it at that point. One way or another, he was going to have a way that he'd communicate it."

It was Walsh's way of injecting something positive into the conversation during a season in which very little was considered positive. It was also one of the myriad psychological devices Walsh used to get his point across. Another was to talk to players through his coaches. It was one of Walsh's preferred tactics, and he used it frequently—and always to his advantage.

"Billie Matthews was the running backs coach, and one day, the running backs were doing something wrong," Billick said. "So [Walsh] said out loud during practice, 'Billie, they need to punch with that inside hand in pass protection. Are you a good enough coach?' Well, the coaches knew what Bill was doing, but the players all of a sudden want to defend their coach. Rather than Bill Walsh walking over and challenging the player, he'd go through the coach."

It was an ingenious technique. Walsh would get his point across to the player, even though he wasn't addressing the player directly.

"Afterward, he'd probably cuddle up to the coach and say, 'Hey, we cool?' And the coach would go off mumbling, 'That motherfucker,'" recalled Billick.

Billick himself felt the sting of Walsh's sarcasm.

"One of my duties was to find a spot for Bill to address the media after games," Billick said. "So we're playing in Oakland, and we get our asses kicked. So I've got to figure out where Bill is going to talk to the media. Bill's not in a great mood, and I had two places where he could go. 'Bill, we need to go here or there. We can go to either place.' Bill says, 'You don't have a place for me? I've got nothing better to do than figure out where I need to go sit and visit with these fuckers?' It was a total dressing down, and it was Bill's way of venting."

The fit of pique didn't last long, though.

"The next day, he'd give me a couple of tickets to a concert or buy me dinner," Billick said. "He was just that way. There was a method with him."

"He just wanted to get everybody's attention, so instead of screaming at the players, he'd scream at somebody else," said Frank Cooney, the longtime football writer for the *San Francisco Examiner* who covered Walsh throughout his career. "He'd scream at the coaches. He'd scream at the trainer. He knew what he was doing."

No source of information was off-limits, and Walsh used every resource at his disposal. Up to and including the people who covered him on a daily basis.

"He'd even get to know what writers were close to what players and what ancillary information he could get from them," Cooney said. "Sometimes he'd be talking to you and putting one over on you, but you didn't realize it until fifteen minutes after you walked away.

Sometimes, you thought he was a bumbling professor, but it turns out you were probably wrong."

Walsh had done a painstaking job in planting the seeds for his eventual success during those first two years, and it was obvious to those who were sharp enough to understand his methods that there would be an eventual turnaround. Even so, having inherited such a barren roster from a collection of failed regimes prior to his arrival, this would not be an overnight process.

"Bill didn't deviate, and he had a great eye for seeing the potential in people," said Tony Dungy, the Hall of Fame coach who turned around the Buccaneers and later won a Super Bowl with the Colts. Dungy, a former college quarterback who played defensive back for the Steelers, was acquired by Walsh in a 1979 trade with Pittsburgh. "More than anything, it was utilizing what guys could do. We didn't have all complete players. Even with Joe Montana, there were things he could do well, and things he didn't do well, and Bill wouldn't put him in bad situations. He was a brilliant strategist, and that's what you could see, even during the course of a 2-14 season."

Dungy had come to the 49ers from the dominant team of the 1970s, a Steelers franchise led by no-nonsense coach Chuck Noll, whose approach was as meat-and-potatoes as it got. Noll believed in playing great defense, establishing the running game, and complementing both with a passing game that Terry Bradshaw led so brilliantly during the team's run of four Super Bowl titles. His practices were intense and physical, a style that was preferred by most teams in that era.

But Walsh had already decided it wasn't necessary to have his players beat one another up with punishing practices and old-school toughness. Oh, he was all for physical practices during training camp as a way to not only condition players in advance of the regular season, but also to weed out those who wouldn't be up to the physical challenges of the game.

"We practiced twice a day in training camp, and we hit each other," Cross said. "Bill was just trying to identify who and what he had."

Dungy was amazed that Walsh would run some practices where the players didn't work in pads—just helmets and shorts. It was unheard-of in the NFL at the time, and certainly something he'd never experienced during his days with the Steelers. In Pittsburgh—as in every other NFL city with every other NFL coach—there was only one way to get players ready for an NFL season, and that was to stage physical practices throughout training camp and into the season. It was routine for players to practice twice a day in pads, full-contact sessions that generally lasted two hours—once at about 9 a.m. and again at 3 p.m. The practices took such a physical and mental toll that most players spent the hour or so after lunch taking a nap. By nightfall, they were exhausted.

The next day: Do it all over again. Six days a week for about six weeks until the start of the regular season.

"I remember getting there from Pittsburgh and calling back and telling my buddies, 'We practice with no pads on sometimes,'" Dungy said. "They were like, 'What?' They couldn't believe it. I couldn't believe it."

Walsh's reasons for backing off on physical practices were twofold: (1) he believed it was best to make sure players remained as fresh as possible, particularly late in the season; and (2) there were so many intellectual challenges to learning his system that choreographing plays without the players hitting one another gave them a better concept of how the plays should work.

It was something Dungy carried with him throughout his coaching career, having seen Walsh disciple Dennis Green adopt many of his practice techniques with the Minnesota Vikings.

"Our practices [in Minnesota] were so short compared to what I had been used to in Pittsburgh," said Dungy, who was the Vikings' defensive coordinator in the early 1990s. "I would go to Denny and say, 'I don't know if I can get all these defenses in.' He'd say, 'No, you will. It makes you concentrate on what you're going to call in the game, and you won't waste time in practice.' It was different for me, but I ended up liking it. We adapted and understood that you could get a lot done in the walk-through. It changed my thinking, and a lot of other people's thinking."

Despite Walsh's preference for not beating his players up with the kind of relentless two-a-day practices that most coaches preferred, he certainly didn't come off as soft. No, his frequent use of sarcasm when addressing his players and coaches was as much a motivating factor for Walsh as yelling and screaming—and stretching the bounds of physical endurance—were for a hard-assed coach.

"Bill had a tenacious way of keeping things on edge," said linebacker Keena Turner, who was drafted by Walsh in 1980. "He knew how to push without confrontation, and set lofty goals for all of us. Yes, he was very detailed in the way we needed to approach getting there. He was a fierce competitor and he was demanding, because he was in a search for perfection without ever using that word."

How obsessed was Walsh with the idea of perfection?

"He would walk down the hallway and straighten the paintings on the wall," Turner said. "It was that kind of discipline that he had, the way that he did everything. I think there was this perception that we were a finesse team, maybe because with our style of offense people wanted to present us as a finesse team. But we were a tough, disciplined team, and that all came from Bill."

There wasn't a person associated with the 49ers whom Walsh did not impact. Not the coaches, not the players, not the owner, not the front office . . . not the secretarial staff.

"Bill had great vision of what a team ought to be like, and he developed a process to bring those visions to fruition," his longtime friend Dick Vermeil said.

Walsh drew from a wide variety of influences to come up with a vision that guided his thinking, a process that expanded over time and would soon provide the foundation for how to successfully operate a franchise.

He referenced George Washington, Gen. George Patton, the Chinese philosopher Confucius, Abraham Lincoln.

"Beware of rashness, but with energy and sleepless vigilance go forward and give us victories," Walsh quoted Lincoln in his 1997 book *Finding the Winning Edge,* cowritten with Brian Billick and James Peterson.

"He who requires much from himself and little from others will keep himself from being the object of resentment" was a quote he used from Confucius.

"Discipline is the soul of an Army. It makes small numbers

formidable, procures success to the weak, and esteem to all," George Washington wrote in 1759.

Walsh even referenced the infamous German World War II general Erwin Rommel: "A commander must accustom his staff to a high tempo from the outset, and continuously keep them up to it. If he once allows himself to be satisfied with norms, or anything less than an all-out effort, he gives up the race from the starting post, and will sooner or later be taught a bitter lesson."

Walsh certainly wasn't endorsing the barbarism of the Third Reich by quoting Rommel. Instead the coach related to the general's principles of how to lead people and maintain a high level of intensity while doing so.

"If you make a mistake, admit it quickly and emphatically, and don't dwell on it," Walsh quoted John Madden.

Tapping into Walsh's mind while writing the book was one of the greatest experiences of Billick's life.

"Bill was retired at the time, and he had an office in Palo Alto," Billick said. "I walked in there, and I'm like, 'Holy shit. Are you kidding me?' There were game plans, notes, lectures. It was like finding the Dead Sea Scrolls."

It was an astonishing compilation of a lifetime of thought from perhaps the smartest man to ever coach in the NFL. Billick was the Vikings' offensive coordinator at the time Walsh asked him to help write the 550-page volume, which is now a hard-to-find book that is arguably the most valuable coaching manual in the history of pro sports.

"Bill approached me one year at the Scouting Combine and said, 'Brian, I want to do this legacy, talk about the structure of the league, the way I look at practice, building an organization, that kind of thing. Do you know anyone who might be able to help me with that?' Bill never did anything directly, but as he's talking, I'm like, 'Holy shit. Bill Walsh just asked me if I wanted to do a book with him.'"

Billick asked if that was what Walsh wanted.

"He was like, 'Oh, yeah, Brian, that would be great,'" Billick said. "I hadn't thought about that."

Actually, he had thought about it, and Billick was just the person he wanted to work with on the book. Billick spent every spare moment he could meeting with Walsh, all this while calling plays for the Vikings and coach Dennis Green, who had been on Walsh's 49ers staff before taking over in Minnesota.

"I've got about forty hours of tape that has all been transcribed, and that is one of my most valued possessions," Billick said. "I put together a 120-page outline so I could prompt questions. I flew out on my free time to San Francisco, there were a lot of phone calls back and forth— I'd get an eight-page fax and notes—and you could see the way Bill's mind works. The first two notes might be on the responsibilities of the head coach and general manager. The design of an offense. What you look for in a quarterback. The next three notes on the design of a certain play."

Each year, Walsh would give lectures to the different parts of the organization. The players. Team management. The secretarial staff. The custodial staff. Every job on the team meant something to Walsh, and he didn't simply concentrate on the football operation. In Walsh's mind, if the team was to be successful, then everyone had to be on the same page.

"My Standard of Performance—the values and beliefs within it— guided everything I did in my work at San Francisco and are defined as follows," Walsh wrote in *The Score Takes Care of Itself.* "Exhibit a ferocious and intelligently applied work ethic directed at continual improvement; demonstrate respect for each person in the organization and the work he or she does; be deeply committed to learning and teaching, which means increasing my own expertise."

Walsh would also learn from the mistakes of others, even going so far as to interpret historic events in ways that weren't always conventional. For example, he was influenced by the experience of the renowned British explorer Sir Ernest Shackleton, whose expedition to Antarctica became a lesson in survival and courage when his ship, *Endurance,* became stuck in ice in January 1915. The ship eventually sank, but Shackleton and all twenty-eight men on the expedition survived more than a year and a half. Shackleton himself led a group of six and rowed across the open ocean to eventually reach land and organize a rescue.

Shackleton's story has been almost universally hailed as one of the great feats of survival in human history, and even Patriots coach Bill Belichick once showed his players a film telling Shackleton's story to promote the lessons of teamwork.

Walsh viewed Shackleton differently.

"Many have been inspired by his exploits; even the name of his ship—*Endurance*—is used for motivation," Walsh wrote of Shackleton in *The Score Takes Care of Itself*. "I also greatly admire his courage, loyalty, and dedication, but in case you forgot, his expedition was doomed; it ended in failure: The HMS *Endurance* was trapped in ice and crushed. Shackleton's incredible commitment to his men ultimately saved them from death . . . I, too, am inspired by his raw drive to save his men. I also keep in mind the loss of his ship and the failure of his expedition."

The lesson of Shackleton had a profound impact on Walsh.

"A leader must be keen and alert to what drives a decision, a plan of action," he wrote. "Among the most common faulty reasons are (1) trying to prove you are right and (2) trying to prove someone else is wrong. Of course, they amount to about the same thing and often lead to the same place: defeat."

Walsh thus demanded of himself a clear-eyed vision of his path forward and excellence from everyone else at every level of the organization, lest his leadership ultimately end in failure—no matter his level of commitment and loyalty.

"If you were lucky enough to receive a 49er paycheck, it meant you were part of an organization that had high expectations of itself and of you, whether you were a superstar or a secretary, manager or maintenance man, athlete, executive, or head coach," he wrote.

Walsh believed in treating every member of the organization fairly, and as long as he felt that approach was being reciprocated, he had no problem with you. But if you crossed the line with him, he stood his ground and made people around him realize that he would not compromise his integrity.

He was tested on this approach during one particular contract negotiation in his second year as the 49ers' coach. Left tackle Ron Singleton was unhappy with his deal heading into the 1980 season, and he wanted a significant raise. But the negotiations had become contentious, and at one point, Singleton and his agent accused Walsh of racism.

"[Singleton and his agent] argued that racism was built into the 49er organization, that we were unwilling to negotiate seriously and give him more money because he was an African American," Walsh wrote. "This was absolutely false. Everyone was treated the same, especially when it came to money; specifically, *nobody* got paid very much, including me (my first-year salary as head coach and general manager in the National Football League was $160,000, probably the lowest in the league—and I had to fight for that). Additionally, Ron was verbally abusive to certain staff members, a very serious breach of my Standard of Performance, which demanded respectful behavior toward all others on the 49er payroll."

After another unproductive negotiating session, Singleton left Walsh's office "and proceeded to walk through our locker room making disparaging remarks about me and the 49ers, throwing in several racially charged comments for good measure, right in front of our equipment manager, Chico Norton, to whom he also made dismissive remarks."

Walsh soon heard about what happened, and called in R. C. Owens, a former 49ers receiver famous for helping to create the "alley-oop" pass. Owens, who had worked in public relations, was told by Walsh to clean out Singleton's locker. "Shoes, shirts, socks, everything," Walsh told Owens. "Put it all in a box and deliver it to his house."

Word quickly spread that Singleton had been thrown off the team.

"It sent out a vitally important message," Walsh wrote. "There are consequences—at times harsh consequences—for ignoring the spoken and unspoken code of conduct that was part of the standards I had established. Ron Singleton was not exempt from my code of behavior just because he was an important component of our future. People got the message: If a top player such as Ron Singleton could be fired for breaking some fundamentally important element of my Standard of Performance, so could anyone."

For Walsh, football had to come first. It was why he threw linebacker Thomas "Hollywood" Henderson off the team in 1980 after just three games. Henderson, the former Cowboys defender who had made a name for himself with his outspokenness during the 1970s but also developed an addiction to cocaine, was acquired in a trade before the season. But Walsh quickly realized Henderson was still on cocaine—the coach found out he actually used the drug when he and his wife visited with Bill and Geri at their home—and released him.

It was another example of how Walsh went through the formative stages of building the 49ers. He used ideas and examples culled from years of study and preparation, through his long apprenticeship as a college and pro assistant, and formed a basic set of principles by which he operated—even if his players didn't always understand that his Standard of Performance would ultimately prove successful.

Yet Walsh himself experienced many moments of uncertainty through the early part of his run with the 49ers. Only a few people in his inner circle knew that beneath the outward show of confidence—and even arrogance—was a man who was at times paralyzed by self-recrimination. That breakdown on the plane back from Miami after the loss to the Dolphins near the end of his second year was the most obvious example. But his close friends knew there were other times when Walsh was filled with anguish and uncertainty.

"The losing killed him," Dick Vermeil said.

Vermeil had always been aware of Walsh's insecurities. They'd known each other almost their entire adult lives, from the time they first met in 1956 as graduate assistant coaches at San Jose State. They worked together as assistant coaches at Stanford in 1965, but always kept in close touch.

In fact, it was Vermeil who'd act as Walsh's coaching psychologist during the early days with the 49ers.

"I remember sitting in my office on a Monday night after a 49ers loss," Vermeil said. "It'd be midnight my time, which was 9 p.m. for him. My coaches would be there, and they'd hear the phone ring, which meant that it would be another hour delay to the meeting."

What were the conversations like?

"It was basically me trying to talk him into not jumping off the Golden Gate Bridge," Vermeil said.

Vermeil proved to be a good listener and a dear friend, but he had his own emotional issues at the time. He had been hired as the Eagles' coach in 1976, inheriting a team that was in many ways similar to the 49ers that Walsh started coaching. The Eagles hadn't had a winning season since 1966, and because of previous trades, Philadelphia didn't have a first-round pick until 1979.

Vermeil felt the only way to transform his team into a winner would be to do so through sheer will and punishing practices. He drove his players with an uncompromising zeal, working them through brutally tough and long practices that weeded out veteran malcontents, but eventually led to a team that put the franchise back on solid footing.

What Vermeil didn't understand at the time was that he was driving himself to the brink, in part because he, too, had an underlying insecurity very similar to Walsh's.

"Bill was an emotional guy, and I know what that's like," Vermeil said. "You take everything too seriously, and you carry the load, and it can wear on you."

Vermeil led the Eagles to the first Super Bowl appearance in franchise history in 1980, but they were beaten by the Raiders, 27–10, in Super Bowl XV. A year later, they made the playoffs again as a wild card team but lost to the Giants in the first round.

But by then, Vermeil was starting to unravel, one of the early victims of coaching burnout. His inability to delegate authority and share his burden with others left him an emotional wreck—even though he couldn't see it for himself.

"People saw what I was doing to myself—Sid Gillman [the former Chargers coach who worked as an Eagles consultant]; Lynn Stiles [an Eagles assistant coach]; my wife, Carol; [Eagles owner] Leonard Tose," Vermeil said. "But I wasn't a good listener. I went to New York and spent a couple of hours with Dr. [Herbert J.] Freudenberger [a psychologist who specialized in stress-related issues]. I remember getting back off the train in Philadelphia, and I asked my wife and some other people if they had talked to him before I got there, because he described me perfectly. It startled me."

By 1982, he was near the end.

His epiphany came later that year.

In a bathroom at Veterans Stadium.

"I remember sitting on the crapper eating my hoagie before I went onto the practice field," he said. "That was a good indication right there it was time to go."

Vermeil would retire after the season, spending the next fifteen years as a broadcaster before finally going back into coaching—at Walsh's urging. Vermeil then led the St. Louis Rams to the only Super Bowl victory in franchise history, presiding over Kurt Warner's magical run through the 1999 season and a win over the Tennessee Titans in Super Bowl XXXIV.

Toward the end of the 1980 season, Walsh would eventually come through his long stretches of self-doubt at around the same time Vermeil was getting his own team ready to launch into the playoffs. While Vermeil was putting the finishing touches on a 12-4 regular season, Walsh had achieved a far more modest goal—albeit a very important one—by winning three of his final five games.

Little did he know how quickly it would all come together, and that his convictions would be validated.

GIBBS

NEARLY FIRED BEFORE HE'D
EVEN WON A GAME

On January 13, 1981, Jack Kent Cooke was positively beaming as he introduced Joe Gibbs as the Redskins' twentieth head coach. Even though general manager Bobby Beathard was the one who had settled on Gibbs, Cooke took credit for the move, and wasn't shy about reminding Beathard.

"He referred to Joe as 'my coach,' back then," Beathard said of Cooke.

It wouldn't be long, however, before Cooke amended that phrase to "your coach."

Cooke's role in Gibbs's hiring was essentially to rubber-stamp Beathard's decision. The day before the hiring was made official, Cooke met for three and a half hours at the posh Waldorf Astoria hotel in Manhattan with both Gibbs and Beathard. Cooke had come into the meeting knowing full well that he would hire Gibbs, but the coach was as nervous as he'd ever been, unsure what decision Cooke would make.

"I had no idea he was serious about hiring me," Gibbs said.

It didn't help when Beathard showed up looking as if he was about to head into Central Park for a jog. The general manager wore sneakers, slacks, and a button-down shirt. No jacket. No tie.

"Bobby, you're going to cost me this job," Gibbs whispered to Beathard.

Gibbs had dressed appropriately for the interview—jacket and tie—carrying with him a legal pad to take notes. They sat down and spoke for a few minutes, and Cooke suddenly looked out the window and pointed to the iconic Chrysler Building a few blocks away.

"Oh, by the way, that's my building," Cooke told Gibbs.

"I went in there not knowing whether I'd get the job, and then he says that and I'm like, 'Oh, man. What am I doing here?'"

But by the end of the meeting, the two men shook hands. Gibbs was Cooke's coach.

By the next day at the news conference at Redskins Park, Cooke was showering Gibbs with praise, making it seem like he'd known him for years, when in fact he'd spoken to him for the first time the day before, when they met at the Waldorf.

"Joe appeals to me because of his obvious dedication to the game," Cooke told reporters of the forty-year-old Gibbs. "I have all the confidence that Joe will provide the Redskins fans with a team that will stir the imagination, win or lose. And I believe his abilities match his ambitions. He's a pioneer in the game inasmuch as he recognized before others the perceptible change in the character of the game."

Cooke was referencing the Chargers' pass-oriented offense, which had achieved unprecedented success with Gibbs as the offensive coordinator. With Gibbs calling the plays in San Diego, the Chargers had become the first team in NFL history to average more than 400 yards offense and have three 1,000-yard receivers in the same season. Gibbs promised to bring that pass-centric offense to the Redskins, whose offense had languished under Pardee.

"I'm thankful to God for the body and mind to get a job like this," he said. "I feel a tremendous sense of responsibility and gratitude to Mr. Cooke. I want him to look back on this and say it was the best decision he ever made. I have a sense of urgency. I am ready and fired up."

Gibbs quickly put together his coaching staff, which soon became a tight-knit group. Gibbs agreed with Beathard's suggestion of making secondary coach Richie Petitbon his defensive coordinator, and he also hired linebackers coach Larry Peccatiello. He brought in noted offensive assistant Dan Henning as his assistant head coach, Joe Bugel as offensive coordinator (a title in name only, since Gibbs would be calling the plays; Bugel's primary responsibility was coaching the offensive line), running backs coach Don Breaux, and tight ends coach Warren "Rennie" Simmons, a former teammate and longtime friend.

While it was relatively easy forming a staff whose loyalty and dedication to Gibbs was sacrosanct, Gibbs had a major issue to resolve, one that had hovered over the franchise throughout the entire 1980 season. Running back John Riggins had expressed unhappiness with his contract during the preseason, and wound up leaving the team and holding out the entire year.

The Redskins still owned his rights, but Gibbs wanted to have clarity about a player who had been so important to the team since coming to the Redskins in 1976 after a four-year run with the Jets.

Riggins had returned to his native Kansas during the holdout, spending the year pursuing two of his favorite avocations: hunting and drinking. Soon after Gibbs got the job, Riggins had agreed to meet with him, and the coach flew out to Kansas to see him.

When Gibbs pulled up to Riggins's home near Centralia, Kansas, the running back was dressed in camouflage hunting gear.

"He has a beer in both hands," Gibbs recalls of the meeting. "He says, 'I figured I was going to get my coach a beer.'" Gibbs didn't drink, so Riggins kept the beer for himself.

Gibbs started talking about how he wanted Riggins to come back and be a big part of the offense, that he wouldn't even have to block. Riggins didn't say anything at first and just listened to Gibbs, who by now was starting to get a little self-conscious because he was doing all the talking.

Then Riggins leaned across the table. "You need to get me back there," he told Gibbs. "I'll make you famous."

Gibbs was mortified.

"He made that statement and I'm thinking, 'Oh, my gosh, this guy's an egomaniac,'" Gibbs said. "'I'm going to get stuck with a fruitcake for ten years.'"

Gibbs listened and told himself there was no way he would put up with Riggins. The only solution was to entice him to return to the team and then trade him.

Two days later, Riggins called Gibbs. "Joe, I've made up my mind, and I'm going to play next season," he told Gibbs.

The coach smiled and thought about when and where he'd trade Riggins.

But Riggins had outfoxed Gibbs on this one: He said the only way he'd come back was if Gibbs gave him a no-trade clause.

Gibbs reluctantly agreed, making perhaps the most important concession of his life.

Riggins returned to the team and promptly served up one of the best quotes in pro sports history: "I'm broke, I'm bored, and I'm back."

Gibbs had thus overcome a significant obstacle by convincing Riggins to play again, but even though the coach had agreed to the running back's demand that he not be traded, he wasn't ready to make Riggins the focal point of the offense. Instead Gibbs planned on installing the pass-centric offense he ran in San Diego under Coryell.

Gibbs had inherited quarterback Joe Theismann, who had come to the Redskins in 1974 after playing three seasons in the Canadian Football League. He had originally been a fourth-round pick of the Dolphins in 1971, but the former Notre Dame star couldn't agree on a contract and elected to sign with the Toronto Argonauts. Theismann, who led the Argos to the Grey Cup championship game as a rookie (Toronto lost to Calgary in the title game), had his NFL rights traded from the Dolphins to the Redskins in 1974 in exchange for a first-round draft pick.

Now, if you want to get a sense of just how unconventional Theismann's career turned out in his early days, consider this: He was the team's leading punt returner in his first NFL season. Imagine a team in today's game trading a first-round pick for a quarterback and using him as a punt returner. It simply wouldn't happen. But because George Allen already had quarterbacks Sonny Jurgensen and Billy Kilmer, there was no place in the offense for Theismann.

But by 1978, after Jurgensen had retired and Kilmer's effectiveness had waned, Theismann replaced Kilmer as the starter. He had modest success running the offense, but was certainly not considered great. In his three seasons as the starter before Gibbs's arrival, Theismann went 7-7 in 1978, 10-6 in 1979, and 6-9 in 1980. In those three seasons, he had 50 touchdown passes and 47 interceptions.

Gibbs liked the fact that Theismann had good mobility and could roll out of the pocket much easier than most quarterbacks, so the coach had grown even more convinced that airing the ball out was the way to go.

"Joe's a new coach, he inherited me, and that's one of the toughest things for people to understand," Theismann said. "When there's a coaching change, you have to earn your place on the team, and it's tougher for you because you're not his. He didn't draft you or sign you. You were there. You were the leftovers after he took over a bad situation."

Gibbs also wasn't a fan of Theismann's bon vivant lifestyle. Theismann was by far the most recognizable player on the team, did a bunch of commercial endorsements, and had an outsized personality that often rubbed teammates the wrong way. Theismann loved to talk. And talk. And talk. Whether it was to reporters. On radio or television interviews. Anywhere. The man was as chatty as they came.

This was anathema to a buttoned-down coach like Gibbs, and there was plenty of adjusting to be done. Gibbs demanded full attention from his players, and he perceived Theismann as spreading himself too thin with his off-field activities. Gibbs wanted players who had football as the central focus of their lives.

Mark Murphy could see that immediately.

"You could tell that Joe was very organized," said the former Redskins safety, who enjoyed a stellar NFL career and years later became president of the Green Bay Packers. "Pardee was a very good football coach. There wasn't anything wrong with him. Gibbs was just an exceptional leader."

Gibbs not only faced a major overhaul in terms of bringing in his system, but he had to change a culture that had been fostered by Allen and then Pardee, both of whom showed deference to the veteran players who comprised the core of the team. Gibbs was about to revamp everything about the way the team did business, from the way they trained, to the way they studied, to the way the players and staff interacted with one another.

Everything.

"Joe minimized the ego," said Rick "Doc" Walker, a Redskins tight end from 1980 to 1985. "Everybody was all in. You have to remember, only a few players were making money back then, and most of us were in the same boat. That's the one thing that poverty brings. There's a sense of community. We were highly incentivized to make more money, and we needed each other to do that, to get to the playoffs and get those additional game checks."

The one thing Walker realized early on about Gibbs was that while the coach was resolute in demanding discipline from his players during meetings and practice, he took into account that everyone had a unique personality, and that they therefore needed to be handled differently. If one player responded better to being told what to do, Gibbs would react accordingly. If another player was more of a self-starter and didn't respond well to criticism, he backed off.

"Every guy on the team was different," said Walker, now a popular radio and television personality in the Washington, D.C., area. "He let John [Riggins] be John. If John needed a little extra slack, Joe let it happen. [Riggins] didn't miss his assignments. He didn't miss practices. He did his job. But Joe let John's personality live. He didn't stifle him, and that's part of his genius for why he was such a successful coach. He didn't have to put his finger on everybody or suppress a guy's personality. The fact is he allowed that attitude to breathe.

"One thing I've learned about coaches is they don't have to micromanage," Walker said. "For some coaches, they've got to run it like a military camp. The best coaches get you to function as a unit. As long as you as a player respect order and respect the rules, you can work with coaches who understand that."

Charley Casserly, a Redskins scout at the time Gibbs was hired, noticed immediately that the coach had a unique way of dealing with people.

"He came across as very straitlaced, but he could adapt to different personalities," said Casserly, who went on to succeed Beathard and was the GM of the Redskins when they won their third Super Bowl title. "He had an ego, but he wasn't an egotist. All the great ones have an ego, but he wasn't a guy that flaunted it."

There was one thing that was a nonstarter with Gibbs, though.

"If he sensed that football wasn't important to you," Casserly said, "that was a line that couldn't be crossed."

And when it came to his vision of how the game should be played,

Gibbs was stubbornly loyal to what he had learned under Coryell. Regardless of the personnel he inherited from the Pardee regime, he was going to use the pass-oriented system, even if it ran counter to the style of offense used in the more conservative NFC East.

In order to do so, however, he knew he needed to retool the offensive line to provide adequate protection for Theismann. As a former offensive line coach himself, Gibbs understood the value of having quality blockers up front, even if they were the most overlooked and underappreciated part of the team.

Beathard was completely on the same page as Gibbs, and as they prepared for their first draft together, they built a consensus on Pittsburgh offensive tackle Mark May for the first round. He was widely acknowledged as one of the top tackle prospects in the country, and Gibbs viewed him as a franchise-caliber left tackle who could play a dozen or so years in the NFL.

The Redskins were also keen on May's Pittsburgh teammate, Russ Grimm, who wasn't as highly regarded as May, but was the kind of smart, tough player who could fit into the interior of the line and figure prominently in the run game.

What the coach didn't know was that May would need time to develop into a quality lineman, and that Grimm would more quickly turn into a significant part of Gibbs's offensive line. In all, the Redskins drafted five offensive linemen in 1981—Gary Sayre of little-known Cameron University was a fifth-round guard (although he never played a game), Rice guard Darryl Grant was a ninth-round pick (and later converted to defensive tackle), and tackle Allan Kennedy of Washington State was taken in the tenth round.

But there was one more rookie who came out of nowhere who would soon figure prominently into the equation along the line.

Joe Jacoby, a mountainous left tackle at six foot seven, three hundred pounds, out of Louisville, went undrafted in 1981, but Casserly had scouted him at Louisville and told Beathard and Gibbs it would make sense to sign Jacoby as a free agent. It took Gibbs a while to realize Jacoby was an offensive tackle, not a defensive tackle. That's how big the guy was; it was extremely rare for an offensive tackle to be as tall as Jacoby.

Jacoby had been expecting a call from the Redskins either in the later rounds or after the draft, but as he waited at home in Louisville, they still hadn't called.

"So Washington was the only team that worked me out before the draft, and I heard from nobody else," Jacoby said. "After the draft is over, I hear from Dallas, Cincinnati, Tampa Bay. They're looking for guys to fill out their 120-man roster. So I'm waiting on the Redskins to call, and the doorbell rings. It was a scout from Seattle, and he's got a three-year contract."

Jacoby wasn't sure what he'd do, and he was tempted by the Seattle offer. But then he finally got a call from the Redskins.

"They said, 'We'd love you to come up,'" Jacoby said. "So I pack a bag, and the guy from Seattle is still there. I tell him I'm going to Washington. The guy goes, 'You need a ride?' So the scout from Seattle drove me to the airport."

Gibbs now had at least the framework of a line he felt could develop into the kind of unit that would be able to handle his offense. With center Jeff Bostic, another undrafted free agent who made the team in 1980; right guard Melvin Jones, a seventh-round pick in 1980; and right tackle George Starke, who had been with the Redskins since 1972, the rookie class would soon fill out the line and provide Gibbs with exactly what he was looking for.

The Hogs were born.

Gibbs's vision for May as the centerpiece of his offensive line didn't immediately come to fruition, though. Nor did May wind up playing the position Gibbs had initially expected. As was typical in that era, first-round draft picks usually held out of training camp to try to gain leverage in contract negotiations, and May was no exception.

May's agent, Ralph Cindrich, remembers some contentious moments trying to hammer out a new deal. And the arguments weren't only with Beathard.

"If I would be going into an area of compromise, Mayday would nix it," Cindrich said, referring to May by his nickname. "I'm like, 'What the fuck do you want me to say?' Bobby would blow up, and I'd blow up on Bobby. Eventually, we got it done."

The missed time in training camp slowed May's development,

and he suffered some nagging injuries and weight loss during the season—to the point that Gibbs decided he wanted May to work out in the off-season to get his strength up and return to his normal playing weight.

"That first year, I went from 285 to 260," May said. "I broke my nose, got a hip pointer, sprained a knee, and still battled to play. So the next year, they change the whole off-season program. They put a ton of money into the weight facility, they want guys to live and train in Washington."

Little did May realize that he had unwittingly led to the eventual explosion of off-season training programs around the NFL. Where players used to go home in the off-season, return for minicamp and then training camp, they would soon train year-round, a practice that continues today.

"I'm the guy," May said. "Blame me. [Former Bills, Panthers, and Colts general manager] Bill Polian said I ought to be in the Hall of Fame because of that. It made it much easier for teams to get their guys to train year-round."

Gibbs felt reasonably optimistic that he and Beathard had put together a team good enough to compete from the start, and they'd get a major test with four straight games against NFC East teams. In Gibbs's debut at RFK Stadium, Tom Landry's Cowboys beat the Redskins, 26–10, as Danny White threw two touchdown passes and Rafael Septien kicked four field goals.

Gibbs's offensive approach was just as he'd promised: a lot of passing and very little running; the Redskins finished with 280 passing yards and just 44 rushing yards.

A week later against the Giants, it was the same formula. And the same result. In a 17–7 loss to the Giants, the Redskins had 284 passing yards and 65 rushing yards.

In subsequent road games against the Cardinals and Eagles, the Redskins lost both, and Gibbs's offense again floundered.

A week later, the bottom fell out.

Facing Bill Walsh's 49ers at RFK in Week 5, the Redskins trailed 30–3 going into the fourth quarter, and only two fourth-quarter touchdowns made the 30–17 final score look respectable.

———

Bobby Beathard picked up the phone in his office. Redskins owner Jack Kent Cooke was on the other line.

"Hey, get your coach and get out to my house," Cooke told Beathard.

"Mr. Cooke, I can't," Beathard told him. "I have a flight, and I'm just leaving. I'm going all around the country to scout players."

"Do you own this team?" Cooke asked.

"No, sir," Beathard replied.

"Then get your coach, and get out to the house."

Beathard and Gibbs thought they were about to be fired. Before Gibbs had even won a game.

Notice Cooke referred to Gibbs as "your coach" when he summoned Beathard for the meeting at Cooke's home at Kent Farms, a 640-acre estate in Middleburg, Virginia, about a forty-five-minute drive from Redskins Park.

"You never knew what Mr. Cooke would do," Beathard said.

"Cooke was tough to work with, because he was a detail-oriented, successful person," said Charlie Taylor, the former Redskins public relations director. "To have to waste your time explaining things when you're already working sixteen-, eighteen-hour days, was tough. If it was out of season, you didn't mind doing it. To give up another two hours out of your day, it was challenging."

Cooke was clearly frustrated and had floated the idea of bringing back George Allen to coach the team. Cooke's son, John, convinced his father that wouldn't be a good idea, and Jack Kent Cooke eventually agreed.

By the time Gibbs and Beathard had met with Cooke—with either or both men expecting to be fired—they were relieved when Cooke actually offered words of encouragement. Of course, Cooke did not mention the part about wanting to rehire Allen before the owner's son intervened.

"We rode back to Redskins Park after the meeting and just laughed about it," Beathard said. "But really, Mr. Cooke was a great owner. He gave us everything we ever needed. We could never blame him for trying, because he really was all about winning."

There had been a somewhat similar meeting between just Gibbs and Cooke a few days earlier, at which Gibbs again thought he would be fired. This one was in Cooke's office at Redskins Park.

"I was sweating bullets every time I saw him," Gibbs said. "He had these accounting books under his arm. One time, he said, 'I just did a deal for $16 million, and now I have to figure out the taxes.' One of his favorite lines is, 'I'm going to try and make some money so you can go throw it away.'"

Cooke offered some words of encouragement. "I'm going to lay down and bleed awhile, and we're going to get up and fight again," Cooke told him, paraphrasing the Scottish ballad about Sir Andrew Barton.

"I will say this about Mr. Cooke," Gibbs said. "He was at his best when things were at their worst."

Cooke's vote of confidence for Gibbs was about to be rewarded.

If Cooke had grown frustrated with the Redskins' problems, it was killing Gibbs.

His team was flailing in trying to learn the offense he had brought with him from San Diego. But unlike Walsh, who stood by his offensive philosophy and made his players adapt to it through constant repetition, Gibbs decided to junk his entire system.

"You always try and fit your offense to your personnel, and Joe had radically changed our offense from the year before," center Jeff Bostic said. "Obviously, Joe hadn't drafted everybody that he had, but he had radically changed our offense. We were throwing like fifty times a game the first five games."

And losing them all.

Gibbs's genius was about to reveal itself.

Gibbs liked to think he was good at making in-game adjustments, yet as Fouts knew, the coach would often be stubbornly attached to his system, even when his star quarterback in San Diego would lobby to change Gibbs's mind.

"Deep down, Joe wanted to throw the football, but he didn't have Dan Fouts, Kellen Winslow, and Charlie Joiner," Bostic said. "He's trying to run the Air Coryell offense, but that wasn't our personnel."

Despite the winless start, Gibbs had nevertheless instilled in his team a sense of camaraderie by maintaining a sense of composure that told the players their coach had not lost faith in them. He was impatient to win, yes, but he was outwardly patient with the process.

"Our team became very close, and a lot of that was Joe Gibbs being able to keep us together," Theismann said. "He had a great way about him, in that he knew what he wanted from his football team, he was very disciplined, but he also had a great understanding of what made different players tick. When you can come through that kind of adversity and be together, it says a lot about what a coach's impact on a team is all about."

Theismann himself was a big part of that equation, and he knew that if Gibbs was to succeed, then the quarterback had to be certain the coach could believe in him.

A few days after the loss to San Francisco, Theismann drove to Gibbs's home off Lawyers Road in Vienna, Virginia. A startled Gibbs answered the door.

"Coach, we need to talk," Theismann said.

The two sat down in Gibbs's living room.

"That was a big meeting," Gibbs said. "We had just lost our fifth game, everything in the world went wrong, and it was a nightmare. I was so discouraged. Joe came in and we talked about a lot of things."

"Joe, I want this more than anything in the world," Theismann told Gibbs. "You tell me what you want me to do, and I'll do it. All I want to do is be the quarterback."

After several minutes, the two men shook hands and Theismann left.

"Joe was highly motivated," Gibbs said. "The guy wanted to succeed. He was really, really bright as a quarterback. He wanted it. That helps when you get somebody like that. After our conversation, we committed to going down the road together."

Gibbs knew he could count on his quarterback.

Gibbs also knew he had to fundamentally change his thinking. So he figured discretion was the better part of valor and decided on a sweeping transformation of his offense: He would make the running game the centerpiece of his attack.

The makeover was astonishing, especially when you consider how much time and energy had been spent installing the Air Coryell attack during training camp and for more than a month during the regular season.

Relying on the speed and power of his young offensive line, Gibbs had Riggins and Joe Washington share the load on the ground, and Theismann, who had dropped back to pass an average of 38 times over the first five games, attempted just 25 passes in Week 6 against the Bears.

Riggins rushed 23 times for 126 yards and 2 touchdowns, while Washington had 21 carries for 88 yards. Gibbs had his first NFL victory, as the Redskins dominated the Bears, 24–7.

"Joe had radically changed the offense, and it showed you just how brilliant of a coach he was," Bostic said. "He started molding his offense to fit the personnel, not the San Diego Chargers' former personnel. He kind of flipped it upside down."

Gibbs's inner offensive line coach came out in a big way, as he introduced a play that would become a signature of his offense.

"Joe had seen this play, called the counter trey, that one college team was running and thought he could implement it," Bostic said.

The blocking scheme was an ingenious one, but required speed and agility from his offensive linemen—even the six-foot-seven Jacoby.

Especially Jacoby.

The play required both the left tackle and the left guard to "pull," which meant that both had to run from the left side all the way to the right to open up the hole for the running back. Jacoby turned out to be the perfect tackle to run the play, because he had exceptional speed for such a big man.

"The counter game," Jacoby said, "if you catch it right, there are some huge running lanes."

The mood was euphoric after the game, even though the Redskins knew they were still in a deep hole at 1-5.

Jacoby wasn't around at the end to celebrate, though. He had suffered a sprained neck in the second half, and had to be taken to a nearby hospital.

"They did a bunch of X-rays, wanting to make sure nothing was broken," Jacoby said.

Meanwhile, the Redskins' charter flight home was on the tarmac at O'Hare Airport, and the players and coaches filed on board. Jacoby wasn't there. As the flight crew prepared the cabin for takeoff, several players refused to let the plane take off.

"We weren't leaving Jacoby behind," Bostic said.

As it turned out, the X-rays were negative, and Jacoby headed for the airport.

"I was in my uniform, in my cleats, still with my pants on, still sweaty, didn't shower," Jacoby said.

He boarded the plane, and the players erupted in cheers when they saw him.

"They were yelling and screaming," Jacoby quipped.

The big tackle smiled and opened the package he'd received from relatives who had come up from Louisville to attend the game. Inside were home-baked chocolate chip cookies.

"I had the food. That's why they held up the plane," Jacoby quipped.

That was not the reason they held up the plane, of course. They held it up because one of their brothers had been left behind, and his teammates refused to go home without him.

"It was touching that they thought of you that way," Jacoby said. "You're in a good organization, and it makes you feel pretty good that they would wait on you. At least I didn't have to take a Trailways bus home."

The symbolism of that moment was unmistakable, and the togetherness would soon bear promising results.

The Redskins lost the following game to Don Shula's Dolphins, 13–10, at the Orange Bowl, but Gibbs once again stuck to his revamped offense and used the running game as the focal point. Three straight wins followed, giving the previously winless team a shot at the Giants to get to within a game of .500.

It would be the most complete game the Redskins had played under their first-year coach, as the Redskins beat the Giants, 30–27, in over-time, on the road.

Theismann threw for 242 yards and 2 touchdown passes. Riggins and Washington combined for 135 rushing yards and one touchdown. And kicker Mark Moseley, a holdover from the George Allen and Jack Pardee years, tied the game with a 49-yard field goal in the final sec-onds of regulation and then won it on a 48-yard kick in overtime.

After an 0-5 start, the Redskins were now 5-6 and tied with six other teams for the NFC's second wild card spot.

"Before today, it was a long shot to think of us being a playoff con-tender," Gibbs said afterward. "Now, to win the last three games against good teams like this, you have to feel different about it. That's what I told my players, too."

Moseley, one of the team's most popular players, was ecstatic in the locker room.

"In the huddle [before the game-winning kick], the guys were ready to go home," he said. "So I said, 'Let's do it.' As a kicker, you cherish the opportunity to get a field goal, but this was something extra special. Every time we play New York, we either seem to win or lose on a field goal."

"I don't think anyone doubted that Mark would win this game," tight end Don Warren said. "He's the best kicker under pressure I've ever seen. None of us ever felt we'd lose, even when they scored at the end. We played too well to lose."

Gibbs was beaming about his team after such an emotional win.

"I don't know how much prouder I can be of this team," he said. "When we were 0-5, we were at the lowest point of any team in the NFL. Now I think we cherish winning more, it means so much to us. To be where we are, after the start we had, it's a testimony to these guys never quitting."

The optimism would be short-lived, though. Gibbs lost for a second time to Landry, as the Cowboys won, 24–10, in Dallas, and they lost the following week in Buffalo. But they did close out the season with three straight wins to finish 8-8, and there was an unmistakable sense that they could build on what they'd done right after the shaky start.

"You could really feel something, the way we got better as the sea-son went on," May said. "And I think Joe knew that having another year together would be helpful."

WALSH

FROM DOUBT AND DESPERATION
TO VINDICATION

From the depths of depression on the flight home from Miami, when Bill Walsh broke down crying after losing to the Dolphins, he was heartened by how his team—and he himself—had responded in the aftermath. With consecutive wins over the Giants, Saints, and Falcons, he'd felt at least a small sense of reassurance that his plan might succeed after all. Season-ending losses to the Falcons and Bills were a disappointment, though, and the 49ers finished the 1980 season 6-10.

Still, it was four wins better than the previous year, and he had found his quarterback in Joe Montana and his go-to wide receiver in Dwight Clark. Those were two gigantic answers for a franchise that had been adrift before Walsh got there, although the roster was hardly complete.

With his offense now showing unmistakable signs of progress, it was the defense that most concerned Walsh heading into 1981. He and chief personnel assistant John McVay knew they needed a significant infusion of talent to address chronic weaknesses in the secondary. The 49ers had the twenty-sixth-ranked defense in the twenty-eight-team league, and the pass defense was next to last.

If his team was to achieve any level of success in the coming years, Walsh knew he'd have to begin a sweeping makeover on defense.

"We were still not a complete team by any means," McVay said. "Bill went through a ton of defensive backs, those first two years, so we knew we needed to upgrade."

McVay trusted that he and Walsh could improve the defensive side of the ball, and their personnel moves seemed promising. They had the eighth overall pick that year, and were concerned that the Seattle Seahawks would take the player they coveted most: USC defensive back Ronnie Lott. But the Seahawks, at fourth overall, instead took Kenny Easley, so Lott was still on the board at number 8.

The 49ers loved Lott's versatility. He was drafted as a cornerback, but the team knew he also projected as a safety, so Walsh had plenty of flexibility with the hard-hitting defender. After taking nose tackle John Harty with the first of two second-round picks, the 49ers selected three defensive backs in a row—Eric Wright of Missouri and then Pittsburgh's Carlton Williamson and Lynn Thomas. Lott, Wright, and Williamson would soon form the nucleus of a much-improved secondary, joining holdover Dwight Hicks, who was with the 49ers since 1979. Hicks had been working at a health foods store outside Detroit when the Niners called him in October that year.

Walsh wasn't done, though. Always in search of talent, the 49ers staged open workouts to see if someone might catch the coach's eye. It was at one of these workouts that Walsh sat alongside McVay and studied a group of free agents.

Walsh noticed a short, squatty player during drills. "Who's that little towheaded guy down there?" he said to McVay.

"That's Billy Ring," McVay told him. "He's a running back."

"Just watch him for a few minutes," Walsh said.

After they watched, Walsh turned to McVay.

"Sign him," Walsh said.

Ring, a five-ten, 208-pound runner out of Iowa, was still a long shot to make the team during training camp, but Walsh saw enough in him to find a way to get him into the lineup as a lead blocker and occasional runner.

"I marvel at the way Bill [Walsh] could just look at players and see the talent in them, sometimes when no one else could," McVay said. "Billy Ring was one of those guys."

Walsh also felt his team needed an infusion of some veteran talent, and he zeroed in on linebacker Jack "Hacksaw" Reynolds, a former first-round pick of the Los Angeles Rams who was embroiled in a contract dispute. The Rams had a number of veteran players looking to cash in with new deals, and they decided that Reynolds was one of the most expendable. Rather than give in to his demands, they instead set an example by simply releasing him.

Reynolds was just what Walsh was looking for—an experienced player who would use his savvy not only in games, but in practice and especially in the meeting rooms. Walsh was as cerebral a coach as you'd ever find, and Reynolds was as meticulous with his game preparation as any player in the league.

With a bunch of newly drafted players like Lott, Williamson, and Wright, as well as second-year linebacker Keena Turner, Walsh wanted someone who could teach his younger players about the meticulousness of football, and how studying even the most minute tendency on film could make a difference on game day.

"Hacksaw Reynolds taught them how to focus," said Frank Cooney, the veteran San Francisco Examiner 49ers beat reporter and columnist. "He'd show up at four thirty in the morning, and he'd have a box full of sharpened pencils. He'd take out a yellow pad and work until everyone else showed up."

"He was overprepared," said Ira Miller, the longtime San Francisco Chronicle 49ers beat reporter and columnist. "Hacksaw used to have a million pencils, and he'd have them sharpened and be ready. When Lott was a rookie, he didn't have any pencils, and he asked Hacksaw for one, and Hacksaw wouldn't give it to him. He said, 'Bring your own.'"

Hacksaw was a unique character who brought with him a colorful history. How he got his nickname really told you all you needed to know about how distinctive an individual he was, and how his intensity was so infectious around any football team he played for.

When he was a senior at the University of Tennessee in 1969, the Volunteers had already clinched the Southeastern Conference title but had one last game against the University of Mississippi ("Ole Miss"). A win, and the Vols would go to the Sugar Bowl.

The year before, Tennessee had walloped Ole Miss, 31–0, so there was an unquestionable feeling of overconfidence. Archie Manning led the Rebels to a 38–0 annihilation of Tennessee, and Reynolds was incensed.

"I played a good game, but was really upset at the outcome," he said years later. "We had an old car—a '53 Chevrolet with no motor—on top of a bluff at the school. We used to push it around with a guy's Jeep and practice driving into things, like a demolition derby. When I got back to school, I decided to cut that old Chevy in half and make a trailer for a new Jeep I had just purchased. It was a good outlet for my frustrations.

"I went to Kmart and bought the cheapest hacksaw they had, along with thirteen replacement blades," he said. "I cut through the entire frame and driveshaft, all the way through the car. I started on Sunday and finished Monday afternoon. It took me eight total hours. I broke all thirteen blades. When I finished, I got one guy from the dorm, Ray Nettles, to witness it. The next day we took the rest of our friends from the dorm up the hill to see it, and when we got there both halves of the car were gone, with just the thirteen broken blades lying on the ground. To this day, I don't know what happened to that car."

And so was born one of the greatest sports nicknames of all time.

Walsh was delighted to be able to get a player of Reynolds's caliber.

"Any time you can get a player the quality of Jack Reynolds, you find a way to do it, and defense has been one of our problems," he said after signing Reynolds. "Football is played two ways—when you have the ball and when the other team has the ball—and you have to be prepared in each instance. The days when an NFL team could rely on eight or nine good defensive players and be competitive are gone. Now you need at least eighteen to have a chance. Even with a first-round draft pick, we couldn't have found anyone with Jack's credentials."

Walsh would later take advantage of a contract impasse involving another veteran defensive player, and his midseason trade for Chargers pass rusher Fred Dean would be instrumental in taking his defense to another level—especially after the struggles on that side of the ball the previous two years.

"I think things really started coming together on the defensive side of the ball," said Keena Turner, a second-round pick of the Dolphins in

1980 out of Purdue. Walsh traded for Turner on draft day, yet another move that would turn out to be a stroke of genius in the ensuing years. "We had that draft with Ronnie Lott, Carlton [Williamson], Eric [Wright], and then [the trade for] Fred Dean. I think it showed some of the possibilities we had."

Turner said his defensive teammates who had been with the team the year before were mindful of Walsh's anger and disappointment, especially during the eight-game losing streak.

"You lose eight in a row, and everybody's looking around and wondering," Turner said. "I was still trying to understand it all, being a rookie, but he put the fear of God in me somewhere in that losing streak. He called me and a couple of guys in. We were just special teams contributors, but the next week, one of the guys got cut in the meeting."

As much as Walsh had hoped there'd be a carryover from the team's resurgence near the end of the 1980 season, they got off to an inauspicious start, losing two of their first three games and continuing to struggle to capture the imagination of 49ers fans.

They drew only 49,520 fans to the home opener against the Bears—a game they won, 28–17—but sandwiched around that were road losses to the Lions at the Pontiac Silverdome and the Falcons at Atlanta–Fulton County Stadium.

Poor attendance at Candlestick Park had really bothered Walsh, especially after he'd gotten the job in 1979. Even with a long history in the NFL, this wasn't a franchise like the Giants or Bears that drew big crowds regardless of the team's record. Walsh had even organized an event at Candlestick his first year with the team in an effort to drive up season ticket sales. The 49ers barely sold any tickets at the event, leaving Walsh dejected. But he also realized there really was only one way to bring people back to Candlestick.

He had to win. And just eight wins in his first two seasons simply wasn't enough.

Walsh felt much better about his roster entering the 1981 season, and with Montana back for a third season and now fully ensconced as the starter, and a defense that finally had some players with enough talent to at least be competitive, there was a legitimate feeling of optimism heading into training camp.

The team had moved its summer practice facility from Santa Clara University to Sierra College in Rocklin, California, a little more than twenty miles outside of Sacramento, where Walsh could take advantage of the remote setting to have his players bond and practice in some brutally hot conditions. Walsh liked the Spartan conditions and the fact that he could have the team's complete attention as he got them ready for the regular season.

Linebacker Dan Bunz, the 49ers' first-round draft pick in 1978, had suggested Walsh look into the Rocklin campus. Bunz grew up in nearby Roseville, California, so he knew the area well and figured it would suit Walsh's needs. Walsh and his trusted assistant, John McVay, toured the area and liked it—although Bunz wasn't exactly a popular player for recommending the move inland. The place seemed like it was in the middle of nowhere, and it was desert hot during the daylight hours.

But it was perfect for Walsh. For three weeks, he could mold his team the way he wanted, and have his players drilled in the fundamentals of his system.

"That first year in Rocklin, there were like ten days of 105-degree temperatures, and Bill had them in two-a-days," Cooney said. "It was brutal, but Bill liked it.

"There were times in those two-a-days when it was brutally hot, and the players were dogging it—as they should have been, because it was so damn hot," Cooney said. "But Bill knew better than to yell at the players. He'd yell at a couple of reporters. You'd be there talking on the sidelines, and he'd yell over, 'Hey, you know, we're trying to work here! What are you guys talking about, where you're going out tonight?!' Bill just wanted everyone's attention. Instead of screaming at the players, he'd scream at somebody else."

Walsh came out of the camp feeling reasonably confident that he had at least the semblance of a good team, surely a better one than the previous two seasons. How good? He just wasn't sure. And by the third week of the season, the doubts had begun to resurface after he lost two of his first three games.

But they righted themselves with a home win over the Saints and then routed Gibbs's Redskins at RFK Stadium. The win in Washington was about as complete a game as the 49ers had played under Walsh, and it left Gibbs at 0-5 and wondering if he'd be fired.

"Everything in the world went wrong in that game," Gibbs said. "I can still see [running back] Terry Metcalf fumble the ball straight in the air. It was a nightmare."

For Walsh, though, it was a breakthrough.

The 49ers built a 30–3 lead after three quarters, and even though Montana had an ordinary day passing (193 yards, no touchdown passes, and an interception), the offense was efficient and the defense, now featuring a major upgrade after a sweeping off-season injection of talent, was superb.

The Redskins scored two meaningless touchdowns in the fourth quarter and, like Walsh the year before at halftime of the home game against the Saints, Gibbs left the field to boos. Walsh even walked over to the Redskins' locker room and briefly met with Gibbs to offer some encouragement.

Walsh had been in Gibbs's shoes before, having struggled badly his first year. In fact, record-wise, it was even worse than Gibbs's start; the 49ers had gone 0-7 in 1979 before Walsh got his first career win. But while Gibbs was still trying to gain his footing with the Redskins, Walsh's system was finally showing meaningful signs of success. The win at RFK was his third in four games and put the 49ers at 3-2 heading into a game against the Cowboys that would be a more definitive barometer for whether or not the results were indicative of true improvement.

For Walsh, 49ers-Cowboys at Candlestick Park on October 11, 1981, would provide an important moment of truth.

The Cowboys were still considered an NFL dynasty, with legendary coach Tom Landry having won two Super Bowls in the 1970s and reaching three others. Landry's team beat Denver in Super Bowl XII after the 1977 season and was beaten by Pittsburgh the following year. Even though the Cowboys hadn't been back to the title game since then, and even though Roger Staubach had retired and been replaced by Danny White, Tony Dorsett was still in his prime, Landry's "Flex Defense" was still in vogue, and the mystique about "America's Team" was still in full bloom.

Walsh, meanwhile, was still trying to establish his team and his system. He felt certain his players were grasping his methods and had warmed to his unique style, which stressed intellect as much as—or even more than—sheer power, but he still needed to know how he stacked up against a team with the kind of institutional success and reputation the Cowboys had at that time.

The Cowboys came into the game with a 4-1 record and were five-point favorites, and America's Team would prove to be a big draw in San Francisco. In fact, the crowd of 57,574 would be the largest yet to see Walsh's team. By comparison, just 37,476 showed for the previous year's regular-season finale at home against the Bills.

It was a typically crisp autumn afternoon at Candlestick, with a game-time temperature of 58 degrees and sustained winds at 18 miles per hour, gusting to 36. Optimal conditions for Walsh to operate his ball-control offense and a perfect chance to test whether his approach—particularly his use of a play-call script of between fifteen and twenty-five plays at the start of the game—would work against a defense that included the likes of renowned defensive linemen Randy White, Ed "Too Tall" Jones, and Harvey Martin; middle linebacker Bob Breunig; safety Charlie Waters; and a promising young cornerback out of Grambling State named Everson Walls, who already had four interceptions in his first five games.

Walsh's idea of using scripted plays early in a game was something he'd come up with during his days with the Bengals under Paul Brown. Walsh had taken to the idea of planning out the first four plays for the Bengals' first series, in part to answer Brown's inevitable pregame question, "What have you got for openers, Bill?"

Walsh never really took it beyond the first series, but something happened during what turned out to be his final game under Brown that changed his thinking forever. The Bengals had put together an exceptional 1975 regular season, going 11-3 to finish second to the 12-2 Steelers in the AFC Central. They qualified for the wild card round of the playoffs and faced the Raiders in Oakland.

By then, John Madden—the man who had taken Walsh's office when he left the Raiders after just one season as an assistant coach to take over as head coach of the minor-league San Jose Apaches—had become the Raiders' head coach and was in the midst of a highly successful run that would eventually result in a Super Bowl championship. It was a raucous atmosphere at Oakland–Alameda County Coliseum, and the game itself was exhilarating. The Raiders had built a 31–14 lead in the fourth quarter, but Bengals quarterback Ken Anderson, who had blossomed under Walsh's tutelage, rallied Cincinnati for two touchdowns to make it 31–28 in the final minutes.

There was still another chance for the Bengals to drive for a field goal and send the game into overtime, but Walsh couldn't come up with the right calls, and the comeback failed.

Walsh choked.

"My job was to figure out how to get us within range of a field-goal attempt quickly," he wrote in *The Score Takes Care of Itself.* "Unfortunately, the severe pressure and absolute pandemonium—thousands of Oakland's fans howling and throwing half-eaten hot dogs, half-empty cups of beer, crumpled-up game programs, and even clothes and shoes up at the booth where I was sitting—destroyed my thinking...I completely forgot the plays we had practiced that would have worked best under those circumstances."

Afterward, Walsh made a promise to himself: "Never again will that happen to me."

He took that vow with him wherever he went, and built upon it during his time with the Chargers, then at Stanford, and finally with the 49ers. Even though the epiphany in Oakland occurred at the end of the game, Walsh understood the importance of creating the right mind-set for dealing with chaotic situations, regardless of when they occurred. Scripting the first several plays at the beginning of a game was a way for him to relax and settle into the game while also probing the opponent's plan of defending those plays and getting ideas for what would work later in games.

His players had never previously been exposed to a coach who scripted any plays, and after a brief adjustment period, they came to love the idea.

"It started out as the first ten plays, then the first fifteen plays, and it would go from there," center Randy Cross said. "He would write them out, put them on a list, and back in those days, we'd use an overhead projector and then go down the list. You weren't going to call those plays verbatim, because you couldn't anticipate third and short or, say, fourth and one. But it gave you an idea of what Bill was thinking. Without saying, 'Here's the game plan,' it was, 'Here's the game plan.'"

Walsh was anxious to see if his script would work in the biggest game of his career so far.

It didn't take long for the answer to reveal itself.

Walsh's script worked better than he could have imagined, and the 49ers absolutely demolished the Cowboys, 45–14. The Niners took a 21–0 lead in the first quarter on a touchdown pass from Montana to Freddie Solomon and scoring runs by Paul Hofer and Johnny Davis. The lead swelled to 31–7 on a 78-yard touchdown pass to Clark, and Walsh's team went on to finish off the biggest win at Candlestick Park in years.

Montana finished with 279 yards and two touchdown passes. The defense intercepted White twice and held Dorsett to just 21 yards on 9 carries. White was atrocious, completing just 8 of 16 passes for 60 yards and 2 interceptions.

"We ate humble pie," Dorsett said a few minutes after the game.

"There's nothing I can say about this game," Landry told reporters. "I would talk all day, I couldn't change a thing. The loss was a combination of everything. Our offense played badly, our defense, our kicking, even our coaching, I guess. We played terrible. I can't explain it."

Walsh was delighted.

"We tried to prove to doubters that we had a competitive team," he said, a dig at some writers who had questioned his team's worthiness in previous weeks. "This win is gratifying for us, because we had everything going our way for a change. It hasn't been that way for us in recent years."

Offering yet another dose of his passive-aggressive commentary, Walsh said, "We've been playing well, despite what you read in the press. The key is maturing."

"We were definitely starting to feel good about where we were heading," Montana said. "We were used to what Bill was about, and I think the fact that we had a defense was a big thing. You can't win games if you don't stop people, and the additions that we made, especially in the secondary, were important. Once you started winning, it became a habit. We started believing that we had a good team."

Walsh had never put a timetable on winning a championship, relying instead on preaching every aspect of his Standard of Performance that he demanded from each and every member of the organization— from the coaches, to the players, to the training staff, the scouting staff, the front office, the clerical staff, even the owner.

"You could see that the players were different as time went along," DeBartolo said. "When Bill came to us in 1979, you could see what he wanted to do, what players he wanted to draft and bring in. He liked very intelligent players, players who could make decisions on the field. So once we got enough of those players, things started to turn around."

The win in Washington, followed by the destruction of the Cowboys at home the following week, proved to be a springboard for the team, and the 49ers stayed on a roll. They beat the Packers on the road and the Rams at home to improve to 6-2 heading into another showcase game against the mighty Steelers, who were less than two years removed from winning their fourth Super Bowl title in six seasons.

Montana was playing near his childhood home of Monongahela, a coal-mining town about twenty-five miles south of Pittsburgh and the place where he starred at Ringgold High School and drew national attention for his all-around athletic skills. Montana was not only a terrific football player, he loved baseball and basketball as well, even calling basketball his favorite sport. In fact, during the college recruiting process, he was offered a basketball scholarship to North Carolina State, and he seriously considered going there to play both basketball and football. In the end, he went to Notre Dame, following in the footsteps of his childhood idol, Terry Hanratty, and going on to a fine career with the Fighting Irish, capped off by that legendary comeback performance in the Cotton Bowl.

While Montana's performance against the Steelers at Three Rivers Stadium wasn't one of his best games, there was some late-game magic nevertheless. After throwing two interceptions, Montana led what turned out to be the game-winning drive, taking the Niners 43 yards in nine plays to grab a 17–14 lead that ended up being the final score.

Walsh seemed nearly as thrilled after this game as he was after the blowout win at home against the Cowboys, and he paid tribute to Montana for coming through despite not playing particularly well for most of the game.

"He's a tremendously resourceful quarterback," Walsh said after the game. "When he makes a mistake, he doesn't get too upset. He played brilliantly."

Walsh said this despite having watched Montana throw an interception that was returned for a 50-yard touchdown by Mel Blount and another to Jack Lambert that set up another Steelers score.

"That shows the maturity of this team," Montana said afterward. "It's a young team, but nobody let down. We were moving the ball. I think we just felt that sooner or later we were going to get it in the end zone."

Montana's numbers the rest of the season were ordinary, sometimes even poor, as he went three straight games without a touchdown pass and had just 5 touchdowns and 4 interceptions over his last six regular-season games. But with a defense that had gotten better as the season went on, and with a reliable running game in which Walsh used a running-back-by-committee approach, the 49ers found ways to beat everyone but the Browns to finish out the season at 13-3 and win the NFC West for the first time since 1972.

Walsh wouldn't tell this to his players at the time, lest they lose the edge they'd developed over the course of the season, but he privately adored this group and couldn't get over how good they'd become.

"He loved that team so much," Geri Walsh said. "He would come home and say, 'Geri, they don't know how good they are.' I always wanted to have a lunch for that 1981 team, and I will eventually have a cake, a big, decadent chocolate cake that says, 'You guys never knew how good you were—Bill Walsh.' They were his guys. They turned that whole thing around."

Walsh had become even more motivated to get the most out of his team, especially as the players responded to his every move. The coach's resourcefulness could especially be found in how he succeeded with an undistinguished stable of running backs that included Ricky Patton, Earl Cooper, Johnny Davis, Walt Easley, and Paul Hofer. Patton led the team with just 543 rushing yards, while Cooper, who played fullback, had 330 yards. Davis was next with 297, followed by Easley with 224 and Hofer with 193. But Walsh used all his backs in the short passing game, with Patton, Cooper, and Hofer combining for 105 catches for 916 yards and a touchdown.

Hofer was one of Walsh's favorite players, one of the few holdovers from before the coach arrived in San Francisco. Hofer was one of those overachieving players that any football coach would love, an eleventh-round pick out of the University of Mississippi in 1976 who once was told by general manager Joe Thomas he didn't have what it took to play in the NFL. But Hofer proved Thomas wrong, became a fan favorite with his hard-nosed style, and impressed Walsh from the start. The coach loved his versatility as a runner and pass catcher—the perfect combination for Walsh's offense—and he also loved Hofer's grit.

Hofer became an even bigger sentimental favorite when he came back from a devastating knee injury that ended his 1980 season. Determined to play the following season, he made it onto the 1981 roster and was used in spot duty by Walsh. But Hofer never made it to the playoffs; he reinjured the knee in the next-to-last game against the Houston Oilers, ending his career just as the 49ers were about to begin the playoffs.

It was a bitter disappointment for Hofer (who eventually sued the team's medical staff for failing to properly treat his knee injury) and Walsh was saddened to see his overachieving running back unable to participate in the team's first playoff berth in nearly a decade. But Walsh knew he had to deal with the ugly reality of injuries, and he pressed forward with a team that now had the opportunity to follow up one of the greatest regular seasons in franchise history with a meaningful playoff run.

By virtue of a 13-3 record, the 49ers had earned a coveted bye week in the first round of the playoffs, giving Walsh's players a much-needed breather and allowing the coaching staff extra time to study the upcoming opponent. As it turned out, another team that underwent an important transformation under a new coach in 1979—the Giants under Ray Perkins—would face the 49ers at Candlestick Park in the divisional round of the NFC playoffs.

The Giants had gone 9-7 in the regular season to reach the postseason for the first time since 1963, a playoff drought that had haunted the once-proud franchise that had endured some of its darkest moments, culminating with The Fumble in 1978. General manager George Young, who had turned down Walsh's offer to be the 49ers' GM, had done an excellent job rebuilding the team.

Like Walsh, Perkins spent his first two years trying to instill the kind of order and discipline required of a playoff team, but by Year 3, the Giants had turned the corner. Simms, the quarterback Walsh had thought so highly of when he was looking for a passer in 1979, had established himself as a capable starter that year. But he suffered a separated shoulder in Week 10, and backup Scott Brunner went 4-2 in relief to get the Giants into the playoffs.

Walsh wasn't concerned so much with the Giants' offense as he was the defense. And one player in particular on that defense: rookie outside linebacker Lawrence Taylor. The number 2 pick out of North Carolina in 1981, Taylor had immediate success as a rookie, thriving under defensive coordinator Bill Parcells. Taylor was the perfect player for Parcells's 3-4 defense, a versatile player who was strong enough to handle the run, and fast enough to rush the passer.

And oh, how he could rush the passer.

Taylor showed early on he was a generational player. His ability to wreak havoc from the outside was extraordinary, and Parcells's use of him was brilliant. Where most traditional defenses had relied on the defensive end position—particularly the right defensive end—to take up most pass rushing responsibilities, Parcells's system revolved around Taylor's ability to create pressure from the outside, where he could go one-on-one against the opposing team's left tackle and use his athleticism against the bigger, slower linemen.

Taylor had revolutionized defenses with his speed and power, and had nine and a half sacks as a rookie, based on film review (sacks didn't become an official stat until 1982). He was not only voted the

NFL's Defensive Rookie of the Year, but he was the league's Defensive *Player* of the Year, too.

Walsh was thus consumed with finding a way to stop Taylor, and he knew it would require some out-of-the-box thinking. Dan Audick was the 49ers' left tackle, and while he had done a commendable job of protecting Montana's blind side during the season, Walsh was concerned he'd have problems dealing with Taylor. Walsh felt the better matchup was to put left guard John Ayers on him. Ayers had a low center of gravity and couldn't be easily knocked back by Taylor. Still, this was a highly unconventional move, having a guard essentially shadow a linebacker.

In the end, though, it proved to be yet another stroke of genius from the coach, because Taylor was hardly a factor during the game. Montana was sacked just once, and the 49ers won going away. They built a 24–7 lead by the second quarter, increased it to 38–17 after Ronnie Lott's interception return for a touchdown in the fourth quarter, and walked off the field with a 38–24 win in Walsh's first playoff game as a head coach.

Up next: a rematch against the Cowboys, who couldn't wait to get back at the 49ers after that embarrassing 45–14 regular-season loss three months earlier.

No excuses this time for the Cowboys. If they hadn't taken the 49ers seriously during the regular season, they surely would now.

As the teams prepared to face each other, Cowboys personnel director Gil Brandt couldn't help but wonder what the game might look like with Montana in a Cowboys jersey. Brandt flashed back to the 1979 draft, when the Cowboys were seriously considering taking Montana in the third round.

When it was the Cowboys' turn to pick, Brandt was ready to make the call—but Landry talked him out of it.

"We never deviated from our draft board," Brandt said. "When it came to the third round, our next guy on the board was Montana, and Coach Landry says, 'Well, you can draft him, obviously, but I'm afraid that I will probably just cut him at the end of training camp.'"

The Cowboys wound up selecting Santa Clara tight end Doug Cosbie.

"It was the only time we jumped somebody on our board," Brandt said.

It came down to a numbers game for the Cowboys, who already had Roger Staubach, as well as backups Randy White and Glenn Carano, a second-round pick out of the University of Nevada, Las Vegas in 1977.

"Our feeling was, we've got three veteran quarterbacks now, and we're not going to carry four," Brandt said. "All we're going to do is take this guy and cut him and let someone else pick him up."

Former Cowboys public relations man Greg Aiello, who was in his first year with the team and was in the draft room, remembered something else Landry said when the subject of Montana came up: "We already have three guys better than him."

Aiello was taken aback at hearing Landry's assessment; after all, the first-year PR official was a Notre Dame alum who was quite familiar with Montana's legacy with the Fighting Irish.

As it turned out, Montana's first year in the NFL was Staubach's last, and the Cowboys transitioned to White, a third-round pick in 1974 who played two years with the World Football League's Memphis Southmen before joining the Cowboys in 1976.

White led the Cowboys to a 12-4 record in his first season as a starter in 1980, eventually losing to the Eagles in the NFC Championship Game, and he got Dallas back to the playoffs with the same record in 1981. White was certainly no Staubach, but he'd done solid work in replacing the legendary quarterback, and here was another chance to get to the Super Bowl.

This time, though, he'd have to do it against a defense that had come together under the watchful eye of defensive coordinator Chuck Studley, who was able to orchestrate a unit that had finally become elite with all the personnel moves made during the off-season, in the draft, and with the midseason trade for defensive end Fred Dean.

The week didn't start out well for the 49ers and Walsh. Torrential rains had pelted the Bay Area for several days, and the fields at the team's Redwood City training facility were simply unusable.

Walsh and McVay arranged for the team to move its entire operation to the Rams' training facility in Anaheim, and the team spent the week in southern California preparing for one of the biggest games in franchise history, and certainly the biggest in Walsh's career.

At the game's outset, things seemed fine. With his play script in hand, Walsh's calls on the 49ers' first drive were perfect. Montana hit Charlie Young on a 17-yard completion, and later found Lenvil Elliott on a 24-yard pass. And he finished the drive with an eight-yard touchdown pass to Freddie Solomon to put the 49ers up, 7–0.

But uncharacteristic turnovers began to plague Walsh's team. Bill Ring, that overachieving running back Walsh once picked out of a group of tryouts and told McVay to sign immediately, lost a fumble at the 49ers' 29-yard line. That set up Danny White's 26-yard touchdown pass to Tony Hill to put the Cowboys in front, 10–7.

Montana had a chance to retake the lead in the second quarter, driving the 49ers to the Cowboys' 27. But he was picked off near the right sideline by Everson Walls, the come-from-out-of-nowhere rookie who made the team as a free agent and intercepted 11 passes in the regular season. Montana, who somehow survived a pass rush that had collapsed the pocket, threw a 20-yard touchdown pass to Clark to make it 14–10. But the Cowboys came back on their next drive to retake the lead, 17–14. White had been intercepted by Lott on what appeared to be a perfectly legal play, but Lott was flagged for pass interference, and this allowed the Cowboys to retain possession. Tony Dorsett finished off the 80-yard drive by taking a pitch from White and running 5 yards around left end for the score.

The back-and-forth continued in the third quarter, as the 49ers drove to the Cowboys' 16. But another turnover ruined the scoring chance, as Montana's pass to Elliott went off the running back's hands and was picked off by All-Pro defensive tackle Randy White.

Dallas came on strong in the fourth quarter with Rafael Septien's 22-yard field goal and White's 21-yard touchdown pass to Doug Cosbie that gave the Cowboys a 27–21 lead. And then came another turnover from Montana, who was intercepted again by Walls, this time at the Dallas 27.

Still, there would be one more chance to go ahead, one more chance for Montana to work some late-game magic. After a Cowboys punt put the 49ers at their own 11 with 4:54 left in regulation, Montana—and Walsh—went to work.

Walsh was at his intellectual best in figuring out a plan that would work against the Dallas defense in a must-score situation. Using a mix of runs and short passes that had become a staple of his offense, Walsh called about as good a series as there could be.

With Elliott grinding out 30 yards on the ground and Montana throwing darts to Solomon and Clark, the 49ers got to the Dallas 13 with 1:15 left. Walsh decided to go for it on first down, having Montana throw to Solomon in the end zone.

Not good.

"I threw it way over his head," Montana said.

Walsh called a sweep left for Elliott, and the blocking was excellent, allowing him to get to the 6 with fifty-eight seconds left. Montana called time-out and went to the sidelines to talk things over with Walsh. The 49ers obviously needed a touchdown to win it, but Walsh wanted to leave as little time as possible on the clock for the Cowboys in the event that San Francisco got into the end zone. So while a touchdown on the next play would give the 49ers the lead, it would also give Dallas another chance to win it with either a touchdown or a field goal.

"We're going to call a Sprint Option pass," Walsh told his quarterback. "[Solomon] is going to break up and break into the corner. You got it? Dwight will clear."

"Okay," Montana said.

"As soon as you see the angle he's breaking, then just drop the ball up there. If you don't get what you want, simply throw the ball away. You know what I mean?" Walsh said.

"Okay," Montana replied.

"Hold it, hold it, not there, away it goes," Walsh said.

"Okay."

"Be ready to go to Dwight. You got it?"

"Okay," Montana said again.

In his head, Montana wasn't convinced the play would work.

"Both Dwight and I thought Bill was crazy," Montana says now of Walsh's decision. "We'd practiced that play for the first time in training camp."

The play is designed to go to Solomon, who lines up to the right of the formation, slightly off the line of scrimmage. Clark lines up outside of Solomon, with his primary responsibility to set a pick for Solomon to get him open past the first-down marker, or possibly into the end zone.

"Joe comes in the huddle and says, 'We're going to run Sprint Option. Freddie, I'm looking for you,'" Clark said. "And then he says to me as the huddle breaks, 'Be ready if I have to come to you.'"

Montana calls for the snap from Cross, but the play quickly falls apart because Solomon slips shortly after he breaks from the line. Clark therefore can't properly set the pick, so he quickly adjusts his route and runs to his left and into the end zone. By this time, Solomon has his footing and continues his route, which takes him close to the goal line near the right sideline.

Montana, meanwhile, rolls to his right and surveys the field, hoping he can find either Solomon or Clark. Montana nears the right sideline, and with three Cowboys defenders bearing down on him, Clark gets to the back of the end zone and quickly makes a U-turn, then heads right with Walls shadowing him the entire way. Montana spots Clark and intuitively knows that the receiver will continue running toward the right corner of the end zone. There's the throw... it's high... so, so high... looking like it will sail over Clark's head and then...

Clark leaps skyward and gets both hands on the ball, momentarily batting it in the air, and then comes down with it.

Or, as it has since come to be known, "The Catch."

The stadium explodes in celebration as the 49ers tie it, and Ray Wersching's extra point gives the 49ers the lead—the sixth lead change of the game.

Montana couldn't see Clark make the most famous catch in franchise history; by the time Clark reached up and grabbed it, the quarterback was on the ground. But he did see Clark's feet come down in the end zone. And, of course, the crowd reaction told him all he needed to know.

DeBartolo never saw The Catch, either.

The man who set in motion the chain of events that would ultimately lead to this moment, the man whose gut instinct told him that Bill Walsh would be the right coach to lead the 49ers out of the abyss and into contention for a Super Bowl run, was blocked from seeing the play.

"I was in the press box near the end of the game, so John McVay and I went down to the field because I didn't know what was going to happen," said DeBartolo, who had to maneuver his way around dozens of people near the sidelines as well as the mounted police who were ready to guard the field after the game. "So we're standing in front of the [San Francisco Giants'] dugout and all I could hear was this gigantic horse next to us. McVay is looking around the side of the horse, and all of a sudden, I hear the screams grow and the policeman looked down and says, 'Dwight Clark just caught a touchdown pass,' and here I am behind a horse's ass."

DeBartolo immediately understood the significance of that moment, and everything that would happen afterward would only underscore his belief.

"That was the beginning of the Bill Walsh mystique and his era," DeBartolo said.

Brandt, the Cowboys' longtime personnel director who had assembled the teams that had produced so many memorable moments over the previous decade, stood in disbelief over what had just happened. Montana, the quarterback the Cowboys had given serious thought to drafting nearly three years earlier, had just orchestrated a comeback that prevented the Cowboys from getting to a sixth Super Bowl.

Brandt remained convinced years later that Montana never intended to complete the pass to Clark.

"I recall that game like it was yesterday," Brandt said, "and I still to this day think Montana was trying to throw the ball away, and Walls had probably the best coverage he had on anybody. Clark just jumped out of the sky."

No, Montana insisted, he was trying to complete the pass.

"I thought it was an arm's length above Dwight's head," Montana said. "I needed to put it in a spot where only he could catch it."

Walsh thought the pass was too high. In fact, a moment after he saw Montana make the throw, he began thinking about what he'd call on fourth down.

Then he heard the crowd, looked at Clark, and realized it wouldn't be necessary.

"Joe knew Dwight would be there on the end line," Walsh told Dennis Georgatos years later in the book *Game of My Life San Francisco 49ers: Memorable Stories of 49ers Football*, "but to find him and throw the ball under that pressure, and to throw it where only Dwight could get it, that was probably Joe's greatest play ever."

Walsh may have unwittingly contributed to the play's nearly impossible degree of difficulty, and acknowledged one simple adjustment in his thinking might have made this a much less challenging throw and catch.

"I thought the play would develop differently, because I was stupid enough to think we could block those guys and Joe would have a chance to run or pass," Walsh told Georgatos. "[The Cowboys] knew that formation. We had used it before and they knew it was coming. My mistake was not changing the formation somewhat so they didn't recognize what was about to happen."

The one change he should have made was something he'd learned years ago in Cincinnati, the time tight end Bob Trumpy lined up on the wrong side of the formation and quickly hustled to the other side.

A similar adjustment against the Cowboys, and maybe Montana would have had a much easier time with this play.

"I probably should have used a man in motion," Walsh said, "but I just used the slot formation."

Things worked out just fine, though, and the artfulness of Montana avoiding the rush and somehow finding Clark turned it into one of the NFL's iconic plays and easily the most transformative moment in 49ers history.

But even after The Catch, the game wasn't over, and Walsh had to sweat through some tense moments.

Because the 49ers had scored instead of bleeding the clock, the Cowboys had nearly a minute to drive for a potential game-winning field goal. And it looked as if they'd do just that when White hit Drew Pearson on a post route over the middle.

"Coach Landry called a deep turn-in route to me," Pearson recalled. "When I did catch the ball, [Carlton] Williamson and [Lott] kind of collided with each other. I thought I was gone."

Pearson had only one man to beat and he was headed for the end zone for what almost certainly would have been the game-winning score. But out of nowhere, Eric Wright came up from behind and grabbed the back of Pearson's shoulder pads and tackled him with one hand at the 49ers' 44-yard line.

On the next play, White dropped back to pass and was about to make a throw before deciding better of it. But as he attempted to bring the ball back to his chest, he was hit and fumbled.

Game over.

The 49ers had conquered the Cowboys yet again.

Walsh had beaten Landry yet again, only this time with a Super Bowl berth on the line.

Guts and genius were on full display on a cool January afternoon at Candlestick Park, where Walsh had planted the flag of his own legacy and put his team within sixty minutes of winning the Lombardi Trophy for the first time in franchise history.

"It was a classic game, I'll say that, and overcoming Dallas that day was huge, huge for our franchise," Walsh said. "Joe's throw and Dwight's catch continued our momentum to our first Super Bowl."

It wasn't just The Catch that Walsh remembered. It was the very foundation he had set from Day 1 with his deep-seated belief in the meticulous plan he had created for success, his Standard of Performance, which was compiled over a lifetime of experience, of trial and error on the football field and in life. Most fans will remember The Catch as the salient moment of that game, but Walsh remembered the totality of purpose that got them to the brink of a championship.

"It was our coaches, players, and team as a whole coming together in the crucible of a pressure game that was central to the ascendancy of the 49ers," he said. "That was the breakthrough for us."

A little more than a year after breaking down on the flight home from Miami after losing to Don Shula's Dolphins, three years after agreeing to become DeBartolo's head coach and being tasked with the job of resurrecting one of the NFL's most moribund franchises, and six years after Paul Brown delivered the soul-crushing news that he would not get his dream job as head coach of the Bengals, Walsh had made it to the Super Bowl.

He would face the team and the coaching icon that had shunned him: Paul Brown's Bengals. There couldn't have been a more symbolic team—and man—to face.

Walsh had already gotten a taste of facing his former team in the regular season, when the 49ers ended the Bengals' five-game winning streak in a

21–3 win at Riverfront Stadium on December 6. The Niners had their way that afternoon, dominating the Bengals with a strong defensive effort and knocking quarterback Ken Anderson out of the game with a toe injury. Anderson had been Walsh's prized pupil when they worked together in Cincinnati from 1971 until Walsh's resignation after the 1975 season.

Even after Walsh left, Anderson continued to flourish, and had his best year in 1981 with career highs in passing yards (3,754) and touchdown passes (29). His coach that year was Forrest Gregg, the Packers' Hall of Fame offensive lineman who had won five championships with Green Bay and then another with the Cowboys.

Until Gregg's arrival in 1980, Brown had had miserable luck with his coaching selections. Passing over Walsh for Johnson was his first mistake, and Johnson didn't even last three seasons. He was a combined 18-10 over his first two years, but lost five straight games to start the 1978 season and agreed to step down. Brown named Homer Rice to take over, but after going 4-7 to finish out his first year, Rice went 4-12 a year later and was fired.

Gregg proved a competent sideline presence and guided the Bengals to a 12-4 record in 1981 and got Cincinnati to the Super Bowl after beating the Chargers, 27-7, in the AFC Championship Game—nicknamed the Freezer Bowl—in brutally cold conditions at Riverfront Stadium. With temperatures dipping to nine below zero and a wind chill of fifty-nine below, the Bengals outlasted Dan Fouts's Chargers to reach their first-ever Super Bowl.

Here was the ultimate chance for payback, a chance for Walsh to beat the man who had given up on him.

Outwardly, though, Walsh showed no ill will toward the Bengals once he knew Cincinnati would be his opponent in the Super Bowl.

"It was a great experience for me to be with the Bengal organization for eight years," Walsh told *New York Times* columnist Dave Anderson. "I wouldn't be where I am now if not for the many lessons I learned in Paul Brown's organization...Working eight years for the Bengals helped put me here. Some coaches change jobs so often all they learn are the names of the players and they're gone. But over eight years in the same system, you learn to refine your ability as a teacher, a technician, and a practitioner."

Walsh acknowledged to Anderson he "had aspirations for the Bengal job, I had hopes. But there was no bitterness toward Tiger Johnson, who was a very competent coach and a very good friend of mine. No bitterness on my part at all, only vast disappointment."

Walsh also told Anderson that Brown's decision to anoint Johnson instead had ruined his chance to become the Jets' head coach. "What hurt my chances for the Jets job, I believe, was the Jets figuring how could I be a very good head coach if Paul Brown has passed me over when he needed a head coach."

Deep down, Walsh was fueled by his anger at Brown, but he had to be careful not to let his personal feelings overpower him in the Super Bowl. Having gotten this far, Walsh knew he needed a solid game plan.

"Everything Bill did was with a purpose," John McVay said. "He didn't leave any stone unturned, whether it had to do with strategy, or getting a special teams player to get his technique just right, or how the team approached a game psychologically."

Psychology was particularly important to Walsh heading into this game, and he wanted to make sure his team wouldn't be overwhelmed by the magnitude of Super Bowl XVI. What he did at the start of Super Bowl week in Detroit was a terrific icebreaker. After the team arrived, Walsh walked into the team's downtown hotel and arranged to borrow a bellman's uniform. What happened next absolutely stunned—and then absolutely cracked up—his players.

There was Walsh, greeting his players, including Montana, as they came off the bus and taking their bags, posing as a bellman—even wearing a cap.

"Bill knew how to prepare us physically, but he also knew how to prepare us mentally," Cross said. "He just had that way about him, and I can't tell you what kind of a difference that made."

After a crisp week of practice, Walsh felt good about the game plan against his old team, and was anxious to see his plan go into action. But his preparation would be tested in a way he'd never imagined in the hours before the game.

With a thick blanket of snow falling on Detroit the morning of the game, Walsh boarded the team bus several hours before kickoff. But the ride didn't go smoothly. Vice President George H. W. Bush was attending the game, and his motorcade interrupted traffic patterns around the Silverdome, even holding up the 49ers' team buses.

Walsh was clearly agitated that his and the team's pregame routine might be negatively impacted, but again, he didn't want his players to see him upset. So he had the bus driver give him the microphone to make an announcement.

"Typical Bill," Montana recalled. "We're on the bus, we're stuck, we've got like twenty-five minutes to get out onto the field, and Bill stands up and says, 'Guys, I just got a call from the locker room. I've got good news and bad news. The bad news is the game started without us. The good news is that Chico just threw a touchdown pass to Cosmo, and we're up, 7–0.'"

The players and coaches on the bus erupted in laughter as Walsh reported that the team's equipment manager, Chico Norton, had thrown a scoring strike to locker room assistant George Cosmo for the early lead.

"It was great," Montana said. "Here we are, all anxious about the game, and Bill just lightens the mood with his sense of humor. It really relaxed everybody."

Once the team did get inside the locker room, Walsh continued trying to loosen the mood, slapping players on the back, even dancing when one player had the Olivia Newton-John hit song "Physical" playing on his boom box. Walsh also engaged in a particular favorite of his pregame rituals: shadowboxing. A former Golden Gloves boxer in college, Walsh often used boxing analogies with his players, and throwing jabs before the biggest game of their lives amped up the mood and pumped up his players.

Despite the outside pressure associated with the game—which would draw a record-setting television rating of 49.1, which to this day remains the highest-rated Super Bowl ever—the 49ers and their coach were ready right from the start.

It wasn't perfect, though.

On the very first play of the game, the 49ers' kick returner Amos Lawrence fumbled on his own 26-yard line, and the Bengals threatened an early score. Ken Anderson eventually got the Bengals to the Niners' 5, but the 49ers' defense came up huge. After a first-down incompletion, Anderson was sacked by Jim Stuckey for a 6-yard loss. On third and goal, Anderson looked for wide receiver Isaac Curtis in the end zone, but safety Dwight Hicks intercepted it at the 5 and returned it to the 32.

Montana then engineered a textbook drive, which included a fake reverse flea flicker that resulted in a 14-yard pass to tight end Charlie Young at the Bengals' 33. Montana's 14-yard pass to Freddie Solomon got the ball to the 1, and Montana scored the 49ers' first-ever Super Bowl touchdown on a quarterback sneak.

The 49ers produced another turnover in the second quarter, as Eric Wright forced a Cris Collinsworth fumble at the Niners' 8. Montana then went 92 yards in 10 plays, finishing off the drive with an 11-yard touchdown pass to fullback Earl Cooper to make it 14–0. The pass to Cooper was yet another example of Walsh's genius. He hadn't called that play in two years, but the element of surprise worked perfectly against the Bengals' defense.

"We didn't know what to expect from them offensively because of Walsh, especially with two weeks to prepare for us," Bengals linebacker Reggie Williams said after the game.

The Niners went on to build a 20–0 halftime lead, the biggest halftime margin in Super Bowl history to that point.

The Bengals finally found their footing in the second half, and Walsh might have unwittingly helped make it a closer game than it had to be. With such a commanding lead, he got just a bit conservative with his play calling, even after the Bengals scored a touchdown on their opening drive of the third quarter. The 49ers were limited to just eight plays and 4 yards for the entire third quarter, while still holding a 20–7 lead.

But as the offense faltered, the defense rose up yet again after surrendering a 49-yard catch to Collinsworth that got the ball to the Niners' 14. Pete Johnson, the Bengals' bruising six-foot, 252-pound fullback, converted a critical fourth-down play to give the Bengals first and goal from the 3. A touchdown here, and it would be a one-score game at 20–14 with plenty of time remaining.

On first down, Johnson bulled into the line and got to the 1. Johnson then tried again on second down, but lost a yard. On third down, Anderson faked a handoff to Johnson and threw a swing pass to halfback Charles Alexander. But linebacker Dan Bunz made a brilliant open-field tackle of Alexander for no gain. Rather than kick a field goal on fourth and goal, Gregg decided to go for it. It was Johnson again up the middle, but Lott and Reynolds—the rookie and the veteran who had keyed the resurgence of the 49ers' defense—along with Bunz, made the tackle for no gain.

Niners' ball.

The Bengals did get to within a score, 20–14, on Anderson's fourth-quarter touchdown pass to Dan Ross, but the 49ers answered with a critical field goal drive to make it 23–14 with five minutes to go. The key play on the drive was a 22-yard pass to receiver Mike Wilson, and again, it was Walsh's forethought that created the completion. He'd noticed on film from the 49ers' regular-season game against the Bengals that a Cincinnati defender would always run stride for stride with the fleet receiver on any route more than twenty yards so he wouldn't get behind the defense. For the Super Bowl, Walsh decided to have Wilson run this particular pattern as if he was going long, but then the route would be cut off at twenty-five yards and Wilson would come back to the ball.

Eric Wright intercepted Anderson's pass on the first play of the Bengals' next drive, and Walsh then went ball-control on offense to run out the clock before Ray Wersching's fourth field goal would increase the 49ers' lead to 26–14 with less than two minutes to play. The Bengals scored once more, but by the time Anderson hit Ross on a 3-yard touchdown, there were only sixteen seconds left. The Bengals attempted an onside kick, but the 49ers recovered.

Fittingly, the man who sealed the win was none other than Dwight Clark, whose epic catch in the NFC Championship Game put the 49ers in position for their first Super Bowl. Once Clark fell on the onside kick, the 49ers had their championship.

Just over thirty-six years later, on June 4, 2018, Clark would succumb to the deadly disease ALS. Only days later, he was surrounded by many of his former teammates and DeBartolo, who said after Clark died that he "lost [his] little brother and one of [his] best friends. Clark was sixty-one, his place in 49ers' history forever remembered. His ashes are buried on DeBartolo's ranch, in the spot next to the original goalpost that stood in Candlestick Park the day he caught Montana's pass to beat the Cowboys. Inscribed on a monument at the gravesite: "The Catch: The dynasty began with you."

Walsh had beaten Brown's team and had done so with the kind of intellectual guile and bold style that had finally blossomed now that he had his chance to run his own team.

"This was one rare moment when a team without great stars and experience raises up," Walsh said after the game. "No one could take us. It was the highlight of my life. Anything can happen now."

The euphoria was intoxicating.

Walsh had persevered through so many challenging moments in his career. His methods had been criticized along the way, his out-of-the-box thinking second-guessed by more conventional coaches and owners. Yet here he was, atop the football world and celebrating the greatest moment of his career.

Walsh finally had his team, finally had his quarterback—Montana—who was selected as the game's Most Valuable Player.

"Montana will be the great quarterback of the future," Walsh said after the game. "He is one of the coolest competitors of all time, and he has just started."

Walsh and the 49ers—minus Montana, who had to remain in Detroit an extra day to be presented with the MVP award—returned to San Francisco and were feted with a parade down Market Street, although Walsh himself was reluctant to take part in the celebration. He was concerned that there wouldn't be many people out on the streets to celebrate the newly crowned champions, and that it might turn out to be embarrassing if the crowds were small.

But as the convertible he sat in alongside DeBartolo and San Francisco mayor Dianne Feinstein turned onto Market, Walsh was overwhelmed by the size of the crowd. City officials had expected about twenty-five thousand people to attend; instead, about five hundred thousand packed the sidewalks and surrounded the cars crawling up the street. People were everywhere, climbing trees and lampposts; fathers hoisted their young children atop their shoulders to get a glimpse.

Many fans couldn't even do that.

"It was the worst parade I never saw," 49ers fan John Sheridan told the *San Francisco Chronicle*. "We won the game and lost the parade."

It was a coronation that was decades in the making—both for the 49ers and for Walsh. It was glorious.

GIBBS

GOING AGAINST EVERY FIBER OF HIS BEING

Walsh wasn't the only one riding high from the 49ers' Super Bowl win. The entire league was energized by the 49ers' campaign and march to the Super Bowl, and with the NFL's popularity growing exponentially after an already dramatic increase through the late 1960s and '70s, this unbridled enthusiasm was translating into a never-before-seen financial windfall. Revenues were now into the billions of dollars, and television networks had seen a huge upswing in their own advertising revenues, with the record viewership for the Super Bowl as only the latest example.

It was therefore an ideal time to strike a new network television deal, and the NFL cashed in handsomely by agreeing to a record $2.1 billion television contract with NBC, CBS, and ABC that would begin with the 1982 exhibition season.

Owners may have been flush with enthusiasm—and cash—thanks to pro football's burgeoning popularity, yet there was growing disenchantment among the players, who wanted a bigger share of the financial pie. Average salaries in the just-concluded 1981 season were $90,102, according to a survey by the NFL Players Association, with quarterbacks enjoying the highest average pay—$160,037.

Salaries had grown by an estimated 14.5 percent over the 1980 season, but players still believed they were vastly underpaid relative to the league's overall financial health. NFLPA executive director Ed Garvey, a fiery Washington, D.C.–based attorney who had organized a 1974 strike by NFL players and who had frequently used the threat of anti-trust violations against the league to secure improved wages and benefits for the players, had told player representatives during the 1981 season to be prepared to escalate their fight with the owners.

That included the possibility of organizing another strike, prompting the union to frequently recommend players save as much money as possible in the event of a work stoppage.

After seeing how lucrative the newly minted television contracts had been, Garvey's battle plan was to not simply seek higher salaries for the players, but to do it within a system where the players earned a set percentage of the league's gross revenues.

Garvey aimed high; he wanted the players to share 55 percent of those revenues, as well as half of the television rights fees. The total: $1.6 billion over four years.

"There was a lot of talk about what was going to happen, and I think the possibility of a strike was a very real one," said former Redskins safety Mark Murphy, the team's NFLPA player rep and a member of the union's executive committee, in looking back at the labor unrest.

Negotiations were often contentious, and many owners cited Garvey's aggressive personality as a major impediment to getting a deal done. But the players were adamant that they were entitled to higher salaries and benefits, and as the off-season and training camp wore on, there was an undercurrent of uncertainty about the possibility of a strike.

Gibbs was certainly aware of the situation, and while he wasn't obsessing about whether there would be a labor stoppage, he was concerned about getting his players to remain closer to the team's training facility in the off-season. It had nothing to do with preparations for a potential strike; Gibbs simply wanted his players more engaged in off-season conditioning, something that no teams had previously done in such an organized way.

In fact, there were no off-season conditioning programs, and the idea of players training almost year-round was simply unheard-of. Once the season ended, players left the team and went home, and off-season workouts were up to the individual players, not the teams.

Gibbs wanted to change that, especially after seeing how his first-round draft pick, offensive lineman Mark May, had struggled during his rookie season to keep his weight up and remain healthy.

"Dan Riley had come in as our strength and conditioning coach, and the Redskins had put a ton of money into the weight facility," May said. "They said, 'We want guys to live in Washington.' Butz and Riggins and those guys, they hadn't done that. Guys were used to going home. I was probably the fault of that, because they wanted us to come in the end of February and start lifting."

It wasn't mandatory...but it was.

"You didn't have to be there," May said, "but there was a lot of pressure on you to be there."

It was an incredible selling job, because the Redskins didn't even offer bonuses for off-season workouts—a standard financial incentive in today's NFL. But most of the players still showed.

"That was something I thought was really important," Gibbs said of having players train together in the off-season. "Building that team feeling between guys, when they're working out there. I think that's where you build a lot of the chemistry, and I wanted guys to be around each other."

The players themselves came up with another way of fostering team chemistry: They called it the 5 o'clock club.

A tradition that actually began when Vince Lombardi came to the Redskins in 1969, a group of players would gather after practice at an equipment shed at Redskins Park as a way to fraternize and drink some beer. Sometimes a lot of beer. Lombardi's 5 o'clock club in Green Bay was a time-honored tradition, when the coach would invite reporters to hang out after training camp practice and the night before road games. Lombardi would have his drink—scotch and water—and reporters would drink beer and just shoot the breeze with the coach. That would be an unheard-of arrangement in today's NFL, where reporters are kept as far away from head coaches as humanly possible, but in those days, there was a much more collegial atmosphere where coaches could trust reporters to respect the rules of engagement: namely, that all conversations would be off the record.

The Redskins' iteration of the 5 o'clock club was eventually a gathering for players and assistant coaches and the training staff, and by the time Gibbs had arrived in 1981, there were several regulars: Riggins, Butz; newcomers Bostic, Grimm, Jacoby, and May; along with most of the other offensive linemen, some defensive linemen, and a handful of coaches and trainers.

"We had officers and everything," Jacoby said. "I was sergeant at arms. Riggins was 'El Presidente.' It wasn't a democracy, though. We did have some coups." Other officers were Grimm, Bostic, and Butz.

Jacoby said it was a good way of releasing tension.

"Yes, there was beer being consumed, but not everybody came in there," Jacoby said. "It was more like a release thing. If you had a bad day at practice, you'd come in there and do all your cussing and complaining, and it stayed there. It was a way to get it off your chest and go home. It was almost like a counseling center."

"It got started before DWI was instituted," Butz said. "We'd give a couple of the security guys money, and we had emptied this old wooden storage shed that had leather tackling dummies in it, these huge things that were hard to lift. It might have been a ten-by-ten shed. We put cardboard around the bottom to keep the wind out, and used a kerosene heater, and we'd sit there and really had camaraderie, tighter than you could ever imagine. Just sit and tell stories."

The ball busting was endless.

"One time I asked Grimm, 'Russ, when's the last time you played a complete game?' He thought and he thought and he said, 'Three years ago.' " The room filled with laughter.

Not everyone was welcome.

"One time we hear a knock on the door and Joe Theismann opens "the door and we just lambasted him. 'Go drink some tea or wine,' " Butz said. "We knew he was a wine drinker. If you're not drinking beer, we didn't want you and you could not come in."

Keeping the quarterback out was good for team chemistry?

Actually, it was.

"That was reserved for John [Riggins] and the linemen, and that was fine. I respected that," Theismann said. "I wasn't a hog, although I did get invited in one time. We were playing the Giants, and Terry Jackson was a defensive back. I handed the ball off to Joe Washington on a sweep, and I blocked Jackson. They made me an honorary piglet for that one day, and I was allowed in. That was their space, and I was fine with it. Our guys could drink."

Especially Riggins, who never hid the fact he liked to drink.

"One time in the meeting room, John asks if I can pick him up in the morning," Bostic said.

"You got car problems?" the center had asked.

"John Boy's going to be drinking tonight," Riggins had told him. "John Boy doesn't drink and drive."

"He had a 1974 canary-yellow pickup truck," Bostic said. "I showed up at his house one time and his pickup truck is right in the middle of his front yard and there's two cowboy boots hanging out the front door. He urinated in the yard and gets in the car. He's an animal. When he's hungry, he eats. When he's thirsty, he drinks."

Gibbs was aware of the 5 o'clock club, but because it had been a long-standing tradition, and because the players clearly enjoyed being with one another, he didn't shut it down. (Had Gibbs been coaching in today's NFL, there would have been no 5 o'clock club, because drinking alcohol at team facilities is prohibited.)

"I knew it was out there, and they kept it under cover," Gibbs said.

John Madden became a frequent visitor to the 5 o'clock club when he met with the Redskins before broadcasting a game on CBS. The players loved having him there.

"We heard a knock on the door, and someone goes, 'Hey, is this the 5 o'clock club?' It's John Madden, and we said, 'Come on in,'" Butz recalled. "He was telling us some of the greatest tales. We ran out of beer, and he takes out what looked like a cobblestone brick phone. Pushes about seventeen numbers, and he says, 'Bill, this is John. Go in the back of the trailer and get all the beer out of the refrigerator.' ... I said, 'I'll be damned. We just had John Madden order us beer.'"

Madden made the mistake of talking about the club on one of his broadcasts.

"I was fine with it until Madden put it on TV," Gibbs said. "That's when I went to John and said, 'You've got to take care of this.' I think John was tipping a few, too."

Something else that brought his team together: Gibbs's use of weekly awards for his players—including the "leather balls" necklace.

"It didn't have to be big things," Gibbs said. "But the most important people to those players are their teammates and their coaches. So when you stand up there and you call somebody up front and give them a Sony Walkman, or a little $150 gift, that means so much to these guys. You wind up having a player of the week who gets his own parking space, defensive player of the week, special teams player of the week. Get a La-Z-Boy chair to sit in [in the locker room]."

And the leather balls award?

"The leather balls award was a huge deal," Gibbs said. "Picture this: You've got guys that are making a million bucks a year, you're playing in one of the most exciting sports, and a lot of them are recognized with their stats, and then you've got the 'leather balls' award."

Yes, it's what you think. The award went to the player with the biggest balls that week. In other words, the toughest guy in a given game.

"It had to be someone that would never back down from anything, and they would literally be the people that would go to war for you," Gibbs said. "There might be only five or six of them given out in a season. But to see a grown guy come to a meeting with the leather balls award hanging from his neck, put them in his car, hanging from the rearview mirror. That's what you love about this game. There's a lot of kid in us, and appeal to that is human nature, how competitive we come into this world. If you define goals, you have rewards, it means a lot to those guys in a world where they got a lot in terms of money and fame."

Gibbs himself had become more financially stable as a head coach, but he was hardly consumed with material rewards. A devout Christian who didn't wear religion on his sleeve but certainly didn't hide his devotion and spoke openly of his beliefs, Gibbs had come to increasingly rely on his faith over the years—especially as the pressures and responsibilities of coaching consumed so much of his time.

"In coaching, there are so many things that can happen to you," he said. "Players can get hurt, you wind up with fumbles, so many things that happen that take you on that ride from the thrill of victory to the agony of defeat. I always felt my faith was the one thing that encouraged me. God made me and let me be a football coach, so it gave me direction.

"I had a feeling of peace," he said. "I was really driven and I went after it hard, but there's always a peace for me knowing that I was in a profession that I couldn't count on things. In football, it's high risk and it's high reward. The life span of a football coach is short, and it's not something you can count on. When you're in a world like that, it makes me depend on God, and I know He's there for me for whatever comes into my life. It does give me a peace of mind."

Murphy could tell that the negotiations weren't going well, and that owners were particularly chafed by Garvey's aggressive style. The owners didn't want to be lectured by the union leader, nor did they want to be intimidated into doing a deal, but Garvey was undeterred and dug his heels in throughout the talks.

The season began with uncertainty, because the players' side wouldn't reveal exactly what plan it had in terms of a strike. But as it became clear there was no middle ground for either side to reach, Garvey and NFLPA president Gene Upshaw, the Raiders' All-Pro guard who drew praise from most of his fellow players for trying to drive a hard bargain with the owners, realized that they had reached the point of no return. By the Friday before the second week of the regular season, negotiations had broken off. The following Monday, just hours before the Giants and Packers were to play a prime-time game, Upshaw announced at a news conference in Washington, D.C., that the players would strike.

"There will be no practices, workouts, or training," Upshaw told reporters. "No games will be played until management abandons its unlawful course and engages in good-faith bargaining. The players of the NFL, as of tonight, will be on strike."

This was uncharted territory for the NFL, because there had never been an in-season strike. Garvey had called a strike in 1974 before the start of that season, but no games were lost. In fact, the '74 strike was a complete failure. Garvey had the players walk out in training camp, demanding that the owners give players the chance to switch teams once their contracts had expired. In all, there were sixty-two demands, including the ability to veto trades and the elimination of the draft.

Within weeks, about 25 percent of veteran players crossed the picket line, and the owners didn't budge on any of Garvey's demands. Even many retired players criticized Garvey's tactics, and when the NFL staged its annual Hall of Fame game in Canton, Ohio, between the Bills and Cardinals, the rookies and walk-on free agents who comprised the teams (rookies weren't members of the union at that point in the season) had flown into Canton just hours before the game and went back almost immediately after the game.

That strike was a complete fiasco, and by the time it ended forty-two days later, on August 10, the players had gained nothing.

But the timing of the 1982 strike was different, because the players had at least some leverage since the season had already begun. The NFL was forced to start canceling regular-season games for the first time, and days turned into weeks, turned into months. The country's only pro football that was played during that time: two AFC-NFC "all-star games"—one of which was at RFK Stadium and the other at the Los Angeles Memorial Coliseum—that were barely attended. Riggins was one of the few marquee players to participate—"I guess I'll do just about anything for money," he cracked.

The strike lasted fifty-seven days before ending on November 16, forcing the cancellation of seven games, with the NFL going to an abbreviated nine-game season upon the resumption of play.

The strike yielded only mixed results, and while the players made at least some progress with the five-year Collective Bargaining Agreement that was eventually agreed to—they won salary increases in the regular season and postseason, and severance packages after players retired—there was major dissatisfaction within the rank-and-file. Garvey was thus unpopular among both owners and players, and he was soon forced out of his position and replaced by Upshaw.

Most teams were hopelessly disorganized when the players returned from the strike, but Gibbs had a major tactical advantage from instituting his unofficial off-season workout program months earlier.

The Redskins won a 37–34 overtime thriller against the Eagles at Veterans Stadium in the opener, as Theismann had his best game under Gibbs with 382 passing yards and 3 touchdowns. And Washington's

21–13 win over the Buccaneers in Tampa gave the Redskins an encouraging 2-0 start before the strike began.

A day after beating the Bucs, Gibbs heard along with the rest of the NFL that the strike was about to begin. But once again, his preparation had paid off; even though the Redskins weren't permitted to practice at the team facility, they practiced nonetheless.

It was Theismann—who had gone the year before to the coach's house and convinced him he was serious about being a leader—who took command of the offense when Gibbs could no longer oversee his team.

"I found a high school field near the Redskins' training facility [in Reston, Virginia], and we'd get a good thirty to thirty-five guys to go over there several times a week," Theismann said. "We didn't have email in those days, so I just called them up and let them know we were practicing."

They'd mimic Gibbs's practice as best they could: warmups, individual drills, run plays—anything they could do to try to stay sharp so they'd be ready if and when the season resumed.

"Some guys don't show up for [off-season practices] nowadays, but here we had a bunch of guys that weren't making anything, and they were willing to show up," Theismann said. "It really created a great bond for us. It was a bunch of guys that cared about one another and cared about the game. There was no obligation to show up, but they did, anyway."

Butz, the veteran defensive tackle, ran drills on defense, and kicker Mark Moseley was in charge of special teams.

"I get to be coach because I'm the only guy who owns a whistle," Butz joked once after an hour-long practice.

Guard Russ Grimm, the team's alternate player rep to the union, was kept up to speed on the negotiations. Or lack thereof.

"Nothing to report," Grimm told reporters after an early practice. "I don't know of any meetings that are planned. It looks like we'll be out a while. I know we'll be out as long as it takes to get management to get serious about negotiating."

Butz knew then it would be difficult to keep up the intensity and enthusiasm in the event of a long strike.

"A week and a half from now," he said, "the mental conditioning will start to slip. We've been going hard since July and training camp, and because it's September, we're conditioned to being involved in football. With no games and no contact, the mental part becomes tougher and tougher. Right now, it hurts the linemen and linebackers, but it'll hurt everyone pretty soon."

Gibbs and his coaching staff faced a different quandary. Even though the strike had dragged on with no apparent end, they had to prepare each week as if the players would be back. That meant watching film and doing game planning for each week's opponent. And each week, when there was no resolution to the strike, those game plans would be tossed.

The first game after the strike began—against the Cardinals—was actually postponed (and would be played a week after the regular season had initially been scheduled to conclude). Then the cancellations began: the Browns, then the Cowboys, the Steelers, the Oilers. Then the 49ers, Bengals, and Vikings.

Finally, after eight missed games, negotiations began to ramp up between the players and owners.

"It was almost a month of negotiating in New York City near the end of the strike," said Murphy, who couldn't be with his teammates for many of their impromptu training sessions near Redskins Park. He was on the NFLPA's executive committee and was thus heavily involved in Collective Bargaining Agreement negotiations. "I remember keeping in shape running through Central Park." He added with a touch of humor, "Running through Central Park at night was very good for my speed."

"Up until that point, there was a real threat that the season would be canceled, and it looked like more and more of a reality," he said. "But we finally got it settled, and went right back at it pretty quickly."

On Tuesday, November 16, the strike was over. The Redskins would resume their season five days later against the Giants at Giants Stadium.

"Once we came back from the strike, our team was still very much together," Theismann said. "There was a genuine closeness among the players, and it was to our advantage that we had practiced together.

As time went on, fewer and fewer guys showed up, but we still had good camaraderie."

The Redskins picked up right where they left off, beating Ray Perkins's Giants, 27–17. The Redskins built a 21–3 halftime lead on two touchdown passes by Theismann and a rushing touchdown by Riggins—proof that the team could stay on a roll despite the nearly two-month labor interruption.

After a 13–9 win against the Eagles, the Redskins hosted the Cowboys at RFK Stadium in an eagerly anticipated game that would renew a years-long rivalry that was one of the NFL's most intense matchups. It would also help determine just how far Gibbs's team had come and whether the Redskins were good enough to compete against a Cowboys team that was still in its heyday.

The answer: Not yet.

The Cowboys dominated most of the way, taking a 17–0 lead into the fourth quarter before Moseley finally got the Redskins on the board with a 38-yard field goal. Theismann hit Charlie Brown with a 17-yard touchdown pass to bring the Redskins to within a score, 17–10. But the Cowboys put it away on Ron Springs's 46-yard touchdown run in a 24-10 win.

It was a brutal day for the Redskins' two biggest offensive players. Riggins was held to just 26 rushing yards, while Theismann had 3 interceptions and was sacked seven times. It was a game the offensive line would not soon forget; the very lifeblood of the Redskins' attack was at its worst against the likes of Harvey Martin, Randy White, and the rest of the Dallas defense.

The loss proved to be the Redskins' only clunker of the regular season, though. Washington reeled off four straight wins to finish with an 8-1 record and, more important, earn the number 1 seed and thus home field advantage in the NFC playoffs.

Because of the strike-shortened season, the NFL devised a sixteen-team playoff—the first and only time that many teams would qualify for the postseason—and the seeding system was done not by division but by conference. In both the NFC and AFC, the teams finishing with the top eight records made the playoffs, with the higher-seeded teams facing the lower-seeded ones in the first round. For the first time in NFL history, two teams with losing records—the 4-5 Browns and Lions—qualified for the postseason.

Unlike traditional playoff years, there was no bye week, so any team that reached the Super Bowl had to win three games to get there.

The Redskins' opening-round game was against the Lions at RFK Stadium, where the atmosphere was electrifying now that the Redskins were in position to win their first playoff game since George Allen's Over-the-Hill Gang went to Super Bowl VII in 1972. It was Washington's first postseason appearance since 1976.

With a promising regular season behind them and Gibbs's moves to foster team chemistry, the Redskins dominated the Lions from the start.

Gibbs was at his play-calling best, leaning heavily on Riggins but also relying on Theismann's arm and an unlikely target in the passing game: five-foot-seven, 178-pound receiver Alvin Garrett, a ninth-round pick in 1980 out of unknown Angelo State who was initially cut by the Chargers, then played for the Giants in 1980 and came to the Redskins late in the 1981 season.

Despite being one of the smallest players in NFL history, Garrett had a knack for getting open, and Gibbs loved having a speed receiver. It was Garrett who starred in the opening playoff game, as Theismann hit him for three touchdown passes in a 31–7 drubbing of the Lions. Garrett finished with six catches—equaling his NFL career total prior to the game.

Riggins, who had been limited the previous two regular-season games because of a sore thigh, rushed for 119 yards on 25 carries against the NFC's top-ranked run defense.

"Alvin Garrett wouldn't be in this league unless he could perform," Theismann told reporters after the game. "He's just never had the chance."

Garrett, who played running back at Angelo State, said afterward, "[I don't] think there is anyone who can cover me. I told [receivers coach] Charley Taylor, if I don't score three touchdowns, I'm not going to be satisfied."

He paused a moment and then said, "I'm satisfied."

Gibbs was delighted with Garrett's production, which was especially significant because the Redskins didn't have Pro Bowl receiver Art Monk because of a foot injury.

"I figured everyone would ask me why we haven't been playing Alvin more," Gibbs cracked at his postgame news conference. "But he sure filled in for us and did a great job...We keep saying it takes a total team effort. That's what is so nice, to have a guy like Alvin fill in for Art like he did."

Next up: the Vikings at home.

To get a sense of where this team was at heading into the game, you had to go back to a meeting Gibbs held with his team late in the 1981 season. Gibbs stood before his players and went through his usual routine of going down a checklist of goals, putting the list on an overhead projector so the players could see it on the front wall of the meeting room.

Center Jeff Bostic was in his customary seat next to Riggins, who was barely paying attention to Gibbs. It wasn't an unusual scene for the veteran running back, because he'd often drift off in meetings. Sometimes he was bored. Sometimes he was hung over. But very rarely did he react the way Bostic had seen that morning.

"It's like Week 15 or Week 16, and I'm sitting there next to John, and Joe is going over his goals," Bostic said. "At one point, Joe says, 'We're not getting the kind of production out of the running back position.' I could tell John was irritated. At that point, we're doing the running-back-by-committee thing, so nobody's 'the man.'"

Word soon got back to Bostic and the rest of the offense that Riggins was so bothered by Gibbs's remarks that he went into the coach's office.

"Coach, give me the ball, and hitch your wagon to me," Riggins told Gibbs.

"John, I appreciate your honesty, and I'll certainly consider that," Gibbs said.

Bostic tells the rest: "After John left the meeting, Coach Gibbs goes to [special teams coach] Wayne Sevier's office and he says, 'You're not going to believe who came into my office and what he said.'"

Sevier asked who met with Gibbs.

"It was Riggins, and he said to give him the ball and hitch the wagon to him," Gibbs told him.

It was too late in the season to change the formula Gibbs had used—namely a collective effort by the running backs in which no single player was the dominant ball carrier. Riggins, in fact, gained 714 yards that first year under Gibbs—a solid total, but certainly not what he'd been used to in the pre-Gibbs years.

Riggins's message resonated with Gibbs, though, and the coach did change his thinking heading into the 1982 season. Riggins became his feature back, and Gibbs gave him an exponentially bigger responsibility in the running game.

Gibbs still never forgot that line Riggins delivered in their first face-to-face meeting in Kansas the year before, when Gibbs convinced Riggins to come out of retirement. "You need to get me back there," Riggins told Gibbs. "I'll make you famous."

That was exactly what was about to happen.

The Redskins were set to host Bud Grant's Vikings, who had finished 5-4 in the strike-shortened season. Minnesota featured a solid defensive front that had limited opponents to just 3.9 yards per carry on the ground during the regular season. And while this wasn't the Purple People Eaters reincarnated, the Vikings were certainly a formidable opponent.

But Gibbs's game plan against Minnesota revolved around Riggins, and the coach showed he had indeed hitched his wagon to the eccentric thirty-three-year-old fullback from Kansas.

Riggins responded with a monster game, rushing for a career-high 185 yards and a touchdown in leading the Redskins to a 21–7 win over the Vikings to put his team one win away from the Super Bowl.

Gibbs had tried a number of different runs with Riggins, but he found the ones that worked best were right up the middle. And yes, there was a healthy dose of the counter trey alignment that Gibbs had once used experimentally but was now a staple of his offense.

"We wanted to run the ball, just like we always do," Gibbs said afterward. "But we never expected to run this well. We just tried different runs, inside and outside, until we saw what worked. We were going up the middle, so we stayed with it."

Riggins was breathtakingly good, powering through the heart of the Vikings' defense and living up to his nickname, "the Diesel."

"Thank God we have John Riggins," Gibbs said. "He's stupendous. It's really remarkable when you think about it. Here's a guy thirty-three years old, but when he says he is going to do something, he is going to do it. And he says he's going to carry the ball for us."

Riggins's previous career high was against the Patriots ten years earlier, when he rushed for 168 yards in his second year with the Jets.

"They said he was washed up three years ago," Redskins linebacker Rich Milot said in the locker room after the game. "If he's washed up, I'd like to be so bad for the rest of my career. We just stand there and cheer for him. All the while, we are resting, and that has to help us play better."

Once it became apparent the Redskins would win and move on to the NFC Championship Game, the crowd of 54,592 broke into a spontaneous cheer that reverberated through creaky RFK Stadium.

"We want Dallas! We want Dallas! We want Dallas!" they roared, jumping up and down so furiously that the stands literally shook and the press box lurched.

"I will never forget that," Bostic said. "It's one of the pinnacle moments that I have as a Redskin. That place was nuts."

The fans would get their wish.

The Cowboys beat the Packers the following day, and it would be Redskins-Cowboys in the NFC Championship Game. At RFK. With a chance for the Redskins to atone for their only loss during the regular season.

For the Cowboys, it was a chance to take some of the pain away from the previous year's conference championship game against the 49ers.

Gibbs remained true to his conviction about using Riggins as his workhorse running back, and Riggins responded with another spectacular effort. He finished with 36 carries for 140 yards and 2 touchdowns, while Theismann, who had thrown 3 interceptions in the regular-season loss, was 12 of 20 for 150 yards and a touchdown pass.

The defense was terrific, too, although their task became much easier after the second quarter, when White had to leave the game because of a concussion.

And just like the week before against the Vikings and the week before that against the Lions, Redskins fans were jubilant, rocking RFK like never before, singing renditions of "Hail to the Redskins" after every score and feting the players and their unlikely coach with unbridled approval.

There would be another Super Bowl appearance—only the second in franchise history.

Riggins confided to reporters afterward that even he couldn't have imagined this kind of moment, and admitted he had thought about not coming back after the strike.

"To tell you the truth, after the strike, I wasn't sure if I wanted to continue the season," he said. "I was ready to pack my bags and head for Kansas. Boy, what a mistake that would have been."

Gibbs was once again a master at refining his offensive approach.

When the Redskins were soundly beaten by Dallas in the regular season, Gibbs used more of a zone-blocking scheme to deal with the Cowboys' talent-laden defensive front that included Randy White, Harvey Martin, and Ed "Too Tall" Jones. This time, though, Gibbs had his linemen use more man-to-man blocking and often double-teamed White to free up the middle.

The results were breathtakingly effective.

The Redskins built a 14–3 halftime lead with a methodical offensive attack and a smothering defense that limited the Cowboys to just a Rafael Septien field goal in the first quarter. Theismann hit Charlie Brown for a 19-yard touchdown pass to make it 7–3 later in the quarter, and Riggins capped a second-quarter touchdown drive with a 1-yard score.

The Redskins' defense was all over the Cowboys, and White would suffer a concussion in the second quarter and not return. He was replaced by rookie third-round quarterback Gary Hogeboom, who initially played well in relief of White.

The teams traded touchdowns in the third quarter, with Hogeboom hitting Drew Pearson for a 6-yard touchdown to make it 14–10 and Riggins scoring his second touchdown to give the Redskins a 21–10 lead. Hogeboom found Butch Johnson later in the quarter for a 23-yard touchdown pass to make it 21–17.

But Hogeboom would eventually succumb to Richie Petitbon's defense. Hogeboom tried to hit Tony Hill down the right sideline, but was picked off by linebacker Mel Kaufman, who made a leaping interception at the Cowboys' 40. Moseley converted the turnover into a 29-yard field goal to make it 24–17.

On the Cowboys' next possession, Hogeboom was again victimized by the Redskins' defense. On a delayed screen pass intended for Dorsett, Dexter Manley tipped the ball and teammate Darryl Grant intercepted it at the Dallas 10. Grant ran into the end zone with 6:55 left, and the Redskins went on to win it, 31–17.

"Dallas said they would take on the Hogs straight up and we wouldn't run on them like we ran against Minnesota," guard Mark May told reporters after the game. "Tell them I hope they have fun watching the Super Bowl on television. This was our revenge. This was the Hogs' revenge."

Gibbs also used a new offensive alignment, as *Washington Post* beat reporter Paul Attner explained in his postgame analysis. In order to confuse the Cowboys and add a new wrinkle to the offense, Gibbs split out tight end Rick "Doc" Walker to use him as a third wide receiver, and put tight end Don Warren in motion and assigned him to block middle linebacker Bob Breunig.

The formation adjustment worked wonders, and the Redskins' running game, which had been so ineffective in the regular-season meeting against the Cowboys, was exceptional in the rematch.

"Joe was such a student of the game, and he realized that making adjustments was the key to his greatness," Walker said. "Whether it was halftime adjustments or altering schemes that didn't necessarily give him the desired effects, that was huge with him. He saw the game, and he reacted to every situation."

"It was just unreal," Gibbs said of making it to the Super Bowl. "You dream about things in your life, and one of my dreams was, if you're a good football coach, you dream to be in a Super Bowl."

His moment was near.

"I felt really good for our coaches and our players," Gibbs said. "So many people put in so much work during that time, and it was gratifying to see them rewarded for it."

But Gibbs knew the reward of getting there would only be worth it if the Redskins could finish the job the following week in Pasadena, where they would face the Dolphins.

It would be Gibbs against Don Shula, a third straight game against one of the NFL's most successful coaches of the 1970s. Shula and Landry had combined for four Super Bowl titles, and Grant had gotten the Vikings to four Super Bowls. Three future Hall of Fame coaches, and now here was Gibbs in just his second NFL season needing to beat all three to win the team's first-ever title.

Shula was now ten years removed from the perfect season of 1972, when the Dolphins became the first and only team to go unbeaten during the regular season and move on to win the Super Bowl. The team they beat that year in Super Bowl VII: the Redskins, and coach George Allen. And while Shula's 1982 team didn't have the likes of Hall of Famers Bob Griese, Larry Csonka, Nick Buoniconti, Paul Warfield, and Jim Langer, the team and its coach were still considered among the elite of the NFL.

The Dolphins came out of the strike season with a 7-2 record, and quarterback David Woodley had done enough during the regular season and three playoff games to make the Dolphins a three-point favorite in Super Bowl XVII.

The fact that Theismann was the Redskins' quarterback provided an interesting twist, since he had originally been drafted by Shula in the fourth round out of Notre Dame in 1971. Theismann dug in his heels during contract negotiations, though, and he ultimately played in the Canadian Football League for two seasons before Miami traded his rights to the Redskins after the 1973 season.

Now Theismann was ready to face Shula's Dolphins with everything on the line.

"We busted our asses," Theismann told his teammates in the

pregame huddle. "We've worked harder than anybody to get here. Nobody can beat us [as] a team, and it's worth seventy thousand bucks and a big ring!"

On a sun-splashed southern California afternoon on January 30, 1983, with 103,667 fans packed into the Rose Bowl—probably the most glorious scene in pro sports in a building steeped in such history and beauty— the Redskins and Dolphins were ready to battle for the ultimate prize.

The Dolphins struck first, as Woodley hit receiver Jimmy Cefalo on a sideline pattern at the Miami 45. Cefalo had gotten in front of single coverage by safety Tony Peters, and suddenly saw open field in front of him. The fleet wideout then raced untouched into the end zone for a 76-yard touchdown to give the Dolphins a 7–0 lead just over six minutes into the game.

But the Redskins gathered themselves, and after trading second-quarter field goals, Theismann hit Garrett for a 4-yard touchdown to finish off an 80-yard scoring drive to make it 10–10 with just under two minutes left in the half.

After the touchdown, Garrett and four teammates gathered in a circle in the end zone and leaped as one with a collective high five, a touchdown celebration that had begun during the playoffs and earned them the nickname "the Fun Bunch." It was a touchdown celebration that would be repeated many times over, until the NFL eventually cracked down on such revelry.

The Redskins' euphoria on this occasion was short-lived, though. Just thirteen seconds after Garrett's touchdown, the Dolphins went back ahead, 16–10, on Fulton Walker's 98-yard return of Moseley's kickoff.

Gibbs was intent on using plenty of misdirection and trick plays against the Dolphins, but he experienced an epiphany late in the third quarter when he had Theismann drop back to pass from his own 18. Theismann was immediately under a heavy rush from the Dolphins' defense—nicknamed the "Killer Bees" because of all the terrific players whose last names started with the letter B (Bob Baumhower, Doug Betters, Kim Bokamper, Charles Bowser, Bob Brudzinski, and brothers Glenn and Lyle Blackwood).

Theismann looked to his right and didn't find an open receiver, then looked over the middle... still no one open. So he spun around in the pocket and rolled to his left, throwing off his back foot from the Redskins' 7. Bokamper was closing quickly on Theismann and deflected the ball into the air. The linebacker got under it and was ready for the interception—which would have been the Dolphins' third of the game—until Theismann dove at the ball and just managed to knock it out of Bokamper's arms at the 3.

A touchdown there, and the Dolphins would have gone up 23–13, making it a two-score game. Instead, Theismann's magnificent save had kept the Redskins within four.

That was it for Gibbs. No more fancy stuff in the passing game. If he was going to win it, he would do it on the ground and not through the air.

Before the Redskins' next possession, he spoke to his players on the sidelines.

"We're going to go back out, and we're going to establish the line of scrimmage," he told them. "We're not going to get impatient. We're going to win the football game by running it."

Just as he had when the Redskins were 0-5 and Gibbs thought he might be out of a job, Gibbs junked that pass-centric concept. This game would be on Riggins. This game would be on the Hogs.

It was back to plays like "40 Gut" and "50 Gut," the go-to inside runs that Riggins had feasted on during his late-season surge and through the previous three playoff victories.

"40 and 50 Gut is John Riggins running out, where he gets the football, he glides to the offensive tackle, and he makes his breaks from there," offensive line coach Joe Bugel said a year after the Super Bowl in an NFL Films documentary. It was Bugel who coined the "Hogs" nickname for his line, once telling Grimm and Bostic in 1982, "Okay, you hogs, let's get running down there."

"This is really our bread and butter, and we were having success running to our left side, because we felt we have the great matchup," Bugel said. "Bokamper was a 250-pounder, a great pass rusher, but Joe Jacoby weighed 300 pounds. We felt in order to beat Miami, we would have to win this matchup and Jacoby was going to have to pound Bokamper."

And so it went, Theismann giving the ball to Riggins, and the Diesel taking it and slicing through and running over the Miami defense.

The moment of truth came with 10:10 left in the fourth quarter and the Redskins still trailing by three, 16–13. The Redskins had a fourth down at the Dolphins' 43-yard line. Gibbs could have elected to punt and pin the Dolphins deep inside their own territory. But the coach also felt he needed to have the guts to take a chance, even if failing meant giving the ball back to the Dolphins and falling even further behind.

It would be Riggins again, only this time, Gibbs's strategic mastery proved genius once more.

Theismann got in the huddle and told his teammates the play.

"Let's go," he said. "Goal line, goal line. I left tight wing, 70 chip, on one."

The Dolphins were expecting a run up the middle, which would be typical of a short-yardage situation like the one they now faced. But Gibbs's offensive line technique would be to have his blockers engage the Dolphins' defensive line and linebackers and try and isolate Riggins on a defensive back in the open field.

"John Riggins knows it's going to be the corner," Bugel said. "John Riggins should beat any cornerback in the NFL."

The cornerback was Don McNeal, and he never had a chance when he met Riggins near the line of scrimmage. The power back had taken the ball and cut to his left, finding exactly what Gibbs had expected from the play—a one-on-one matchup against McNeal.

McNeal tried to grab Riggins around the waist, but he was no match for the Diesel. Riggins shook off McNeal and raced upfield.

He was gone. He went 43 yards for the touchdown, putting the Redskins ahead, 20–16. Theismann added another touchdown pass to Charlie Brown to finish off the win.

Gibbs had done it again, conquering a murderers' row of coaching icons by beating Bud Grant, Tom Landry, and now Don Shula to give the Redskins the first Super Bowl title in franchise history.

"I was so thrilled afterwards," Gibbs said. "Once you get it, you realize that the owner gambled and Bobby [Beathard] gambled. You got coaches who moved to a new city, and they're all busting themselves, and then the fans. You realize that adds a lot of pressure to a coach. You lose football games. You start out 0-5. I'm letting all these people down.

"So when you win something like that Super Bowl the first time, it was just such a thrill to see all those people get to go with you. That feeling is just hard to put in words, really."

Gibbs wanted to share the moment with his wife, Pat, who had been by his side every step of the way, through every assistant coaching job, from the graduate assistant position under John Madden and Don Coryell at San Diego State...to Florida State...then USC... Arkansas...the Cardinals, Buccaneers, and Chargers...and finally to the Redskins only two years earlier.

"She grew up coaching with me," Gibbs said. "We were high school sweethearts. She was a coach's wife. She understood it. She was just so good and so supportive. She did such a good job with the boys [sons J.D. and Coy]. She ran the show. Thank goodness she was there, because she did such a good job."

Gibbs looked around the stadium for Pat.

"I lost my wife, couldn't find her, got all mixed up," Gibbs said. "We finally wound up at about 3 a.m. at a Bob's Big Boy and had our little celebration there. I was just so happy. It was just an unreal experience."

It wasn't just Gibbs who had a hard time wrapping his mind around what had just happened. His players were overcome with excitement at having accomplished so much so quickly. In just two years, a team that had undergone a major transformation not only in terms of going from Jack Pardee to Gibbs, but also Beathard's roster upheaval, which brought in a wave of new players in the first two years of Gibbs's tenure, had risen to the pinnacle of pro football.

"There was so much that happened that week, being in California, so many personalities out there," said Dexter Manley, the outspoken and colorful defensive end. "Walter Payton came up and talked to me at that Super Bowl. That was really different, because I liked Payton so much growing up, and now, I'm talking to this guy at the Super Bowl. I just couldn't believe it. It didn't seem real."

If the game itself, not to mention the outcome, felt surreal, what happened early the morning after the Redskins' win was even more mind-blowing for Manley. He and teammates Mark Murphy and Joe Jacoby were asked to appear on NBC's *Today* show.

"We were staying in Costa Mesa, so there was a limo that picked us up around 4 a.m.," Manley said. "We were taken to the top of the NBC building in Costa Mesa, and then we took a helicopter ride to Burbank and landed on top of the NBC building there, and we all went on the *Today* show. I thought, man, I've never experienced anything like that before. I'm a kid from the ghetto out of Houston, Texas, and now this is happening? I felt like I had arrived, and it was because of the Super Bowl and that win. And then I'm getting a ring on top of it? It was surreal. One of the greatest days of my life."

"I don't know if I slept at all that night we won the game," Murphy said. "Everything was like a whirlwind. Everything that whole season was like that, and it just never stopped. We just kept it going."

Meanwhile, back in the greater Washington, D.C., area, fans had erupted with pent-up joy thanks to the team's first NFL championship in forty-one years. Even President Ronald Reagan and First Lady Nancy Reagan showed up to greet the team when the Redskins returned on their DC-10 jet to Dulles Airport just a few miles from Redskins Park. A makeshift banner hanging on the side of a fire truck read, WELCOME HOME, WORLD CHAMPIONS.

Team buses shuttled the players, coaches, and executives back to Redskins Park, where an estimated five hundred fans showed up to welcome them home. Gibbs, with the Lombardi Trophy in hand, walked across a street and approached the fans.

"This is yours!" he yelled, lifting the trophy in one hand and raising his other hand with his index finger pointed to the sky. The fans screamed their approval.

Two days later, the Redskins would be feted with a parade up Constitution Avenue.

Nearly all the players, except those who were to play in the Pro Bowl in Honolulu the following week, including Theismann and kicker Mark Moseley, participated in the parade. The one prominent no-show: Riggins.

He had remained in southern California after the game to accept the MVP trophy at a Monday morning press conference, and he didn't arrive back to his home in Virginia until later that night. He was anxious to be in the parade, and he called Redskins Park to find out details.

No one picked up the phone.

Riggins turned on the television and was mortified when he saw the parade had already started. So Riggins called local television producer Ernie Baur to see what was up. Baur then figured he had the makings of a good story here, so he told Riggins he'd drive him to the parade on the one condition that he allow a reporter to tag along and get a story out of it.

Riggins said sure. He barely made it to the end of the parade. He explained he was still on West Coast time and had incorrectly set his alarm clock.

Riggins's late arrival couldn't tamp down the euphoria that swept through the region. The Redskins were back, and Gibbs had become the most beloved sports figure in town.

"What a great time," Gibbs said. "Just unbelievable."

PARCELLS

FIGHTING BACK WHILE RISKING IT ALL

Phil Simms was furious with Bill Parcells.

Late in August 1983, Parcells's first year as the Giants' head coach, he told Simms he would not be his starting quarterback.

"Phil, I've decided to go with Scott," Parcells said of his decision to have Scott Brunner as his starter heading into the season.

There was silence for a moment, and Parcells said to the twenty-seven-year-old Simms, "You have anything to say?"

"Sure, I have something to say," Simms said.

"You want to get out of here?" Parcells said.

"You're damn right I do," Simms said. "Go ahead and trade me. Get me out of here."

"Give me three teams where you want to go, and I'll think about it," Parcells told Simms, the Giants' first-round pick in 1979. Then Parcells pissed Simms off even more. "What are you running away from, the competition?"

Red-faced with anger after a conversation that lasted no longer than thirty seconds, Simms brooded for weeks about the decision.

Brunner was the team's sixth-round pick out of Delaware in 1980, and he laid claim to the starting job in 1982 after Simms had suffered torn knee ligaments in the preseason, and now again in 1983. Parcells saw nothing in training camp to change his mind about going to Simms as his starter.

"I had seen more of Brunner," Parcells said in looking back on the decision. "Phil had been hurt the two years when I was there [in 1981–82 as defensive coordinator], and I know that Perkins had confidence in Brunner. When we went to camp, I talked to my coaches, and there was nobody banging on the table for Phil to start."

It was the first major decision of Parcells's fledgling NFL head coaching career, and he would eventually come to regret the move. But it was one of many difficult moments in what turned out to be a calamitous year for the forty-two-year-old coach.

On and off the field.

Things started out well enough, with the Giants going 2-2 over the first month of the season with wins over the Packers and Falcons and losses to the Rams and Cowboys.

Then the bottom fell out.

In every way imaginable.

Just two days after a 41–34 loss at home to the Chargers—and a week before the October 11 trade deadline—Simms went public with his frustration over not starting and told reporters what he had told Parcells after the coach named Brunner his starter.

"I think it would be best for me and everyone concerned if [a trade] happened," Simms said. "If I stay, I'll work hard. But how long can I wait? We're pretty deep into our season. They've made a commitment to Scott Brunner. They have to play him. It's been six weeks since I've had a good look at anything."

Parcells didn't comment to reporters, but he seethed over Simms telling the media he wanted to be traded. General manager George Young, who had lived by the courage of his convictions in taking Simms in the draft and ignoring the criticism that came with it, told reporters he hadn't discussed trading Simms with any other teams.

But Young appeared to hint that he might consider a trade.

"We have to do what is in the best interest of the franchise," he said. "I'm not saying we're insensitive to people."

The Houston Oilers were the most frequently mentioned team that might be interested in Simms, and one way or another, the quarterback wanted out. Even if he did stay with the Giants, Simms suggested there was no motivation for the team to play him.

"Why would they put me in if they know I don't want to be here?" he said.

Simms felt the Giants wouldn't consider playing him, especially after Brunner had played so well against the Chargers, albeit in a losing cause. He was 31 of 51 for 395 yards and 3 touchdowns.

"I think I could be happier in other places not starting," Simms said.

Simms finally did get his wish to play, though. With the Giants playing listlessly in a home game against the Eagles less than a week after Simms vented to the media, Parcells replaced Brunner with Simms.

In the third quarter, with the Giants trailing 14–6, Brunner threw an interception, and fans started chanting, "We want Simms! We want Simms!"

They got him.

Parcells pulled Brunner and inserted Simms, who completed his first four passes for 78 yards and led the Giants to a touchdown drive to bring them within a point, 14–13, early in the fourth quarter.

But just minutes later, Simms hit his right thumb on Eagles defensive lineman Dennis Harrison, and his thumb was momentarily stuck in Harrison's face mask. Simms looked down and saw that his thumb had been bloodied and broken, with a bone protruding through the skin.

His season was over, with yet another injury forcing him out of the lineup in what had been a disappointing career to that point. The year before, he suffered a knee injury when he was sandwiched by Jets linemen Joe Klecko and Abdul Salaam. Two years earlier, Redskins defensive tackle Dave Butz sacked him and caused a shoulder separation. Another shoulder separation ended his 1980 season prematurely.

A week after Simms's latest injury, the Giants were walloped, 38–17, in Kansas City, and then played to a 20–20 tie in a Monday night game in St. Louis. It was an absolutely miserable game—one of the most poorly played games you could imagine.

But the losing—and tying—was just part of the problem for Parcells.

In the two years before he'd been named to succeed Perkins, Parcells was an affable defensive coordinator—and before that a position coach—who was beloved by his players. Oh, he had a mean streak in him, and he was demanding. But he didn't separate himself from the players the way other coaches did, and he would take the same approach when he became the head coach.

But he eventually learned—almost too late—that being a head coach was far different from being a coordinator, and with tough decisions having to be made, there was simply no way of pleasing everyone, no matter how much he wanted to.

"Retrospectively, I brought a little bit of it on myself, because I was acting like I thought a head coach should act, instead of just being Bill Parcells, and some of the veterans on my team, they were used to losing," he said. "We had 1981 when we went to the playoffs, but that's the only year they'd won since 1974. So they weren't on board. Once it goes bad, some of those guys, they're sour. It's a learned behavior. They're used to getting beat."

Now that he was the head coach, Parcells was taking heat like he'd never experienced before, and he didn't handle it well.

"I was a little more detached," he said. "I wasn't as hands-on. I was worried about shit that wasn't pertinent."

His players noticed.

"Early on, we have two groups of guys," linebacker Harry Carson said. "We had guys who had the heart but didn't necessarily have the talent, and then we had guys who had the talent and not necessarily the heart. The team needed to learn how to win and be disciplined, and Ray Perkins brought us that discipline, and then Parcells did, but not until he started coaching the way he wanted to coach. In '83, it was different, because he didn't really know how to do it necessarily as a head coach. He had to learn to do that."

Parcells had plenty of talented players—Lawrence Taylor, Carson, defensive end George Martin, cornerback Mark Haynes, and linebackers Brian Kelley and Brad Van Pelt among them—but the coach didn't have enough reliable ones to count on. That kept hitting home week after week as the losing continued, and he knew that eventually changes had to be made.

The constant losing wore on Parcells. Self-doubt had crept in, and there were no easy answers, especially with a team that had too many players who were too used to losing and too many players not playing at all. By season's end, there would be twenty-five players—virtually half the team he came into the season with—on injured reserve.

But it wasn't just what was happening on the field that rocked Parcells. Personal tragedy hit hard.

First it was the death of running backs coach Bob Ledbetter in September.

A few weeks later, the Parcells family dog, Buckles, died at age thirteen.

"She went everywhere with us," Parcells said of the golden retriever–yellow Labrador mix. "She was a good dog."

Losing a family pet may not rise to the level of mourning a loved one, but anyone who has grown attached to an animal, particularly a dog who lived for so long and who was such an important part of the family experience, can attest to the sadness over its death.

"We all loved that dog," Parcells said.

For Parcells, the heartache only grew from there. His father was hospitalized in October to undergo heart bypass surgery, and there were complications. Charles Parcells was supposed to be out of the hospital within a few days. Within four months, he was dead.

At the same time Parcells's father was being treated for his heart problems, his mother, Ida, was diagnosed with a cancer of the blood.

By December, she died.

"The funeral was two days before the last game," he said. "I knew she was sick. It's just what happens. It's hard to explain what your emotions are. It was a very, very difficult time."

"My dad, he wound up dying in February," Parcells said. "He was in the hospital and was getting ready to get out. I had gone to the Senior Bowl, come right back from Newark Airport to Hackensack Hospital. They planned on releasing him in two or three days. The day I got there, he had this infection that was causing him to be very ill. Then it subsides, and right before I got to the hospital, it came back. He was vomiting and very ill. He had just gone to sleep when I went to the hospital, and apparently it had been a long procedure to get him back to sleep."

Charles Parcells needed more surgery, and he was transferred to Columbia University Medical Center in Manhattan.

Parcells and his two brothers and sister saw him before the surgery. Charles told them he had lived a good life, had raised a good family, and was at peace in case he didn't make it. His children grew emotional and told him he still had a lot to live for, that he would soon return home.

They got the news shortly after the operation.

"It didn't work," Bill Parcells said.

His father fell into a coma and died within days.

In late December, there was another funeral for a member of the Giants' family: Popular running back Doug Kotar, who played from 1974 to 1982, was diagnosed with a brain tumor just weeks after retiring. Sixteen months later, on December 16, 1983, he was gone at age thirty-two, leaving behind his wife and two children.

As if dealing with all the personal heartache wasn't difficult enough, Parcells's professional life had begun to unravel as well. By late in the season, the Giants' front-office executives had become so concerned that there were serious discussions about finding a different coach.

Young held several meetings with the team's co-owners, Wellington and Tim Mara. (Young would meet separately with the feuding Mara family, since Wellington and Tim were not on speaking terms.) By December, a consensus had been reached to fire Parcells.

"George was the one pushing to make a change," said Wellington's son, John Mara, a labor attorney during that time. He was kept abreast of team-related issues through daily talks with his father.

"We were in the process of talking to people about buying out my cousin Tim," John Mara said. "So people were coming to us to express interest in the team. [Dolphins Hall of Fame linebacker] Nick Buoniconti brings a group of bankers for a meeting, and I remember him saying, 'The first thing is you have to get a new head coach, because that guy [Parcells] is terrible.'"

Young had targeted University of Miami head coach Howard Schnellenberger, with whom Young had worked as an assistant coach when Schnellenberger was head coach of the Colts in 1973–74. Schnellenberger was in his fifth season at the University of Miami, and had completed a 10-1 regular season to qualify for the national championship game against unbeaten Nebraska in the Orange Bowl—a game

Miami had won to earn the Hurricanes their first-ever national title. He had taken over the Hurricanes a few years earlier, when the program had nearly been dropped by the school, but he built the team into a national contender by bringing a pro-style offense and a hard-nosed style he learned while working for Bear Bryant at Alabama and Don Shula with the Dolphins.

Schnellenberger was the hottest coaching prospect out there, and the Giants were in disarray. Rock bottom came on December 4, when the Giants lost to the lowly Cardinals, 10–6. Only 25,156 fans showed up at Giants Stadium, meaning there were more than fifty thousand no-shows.

But when Young reached out to Schnellenberger, the coach told him the timing wasn't right and that he wouldn't take the job. Schnellenberger had already been contacted for several other coaching gigs—he even got a call from New Jersey Generals owner Donald Trump to coach the United States Football League team—and he eventually decided to take over the USFL's Washington Federals, which planned to relocate to Miami. (That deal eventually fell through, leaving Schnellenberger without a job in 1984.)

"I can't get him this year," Young told the Maras, "but I may be able to get him next year."

The Giants decided to give Parcells one more year to turn things around, and if the team continued to flounder, Young would try Schnellenberger again.

Unbeknownst to Young, Parcells had found out about the back-channel contact with Schnellenberger when he received a call from his agent, Robert Fraley.

Shortly after turning down the job, Schnellenberger had called his agent to let him know the Giants had reached out.

Schnellenberger's agent: Fraley.

"My agent called me and told me that Schnellenberger had told him that the Giants were shopping the job," Parcells said. "The Giants didn't know Schnellenberger had an agent, and it was the same agent I had. Listen, they'd seen enough. I think both owners were on board with it, and Schnellenberger was good about it by telling Fraley. He became my ally."

Bill Walsh (left) got his first job at Washington Union High School in Fremont, California. He inherited a team that had lost twenty-six of its last twenty-seven games, and they won the league championship within two years. He also drove the team bus. *Courtesy of Washington Union High School*

Walsh was an assistant coach in Cincinnati for the legendary Paul Brown. After Brown retired, he passed over Walsh and chose Bill "Tiger" Johnson as his replacement, a devastating blow for Walsh, but a moment that ultimately transformed his career and led to the greatest coaching tree in NFL history. *Getty Images: Nate Fine/Contributor*

In his final game at Stanford before being hired by the 49ers, Walsh presided over a dramatic second-half comeback win over Georgia in the Bluebonnet Bowl. Niners owner Eddie DeBartolo Jr. watched the game from his home in Youngstown, Ohio, and became convinced Walsh would be his next coach in 1979. *Courtesy of Stanford University*

Walsh had initially zeroed in on former Stanford quarterback Steve Dils in his first draft with the 49ers. But Sam Wyche convinced him to personally work out Joe Montana, and one of the great coach-quarterback relationships was soon created. © *Michael Zagaris*

Walsh's first Super Bowl victory came against the Bengals and team owner Paul Brown, and was the culmination of decades of preparation. *Getty Images: Focus On Sport/Contributor*

Walsh was so confident in his game plan leading up to Super Bowl XIX against the Dolphins that he lay down on the floor of the team's locker room not long before his players took the field. The 49ers crushed the Dolphins, 38–16, with Walsh saying it was as close to a perfect game as he'd ever called. © *Michael Zagaris*

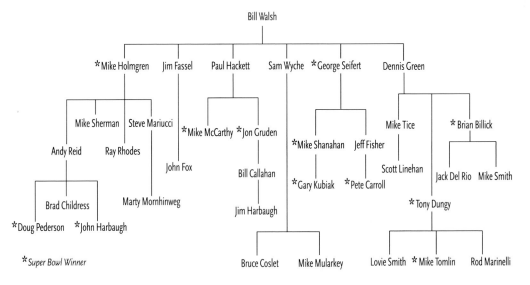

Bill Walsh

*Mike Holmgren · Jim Fassel · Paul Hackett · Sam Wyche · *George Seifert · Dennis Green

Mike Sherman · Steve Mariucci

*Mike McCarthy · *Jon Gruden

Mike Tice · *Brian Billick

Andy Reid · Ray Rhodes

John Fox

*Mike Shanahan · Jeff Fisher

Scott Linehan

Jack Del Rio · Mike Smith

Bill Callahan

*Gary Kubiak · *Pete Carroll

Brad Childress

Marty Mornhinweg

Jim Harbaugh

*Tony Dungy

*Doug Pederson · *John Harbaugh

Bruce Coslet · Mike Mularkey

Lovie Smith · *Mike Tomlin · Rod Marinelli

* *Super Bowl Winner*

Walsh coaching tree. *WikiCommons*

Joe Gibbs inherited Joe Theismann after getting the Redskins head coaching job in 1981, and Gibbs wasn't sure he could count on the flamboyant quarterback until Theismann showed up at Gibbs's house one night to convince the coach to believe in him. They wound up winning the Redskins' first Super Bowl championship the following season. *Getty Images: Nate Fine/Contributor*

Gibbs's first major move was talking John Riggins out of retirement in 1981. His plan was to trade Riggins, but the running back agreed to return only if the Redskins agreed to a no-trade clause. Riggins became a star in Gibbs's offense, and ran for one of the most memorable touchdowns in franchise history when he got past Dolphins defensive back Don McNeal for a 43-yard score in Super Bowl XVII. *WikiCommons*

Gibbs had agreed to trade Doug Williams to the Raiders shortly before the 1987 season, but abruptly reneged on the deal, thinking he might need the veteran backup. That turned out to be exactly the case, as Williams led the Redskins to the championship and became the first African American quarterback to win the Super Bowl. *Getty Images: Icon Sportswire/Contributor*

Gibbs became the only NFL coach to win three Super Bowls with three different quarterbacks, as the Redskins beat the Buffalo Bills, 37–24, in Super Bowl XXVI. A year after Mark Rypien helped the Redskins win the title, Gibbs announced his retirement. *Getty Images: Focus On Sport/Contributor*

Gibbs was talked out of retirement in 2004 by Redskins owner Daniel Snyder, and he coached four seasons before walking away from the NFL for good. *WikiCommons*

Gibbs loved racing cars while growing up in southern California, and he turned that passion into a second career by forming the Joe Gibbs Racing team. He still runs the NASCAR racing group. *WikiCommons*

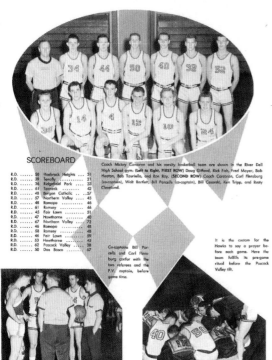

SCOREBOARD

R.D.	50	Hasbrock Heights	31
R.D.	39	Tenafly	21
R.D.	36	Ridgefield Park	33
R.D.	51	Teaneck	42
R.D.	48	Bergen Catholic	57
R.D.	57	Northern Valley	45
R.D.	48	Ramapo	46
R.D.	61	Ramsey	46
R.D.	45	Fair Lawn	51
R.D.	47	Hawthorne	40
R.D.	67	Northern Valley	72
R.D.	48	Ramapo	48
R.D.	58	Ramsey	46
R.D.	46	Fair Lawn	59
R.D.	53	Hawthorne	45
R.D.	62	Pascack Valley	38
R.D.	50	Don Bosco	67

Coach Mickey Corcoran and his varsity basketball team are shown in the River Dell High School gym. (Left to Right, FIRST ROW) Doug Gifford, Rick Fish, Fred Mayer, Bob Heaton, Bob Tauriello, and Ron Roy. (SECOND ROW) Coach Corcoran, Carl Flensburg (co-captain), Walt Bartlett, Bill Parcells (co-captain), Bill Cesorski, Ken Tripp, and Rusty Cleveland.

Co-captains Bill Parcells and Carl Flensburg confer with the two referees and the P.V. captain, before game time.

It is the custom for the Hawks to say a prayer before each game. Here the team fulfills its pre-game ritual before the Pascack Valley tilt.

River Dell High basketball coach Mickey Corcoran (top left) was the greatest influence on Bill Parcells (number 50) as a young athlete and a coach. The two remained close throughout Parcells's career, and Parcells regularly sought advice from Corcoran. *Courtesy of River Dell High School Athletic Department*

Parcells was the linebackers coach at Army under Tom Cahill, his former high school football coach. At West Point, Parcells befriended basketball coach Bobby Knight, who went on to a Hall of Fame career at Indiana. The two have remained friends ever since. *Courtesy of the United States Military Academy*

Parcells's first head coaching job was at Air Force, where he coached for just one season in 1978 before being recruited by Giants coach Ray Perkins to become the team's defensive coordinator. Parcells resigned before the season, but later returned in 1981 and eventually became head coach in 1983. *WikiCommons*

Parcells and quarterback Phil Simms (number 11) often had a combative relationship, but Parcells brought out the best in his quarterback. The two won the Giants' first Super Bowl championship after the 1986 season. Parcells won his second Super Bowl with Jeff Hostetler (number 15). *Getty Images: Focus On Sport/Contributor*

Parcells's 3-4 defense was one of the best in NFL history, thanks in large part to linebacker Lawrence Taylor (number 56), who credits Parcells with helping to turn him into a Hall of Fame players. Carl Banks (number 58) was another cornerstone linebacker for Parcells's two Super Bowl championship teams. *Getty Images: Focus On Sport/Contributor*

Parcells won Super Bowl XXI just three seasons after he was nearly fired. Following a 3-12-1 season in 1983, Parcells turned his team—and his career—around with the kind of Jersey-guy intensity that eventually put him in the Hall of Fame. *Getty Images:* New York Daily News *Archive/Contributor*

Parcells was furious when he found out what had happened, and almost immediately placed a call to one of his most trusted contacts in the league.

Raiders owner Al Davis had known Parcells since 1963, when Davis was the Raiders' coach and Parcells played for him in a college all-star game. The two grew close over the years, and Parcells regularly consulted Davis. This was one of his most important calls.

"Al really helped me with this," Parcells said. "He said, 'Listen, you've got to put yourself in the position of the owner and the general manager. You're raising hell here, and it's causing trouble. You've got to understand, this guy owns the team, this guy's running the team. You've got to do what you do. You coach the team. If you win, things will go well for you.'"

Davis told Parcells he'd take care of the rest.

He then put a call in to CBS analyst Jimmy "the Greek" Snyder, who reported the news that the Giants had reached out to Schnellenberger to replace Parcells, prompting Young to deny the story. Schnellenberger admitted he'd had contact with the team, although he wouldn't say it was with Young.

Parcells didn't say a word to Young, but he would never let go of the anger he felt over such a betrayal. The coach then heeded the advice of his mentor.

"Al's words were very helpful," Parcells said of his talk with Davis. "I knew for a fact that if I could just win games, that would take care of everything. So I got into a mind-set to just worry about winning."

Near the end of Parcells's nightmare first season as head coach, he sat down with Giants beat writer Vinny DiTrani of the Bergen County (New Jersey) *Record*, ostensibly to discuss what the coach planned to do to get out of the mess he found himself in.

"Put your pen down," Parcells told DiTrani.

Parcells wanted to go off the record and knew he could trust DiTrani, a widely respected reporter and writer who lived not far from where Parcells grew up in Bergen County. From one Jersey guy to the next, Parcells laid out his plan.

"I wanted to do the usual 'what the Giants need to do' type of story," said DiTrani, who was nicknamed "the Sage" by Parcells, a nod to DiTrani's football intelligence. "One day after practice, he takes me into the coaches' room and showed me this seven-point plan and said, 'If I can do these things, we turn this franchise around.'"

The list included an upgrade of the team's weight room, which was embarrassingly small and without the latest training equipment. Parcells confided he needed to get rid of several players and replace them with players more to the coach's liking—tougher and tougher-minded than many of the ones on the current roster.

"The whole thing, right across the board," DiTrani said. "He's giving me all these things, and I'm like, 'Why can't I write this?'"

"Because I haven't told George Young," Parcells said, "and I don't want him reading it in the paper."

Not long after their meeting, DiTrani had an off-the-record conversation with Young about Parcells's shaky situation.

"Well, [Parcells] came in and told me what he wanted to do," Young told DiTrani.

"Oh, you mean his seven-point plan?" DiTrani asked.

Young looked at DiTrani.

"How'd you know that?"

DiTrani smiled and told him about his conversation with Parcells.

"That helped sway George," DiTrani said of Parcells's checklist of priorities. "George became convinced the guy has a vision, so let's let him try it."

Parcells's first major move was hiring a strength and conditioning coach, and he settled on a noted college trainer named Johnny Parker. Parker was on the cutting edge of training techniques at LSU and Ole Miss, even traveling to Russia to study what had then been considered the world's most advanced weightlifting program.

Parcells was desperate to improve his team's collective health after a hellish run of injuries the year before, and Parker told him he could help. He did have some reservations, though.

"I didn't know if pro players would work hard," he said.

So Parker called Giants defensive end Leonard Marshall, the team's second-round pick in 1983 and a former LSU pass rusher who had trained under Parker in college.

"Leonard, I'm thinking about doing this," Parker told Marshall in his thick southern accent. "They might run me back to Mississippi on the first day. But if I've got one player that will do what I ask, then maybe I can get some more."

"I'll do anything you tell me to do," Marshall told him.

Parker took the job, and thereby gained insight into how Parcells was going to handle his team moving forward.

"Last year, I tried to be the head coach of the Giants, and that didn't work," Parcells told Parker. "This year, I'm going to be Bill Parcells. If the players get me, they get me. They're going to get me doing it my way."

Parker's off-season conditioning program was intense, and focused on a weightlifting system using free weights, a departure from the Nautilus system that many teams had been using.

"We were going to do what was the best thing for football players, and that is explosive lifting, doing it with heavy weights and lower repetitions," he said.

One of Parker's most diligent weight room workers was running back Joe Morris, a short, powerfully built tailback who came to the Giants in 1982 after a standout career at Syracuse.

"We were working out with the offensive linemen," Morris said. "Those guys had to push themselves to get stronger. If I'm stronger than they are, they're not doing their job. If Phil Simms and Joe Morris could lift more than they could, they're just not doing their job. We were trying to make guys stronger."

Another prized pupil: Simms, who only a few months earlier had demanded a trade, now focused his energy on rebuilding his injury-plagued body by adding muscle in hopes of finally staying on the field.

"Johnny Parker had this great enthusiasm and this great desire," Simms said. "I'd say, 'Johnny, I have something to do with my wife today and can't get to the stadium till late.' He'd say, 'Phil, I'll be here. If it's midnight, I'll wait on you.' There would be nights if I had to visit with my family in Kentucky, I'd get in at nine, and Johnny would be waiting for me. We'd run, I'd go home, sleep, and come back the next day. It was the first time I'd been in something so organized and felt good about it. So many other players bought in, and I do think it made a tremendous difference."

Parcells was a frequent visitor to the weight room, cajoling his players into working harder with the kind of ball-busting personality he'd had when he was a position coach and defensive coordinator, the personality he'd vowed to show.

"Johnny and Bill worked great together, because Johnny was like an extension of Parcells," former Giants guard Billy Ard said. "I'd go into the weight room no matter what time of the day, and Johnny would be there."

Ard had been nicknamed "Biff"—after Braves catcher Biff Benedict Pocoroba—and he wasn't a fan of the moniker. "One day I told Johnny, 'You can call me anything you want, but don't call me Biff.'"

Parcells found out about it, and needled Ard. From then on, he'd call him Biff—just because he knew it bothered Ard.

Another of Parcells's foils was nose tackle Jim Burt, a short, squatty defender who had made the team in 1981 as a free-agent walk-on out of Miami. Undersized at six-one, 260, Burt willed himself onto the roster with a work ethic that was off the charts. Motivated by a constant fear that he might be released at a moment's notice, Burt was the ultimate self-made player who essentially made it impossible for the coaches to keep him off the team.

"I barely slept in that first training camp," Burt said. "It was a horrible experience. They have five linemen in camp, and I was a real long shot to make the team."

Early one morning that first year, Burt got a knock on his dorm room door at the Giants' training camp. Burt knew it could mean only one thing: He was getting cut.

Locker room attendant Vinny Swerk—known in training camp as "the Turk" because he was the one to tell players they were being released—opened the door and said, "Bring your playbook. You need to see the coach."

Burt nearly cried with relief when he realized it was his roommate who was getting cut.

Parcells, who was in his first year as Ray Perkins's defensive coordinator, knew there was no way he could cut Burt. This was exactly the kind of player he needed for his 3-4 defense—a gritty nose tackle who could engage opposing offensive linemen and thus clear the way for the linebackers to make the tackle, particularly in the run defense.

But Parcells rarely offered outward praise for Burt, choosing instead to appeal to the tackle's competitive instincts as a way of getting the best out of him. Sometimes, it would drive Burt crazy. He remembered the time after the Giants' 1981 playoff game against Walsh's 49ers at Candlestick Park. The Giants lost the game, 38–24, but even in defeat, Parcells could appreciate the team's improvement.

So he went around the cramped, sweaty locker room beneath the end zone stands at Candlestick to all of his defensive players, shaking their hands and praising them for a job well done.

When he got to Burt, he scowled.

"Let me tell you something, you little bastard," Parcells said. "I'm gonna find four guys next year to take your spot."

Burt was so taken aback by Parcells's remarks that he thought the coach might be joking. When he realized Parcells was serious, Burt became furious.

"I wouldn't have it any other way," Burt said. "Go ahead and bring in whoever you want."

Burt remembers the moment like it was last year.

"He was a dick, man," he said of Parcells. "I was really pissed off. I was ready to throw down."

Burt was the perfect player for Parcells: hungry, motivated, determined, and competitive. Oh, so competitive. There was a chip on his shoulder that drove him, just as there was a chip on Parcells's shoulder that made him so determined. Maybe Burt didn't have all the measurables, but he was willing to work relentlessly to get better and make the players around him better.

Parcells knew in that off-season of 1984 that Burt was, as he said, "one of my guys," a guy he could always count on, especially when the team—and the coach—needed him most.

He also knew the guys he had to get rid of, the guys he couldn't count on. Even if they had talent.

His two biggest targets: linebackers Brian Kelley and Brad Van Pelt.

They were among the most popular players on the team, part of the vaunted "Crunch Bunch," the core of linebackers that featured Lawrence Taylor and Harry Carson. But Parcells knew there were internal problems on the team, and that Kelley and Van Pelt were at the heart of them.

While the two sure-handed tacklers were excellent game-day players, their partying off the field was creating a problem. And it was impacting Taylor, who Parcells realized during the 1983 season was drinking heavily and using cocaine. Being around Kelley and Van Pelt was only enabling Taylor, whose reckless off-field lifestyle would eventually become public.

"Brad and Brian played well on the field, but they had stuff going on off the field that may have contributed to them not being all-in and contributed to steering Lawrence in the wrong direction," Harry Carson said. "As a group, they were the little devils that were on one shoulder of Lawrence's, and I was the angel on the other side.

"We'd go out and go to a bar, and I'd be drinking ginger ale, and they'd be having shots of whiskey, gin, vodka, or whatever. Those guys [Kelley and Van Pelt] were part of an old crew," Carson said. "When I first got to the Giants [in 1979], there were guys that hung out at Foley's bar in Pleasantville. They'd drink, come to practice with a hangover, and you could smell the alcohol coming out of their system. As the years went by, those players became less. You took on a player that would go to McDonald's, not bars. You had these older guys who'd go into bars, and they smoked and drank heavily, and they could hang out all night. I was never one of those players who could do that. I had to get my rest. I didn't drink. There was only one vice I had, and that was something I kept to myself. I dated a lot of people. In terms of being able to play, nobody could accuse me of not being ready to practice because I'm hung over."

Kelley never made it to the opening-day roster in 1984, and he was out of the league after an eleven-year run with the Giants. Van Pelt was traded to the Vikings just before the start of their training camp, and the Giants got third-down back Tony Galbreath in return.

"I needed to get some of them out of there," Parcells said. "That trade with Van Pelt, you'd think I had traded the messiah. But we needed a nucleus of players we could count on. There were a couple of holdovers. Harry was one. George Martin was another. There was Burt and Taylor and Leonard Marshall, Terry Kinard, Perry Williams, Andy Headen, some of those guys."

Parcells knew he could win only if he had players who were completely committed to winning and to making the sacrifices—both physically and personally—to turn the team around. Young had drafted linebackers Carl Banks, a first-round pick out of Michigan State, and Gary Reasons, a fourth rounder out of Northwestern State University of Louisiana, to replace Kelley and Van Pelt. And with nearly two dozen other players dropped from the team, the coach was starting to feel like he had enough of the "my guys"–type players to at least have a chance of winning.

And Parcells drove them hard.

"Those 1984 players, they're the ones that went through a torture chamber, because I had a whole new attitude, a resolve," Parcells said. "I was close to being over the edge in terms of pressuring these guys, practicing hard, contact, training camp. No fuckin' around."

Simms could tell the difference in Parcells's demeanor as soon as he interacted with the coach after the 1983 season.

"Bill changed from '83 to '84," Simms said. "He became Bill Parcells, this tough, acid-mouthed guy, and whatever came out of his mouth was the truth. He did it with sarcasm and humor, but it still drove the point home. It just changed us. Right from the start, we were a changed team. You could see it."

Once training camp began, Parcells was unrelenting. He had his players practice in pads six days a week, twice a day—which was actually standard operating procedure for most teams, but with Parcells, he was particularly brutal.

If Parcells was going down—and there was that very real possibility, especially if he got off to a poor start—he would do so on his own terms.

"Every day was a war," Billy Ard said. "Absolutely, it was a war."

The players dressed in a cramped locker room by the field—just the atmosphere Parcells wanted.

"It was definitely Spartan. It was horrible. You couldn't bend over, couldn't move around in there," Ard said. "Plus, you had 110 guys in camp, and it was like a prison cell. But that's exactly what he wanted."

Each morning after stretching, Parcells would blow his whistle and send the players to their first drill: They called it the "Pace Party." This was no party, though. This was the "Oklahoma drill," one of the most brutal football practice drills ever, and one that is not often used any longer because of its barbarity.

The drill was named after the great Oklahoma coach Bud Wilkinson, who won three national championships and once had a streak of forty-seven straight wins—a record that still stands. The drill involves two players lined up a few yards opposite each other, with blocking bags on each side to create a lane inside which the drill takes place. At the whistle, the players come at each other and engage until one player is either on the ground or outside the lane. A runner can also be used in the drill, and the defensive player's goal is to shed the block of the offensive player and hit the running back.

Parcells had renamed the Oklahoma drill the "Pace Party" after the college hosting the Giants' training camp.

"We did it every day," Ard said. "I'm sitting there running into Harry Carson from seven, eight, nine yards away. It's just attack, like two rams. It was brutal."

But for Parcells, it was necessary.

"In football, the only way to have fun is to kick the guy's ass in front of you and win games," Ard said. "That's Bill. You've got to kick someone's ass, and you have to win, and you have fun."

Parcells would not screw around with his quarterback situation this time, installing Simms as his starter and hoping that the volatile quarterback, whose career had been stunted because of injury, could stay on the field and live up to his potential. He had added muscle after an off-season in Parker's weight-training program, and there would be no Simms-Brunner training camp competition. In fact, there would be no Brunner, as the Giants had moved on from him and gone with Jeff Rutledge as the backup and Jeff Hostetler, a third-round pick out of West Virginia, as the number 3 quarterback.

Parcells had done all he could in training camp to create the circumstances under which they could succeed during the regular season. But he still felt he needed to underscore what was at stake. After a practice near the end of training camp, Parcells gathered his players around and showed a side of himself they'd never seen.

"To this day, I've never seen him more vulnerable in terms of putting his heart on his sleeve and being as unguarded as he was in order to connect with our team," Banks said. "That was the birth of 'the Parcells guy,' because after that speech, he got everybody up."

"Look, they're going to fire my ass if I don't win around here this year," Parcells told them. "I'm going to make some tough decisions. I need to know the guys on this team are my guys. I need you guys. You give me everything you got, and I'll give you everything I got."

"That was a seminal moment with his players and with his team," Banks said. "I don't think any coach could have been more vulnerable. We bought in, he did things his way, and we responded."

The Giants responded with as perfect a start to a season as imaginable. They beat the Eagles and Cowboys at home, and Parcells had some proof that he could turn this thing around. Two games, and already he had nearly as many wins as the entire 1983 season.

But trouble was not far off.

They lost three of their next four—including blowout losses to Gibbs's Redskins and Walsh's 49ers. The loss to the 49ers was particularly hideous. In a Monday night matchup at Giants Stadium, Parcells's defense was absolutely miserable in a 31–10 loss. The 49ers built a 21–0 lead just 7:33 into the game, as Joe Montana executed Walsh's game plan perfectly.

At 3-3 and with a road game up next in Atlanta against the 3-3 Falcons, Parcells's season was again threatening to unravel.

DiTrani, the *Record* sportswriter Parcells told had confided in and told his plan to rebuild the team after the previous year's 3-12-1 disaster, sat in his press box seat at Atlanta–Fulton County Stadium and thought he was witnessing the beginning of the end for Parcells in the first quarter.

"Early in the game, Steve Bartkowski hits Stacey Bailey, and it looks like it's going for a touchdown," DiTrani said. "Bailey is running down the sidelines heading for the end zone and I'm thinking, 'Oh, here it goes.'"

But seemingly out of nowhere, Giants cornerback Perry Williams, a former college sprinter at North Carolina State who had qualified for the 1980 U.S. Olympic 4×100 relay team, caught Bailey from behind and tackled him at the 1.

It was a brilliant play, but still the Falcons should have had an easy time getting into the end zone on first and goal from the 1.

But the Giants' defense, featuring rookies Banks and Reasons, stuffed the Falcons on four straight plays to turn the momentum around. Banks sacked Bartkowski for a 1-yard loss on fourth down, and the Giants went on to win, 19–7.

"I think that was the turning point of Parcells's entire career," DiTrani said. "If he'd lost that game, I don't know what would have happened, but I always think of that game as the one that turned everything around."

Parcells agreed.

"Even going into that 1984 season," he said, "I was probably a loss from getting fired. I think if we'd lost that game in Atlanta, there's a chance there could have been a change."

The win in Atlanta proved to be the spark Parcells needed. His team won five of the next seven games—including a 37–13 thumping of the Redskins at RFK—and wound up going 9–7 to make it into the playoffs as an NFC wild card team.

Parcells was starting to feel his oats, and the Jersey-guy confidence—bordering on cockiness—started to come out. He even had words with the Giants' radio analyst, Dick Lynch, who had openly criticized the coach the year before but now tried to cozy up to him.

"There was a guy where my relationship got fuckin' ruined with him, and it was Dick Lynch," Parcells said of the former Giants and Redskins cornerback. "And listen, I deserved it. That first year, particularly, but then we started to win some games, and now he's trying to ingratiate himself, and I couldn't turn the other cheek. I told him, 'Look it, you're just a guy that played twenty years ago. Nobody's gonna confuse you with anybody that knows what's going on.'

"It was stupid on my part," Parcells said. "Because now, we've got to live with each other for all those years."

But the interaction stayed with Parcells and taught him a valuable lesson about people. And about himself.

"When somebody shows you who they are, believe them," he said. "If someone shows you they're a crook, believe them. If someone shows you they're dishonest or unscrupulous, believe 'em. He kind of showed me he was something, and I never did let it go, which probably wasn't the right thing."

More than thirty years later, Parcells still regrets the way he dealt with Lynch.

"My father was a bright guy, and his wisdom resonates with me every day of my life," Parcells said. "He said if a man reaches his hand out to you and you don't take it, then it's your problem. If someone is trying to make amends and he tries to do that and you're not accepting of it, that's your problem, not his problem. I probably should have reacted a little differently, but I was so pissed at the guy that I couldn't see it."

But that combination of competitiveness and combativeness also drove Parcells, and now he had legitimately turned things around. It was Parcells's own unique brand of guts and genius.

The Giants were in the tournament again on Parcells's own terms, and his players responded as well as he could have hoped. Simms had made it through the entire season without missing a start for the first time in his career. Morris had begun to flourish with more time in the running back rotation. Even free-agent walk-on Bobby Johnson, given a chance by Parcells as a rookie, led the team with 795 receiving yards and 7 touchdowns.

Parcells had made the correct move to replace veteran linebackers Kelley and Van Pelt with Banks and Reasons. Taylor produced what was then a career high with $11^1/_2$ sacks. Carson and Martin were now his unquestioned leaders in the locker room.

And Parcells's coaching staff, which included his run-centric, meat-and-potatoes offensive coordinator Ron Erhardt and a defensive staff that featured a bright young linebackers coach named Bill Belichick, had taken shape.

Parcells's team and his coaches were just the way he wanted. They were tough, and they were tough-minded.

His first playoff test would take him to the West Coast against the Rams in Anaheim in the wild card round. Los Angeles featured Eric

Dickerson in his prime, as the chiseled running back with the trademark black goggles and high-stepping style was coming off an NFL-record 2,105 rushing yards in the regular season—a mark that still stands.

So there would be no secrets to how the Rams would attack the Giants, nor would there be any doubt that this would be the ultimate test for Parcells's retooled defense. Irresistible force against the immovable object? Absolutely.

Advantage Giants.

"You can't stop him," Belichick said. "You just try to keep him under control."

Dickerson got his yards, but the Giants got the better of Dickerson. He coughed up a first-quarter fumble that the Giants converted into a touchdown, and Dickerson was held to 107 yards on 23 carries. He did score a third-quarter touchdown to bring the Rams to within a field goal, 13–10, but the Giants wound up winning 16–13 after keeping the Rams out of the end zone on a key fourth-quarter series.

Early in the final quarter, Dickerson broke into the open field and appeared headed for the end zone, but second-year free safety Terry Kinard caught him from behind at the Giants' 34. Dickerson helped power the Rams for a first and goal at the Giants' 7, but a key defensive stand held the Rams to a field goal. Dickerson ran only once more for 3 yards, the Giants tackled Dwayne Crutchfield for a 3-yard loss, and quarterback Jeff Kemp's third-down pass fell incomplete, forcing the Rams to settle for Mike Lansford's 22-yard field goal.

The Rams had one more shot late in the fourth quarter, and were down to a fourth and six at their own 30. Martin turned to Taylor just before the Giants broke the defensive huddle.

"Meet me at the quarterback," Martin told him.

"See you there," said Taylor.

They did as promised, combining for a sack and forced fumble to seal the Giants' 16–13 win for Parcells's first postseason victory.

Up next: Bill Walsh and the 49ers at Candlestick Park.

Parcells had already decided he'd keep his team in California in the event of a win over the Rams, especially with the divisional-round game in San Francisco set for a Saturday afternoon. The Giants practiced in Fresno, moved Friday night to a hotel in Berkeley, and then went to Candlestick for a rematch against a team that had humiliated them earlier in the season in a 31–10 Monday night shellacking at Giants Stadium.

Montana had scorched the Giants' defense in that one with three touchdown passes by the midway point of the first quarter, but this game would prove more difficult for the star quarterback, who only three years earlier had won his first Super Bowl.

Montana did produce three more touchdown passes in the early going, but the Giants intercepted him twice in the first half—including a pick that was returned 14 yards for a touchdown by Harry Carson to bring the Giants to within four, 14–10. Montana had one more touchdown throw to Freddie Solomon, but that was it.

The 49ers won the game, 21–10, leaving Parcells disappointed, yet certainly not demoralized. After all, the 49ers had already established themselves as Super Bowl worthy, and they were coming off a 15–1 season as the NFL's top team.

The Giants drove into 49ers territory several times in the second half, but never came away with points, thanks to San Francisco's smothering defense. The 49ers limited Simms to 218 passing yards and intercepted him twice.

"We had our chances," Parcells said afterward. "We got down there three or four times and couldn't get it in. That's the difference right there. I'm proud of my players. We are all disappointed."

Simms, who was sacked 6 times and lost a fumble in addition to his two picks, acknowledged the 49ers were the better team and deserved to win, but he remained defiant about his team's capability.

"I still think we can play with them," he said.

Someone else who was impressed by the Giants' performance, even in a losing effort: Walsh himself.

"The Giants," he said, "are definitely a team of the future."

Those words would soon prove prophetic.

WALSH

A FALL FROM GRACE

Mike White picked up the phone in his hotel room in Honolulu a few days before the 1983 Hula Bowl. Bill Walsh was on the other end, and White could tell something was wrong.

Walsh told White he was ready to quit as the 49ers' coach, and he wanted White to take over the team.

White sat in stunned disbelief as he listened to his best friend tell him he was done.

Only a year earlier, Walsh had been carried off the field at the Pontiac Silverdome after winning the Super Bowl. He had taken the 49ers from the bottom of the NFL in 1979 to a world championship after the 1981 season, and now he was ready to step down as coach?

White was both astonished and confused.

But as the two men spoke, White understood Walsh's angst and realized what was happening.

Walsh's world had again begun to unravel, and the self-doubt he had frequently experienced during his long and difficult journey to the top of the NFL had begun to creep in once more. The reason for the latest bout of uncertainty rested with the team's failure to make the playoffs the year after winning it all.

Even though the 1982 season was interrupted by an unprecedented player strike that negatively impacted so many other teams, Walsh felt he was the reason for the team's 3-6 record, and he felt it would be better to remove himself from the sidelines and let someone else lead the team while he continued as general manager. Walsh was so despondent after losing to the Rams in the final regular-season game—a win would have gotten him into the playoffs—that he went into hiding for several days.

"Mike, I want you to be my coach," Walsh told White, who was head coach at Illinois and serving as a coach in the annual East-West college all-star game in Honolulu. "I'm going to go to Eddie DeBartolo and tell him that you should be the head coach, and that I want to be the general manager."

White, who had known Walsh when the two were assistants for Marv Levy at UC Berkeley more than two decades earlier, patiently listened to Walsh as he explained his reasoning and revealed his despondency over not being in position to defend his Super Bowl title.

"Bill, I'm not going to be your coach," White told him. "You can't leave now. What you've accomplished, you have all the ability in the world. Those kids are depending on you."

The two men spoke for about thirty minutes, with White offering his friend a dose of support at a time Walsh needed it most.

"Bill was just one of those guys that, if something just wasn't going right," White said, "that's when he'd really start battling himself."

Word eventually filtered out that Walsh was seriously considering giving up his head coaching duties, and he even told his assistant coaches they were free to look for jobs elsewhere. Walsh told DeBartolo of his indecision, and after the two men spoke extensively about the situation, it was decided that Walsh would stay on as head coach.

"In just three years he took us from a floundering franchise decimated through trades and other questionable player development to a great regular season and the world championship," DeBartolo said in a statement shortly after his meetings with Walsh. "Last season was just one for the history books. With Bill returning to the sidelines, we will continue to have the formula we've developed for championship football. We'll be back."

Once Walsh got over his indecision, something had changed in him. After days and weeks of reflection, he understood the reasons for his team's failure during the strike season. And while some of it could be justified by the fact that a two-month layoff from the strike was difficult for any team to overcome, he also knew he had to change because of how his players had reacted to winning a championship.

Walsh realized he could no longer be friends with the players he coached.

"We had an inordinate amount of fun after the Super Bowl in that off-season," longtime 49ers center Randy Cross said. "Between the strike and the fact that we were so bad and we didn't make the tournament, nothing was the same. Bill and the coaches used to come to our team parties after games, and it would be great. But that changed in 1983."

There were rumors of drug use, something Walsh alluded to at the time, although he never specified which players or how many players might have been involved with drugs. And there were no arrests—something Montana pointed out to anyone asking whether there was a pervasive problem in the locker room. But there were a number of roster changes after the 1982 season; more important, there was a change in Walsh's demeanor.

With a failed season in his immediate past, Walsh went from gregarious players' coach to no-nonsense taskmaster who would never get as close to his players as he once had. The man who once commandeered a bellhop suit to welcome his players to Detroit before Super Bowl XVI would now put a wall up between himself and his team.

"We betrayed his trust," Cross said, "and he never treated us the same after 1982."

Walsh still felt deeply about his players and was still fiercely loyal to the ones who meant so much to his success. But coming off such a miserable year—the strike interruption notwithstanding—he had to recalibrate his style to put his team back in position to be a championship contender.

"Bill was a no-nonsense guy, and while he still had his heart side, I think he adjusted his approach to the situation and to the players, in that vein," said John McVay, Walsh's trusted personnel man. "He would come across every now and then and be relaxed and engaging, but if the situation demanded it, he would come across as very, very stern. He was under a great deal of pressure, most of which he brought on himself. He was anxious to be successful and to prove himself to anyone who might have thought he wasn't up to it."

With the labor situation resolved for the moment and no threat of a strike for the foreseeable future, Walsh found his bearings after his own moments of self-doubt.

An uncertain off-season nearly veered off into a franchise-shaking decision.

In the run-up to the 1983 draft, with a vaunted quarterback class that included John Elway, Dan Marino, Jim Kelly, Ken O'Brien, Tony Eason, and Todd Blackledge, Walsh briefly dabbled with the idea of going after the number 1 pick to take Elway.

The two had already crossed paths in 1978, when Walsh targeted Elway for Stanford.

"That was before Bill went to the 49ers," Elway said. "Bill was there in the beginning of the recruiting process, and then he ended up getting the [San Francisco] job. So Rod Dowhower [who was on Walsh's Stanford staff] ended up getting the head job at Stanford."

Elway's agent, Marvin Demoff, who also represented Marino, kept a journal before the draft and made a note that Walsh had expressed interest in the Colts' number 1 pick to take Elway. This after Montana had won the Super Bowl less than fifteen months earlier.

Ernie Accorsi, the Colts' general manager, briefly discussed a potential deal with Walsh, who was likely interested in drafting Elway while still keeping Montana.

"I think Bill may have wanted to keep Elway out of Oakland," Accorsi said.

Accorsi seemed interested, but only on one condition.

"There's only one guy in America that I'd trade for, and that's Joe Montana," Accorsi said. "And I'll never forget what Walsh told me. He said, 'I could never do that to Joe for all that he's done for me.'"

The talks ended there.

But Walsh did end up with an important new addition to his offense that year.

Roger Craig, a high-stepping fullback out of Nebraska, would join Wendell Tyler in the 49ers' backfield and produce the kind of one-two punch that Walsh had never truly had until now. Craig would be the perfect all-purpose back for Walsh's system.

Walsh had maneuvered in the draft to get Craig in the second round. Having acquired pass rusher Fred Dean from the Chargers in

1981 for a second-round pick, the 49ers reacquired that pick in a trade that saw the Chargers send two second-round picks to San Francisco in exchange for the 49ers' first rounder.

Craig had played fullback at Nebraska, with Mike Rozier as the I back, but Craig was much different from the traditional blocking fullback. At six feet, 222 pounds, he could block, he could run, and he could catch passes out of the backfield—a combination that perfectly suited Walsh's offense.

"When I came out, there weren't a lot of running backs catching passes out of the backfield," Craig said. "There were mostly pure runners, like Walter Payton, Eric Dickerson, Ottis Anderson, Joe Morris. And of course, you had John Riggins. So it wasn't like running backs were catching a lot of balls out of the backfield. But in our system, we all had roles, and Bill gave me a role where I would block some, run some, and catch passes."

One of the earliest messages Walsh imparted to Craig, as well as the entire team, was one of interconnectivity. It was especially important that Walsh communicate that early on in 1983, because he needed his players to understand they were dependent on one another, and that one of the biggest reasons for their failure from the year before was the loss of that harmony.

"Bill used to always call us being an extension of one another," Craig said. "When he gave us motivational talks, he'd say we all had roles, and we all had to carry out those roles as well as possible, and that was the only way to do things. For example, I was an extension of the play-action fake so the receivers could catch these slant passes. So I had to sell the fake like I'm running the ball. And if I didn't sell that fake, I felt like shit. My goal was to sell that fake like I was running the ball, and I might have gotten my helmet knocked off a few times because the defense thought I had the ball, but if I looked up at the scoreboard and we got 6 [points], I knew I did my job."

Walsh's vision was rewarded with a dynamic start to the season, as the 49ers recovered from an opening-day loss to the Eagles and won six of their next seven games to reestablish themselves by midseason. Craig had proven to be a quick study in the offense, and he and Tyler were just what Walsh was looking for—reliable runners and blockers who were just as adept in an offense where the swing pass was every bit as effective as an off-tackle run. In fact, the short passing game was an extension of the run, and when executed properly, it was difficult for any defense to contain it.

By season's end, the 49ers had gotten back to the playoffs with a 10-6 record. Craig had 725 rushing yards and 8 touchdowns, adding 427 receiving yards and 4 touchdown catches, while Tyler led the team with 856 rushing yards, adding 4 rushing touchdowns and 2 receiving scores. And Montana had his best year yet, throwing for 3,910 yards, 26 touchdown passes, and 12 interceptions.

"I think we all felt pretty good going into the playoffs that year," Montana said.

After earning a bye week, the 49ers faced the Lions in the NFC divisional round and needed some more Montana fourth-quarter magic to get past a stubborn Detroit team.

The 49ers were back in the NFC Championship Game for the second time in three years. The opponent: the defending Super Bowl champion Redskins and coach Joe Gibbs.

There was no better team in the regular season than the Redskins, who had produced one of the most dynamic offensive performances in NFL history. Their 541 total points set a record for most in a season, and they led the NFL with an astounding 209-point differential.

This would be the ultimate test for the 49ers' defense, which was the league's fourth-best unit in the regular season. Washington's defense under defensive coordinator Richie Petitbon had also been strong, especially against the run, having allowed the fewest rushing yards and tied for the fewest rushing touchdowns.

The Redskins had their way through three quarters, building a seemingly insurmountable lead on two rushing touchdowns by Riggins and a 70-yard touchdown pass from Theismann to Charlie Brown to give Washington a 21–0 lead.

But then Montana got to work, firing off two touchdown passes to wide receiver Mike Wilson, who was filling in for the injured Clark. The 49ers had lost their top receiver to a knee injury in the regular-season finale against Dallas. Montana also hit Solomon, and the 49ers were now all even at 21–21 coming down the stretch.

The Redskins had one last chance to win it at the end, even if it meant putting the game in kicker Mark Moseley's hands. He had already missed four field goals that would have put the game away, and it looked as if it would come down to one last attempt.

It did, but not before two controversial penalties against the 49ers—penalties that still infuriate many of their players to this day.

First, Eric Wright was called for pass interference on Art Monk's sideline pattern, a call the 49ers argued because it appeared the ball was uncatchable at the time Wright made contact. The call stood and gave the Redskins possession at the 49ers' 18. Three plays later, Theismann threw an incompletion in the end zone, but away from the play, Lott was called for holding on Brown. Lott had earlier been called on a key pass interference on Monk, a play that led to a Redskins touchdown.

The final penalty gave the Redskins a first down at the 49ers' 8, and Moseley stepped onto the field for one last try with the game on the line.

"Before he went out there, I was going to offer him a blindfold and a cigarette," Riggins cracked after the game. "Actually, I was just hoping we could give ol' Mo one more chance before they fired him."

Moseley made the 25-yard attempt to put the Redskins into the Super Bowl and send the 49ers home.

Afterward, Walsh was livid at the officiating.

"I thought we played extremely well. We just came up short," he said. "Right now, I'm just bitter about the officiating at the end of the game."

The penalty on Wright was particularly galling. He described the play to Monk as a pass "that could not have been caught by a ten-foot Boston Celtic."

All these years later, there are still hard feelings about the penalties.

"We were robbed by the referee," former 49ers linebacker Keena Turner said, his voice rising in anger as he thought back on that game. "That was a very, very tough deal for us. Theismann would agree with me on those penalties."

Actually, he wouldn't. Nor would Gibbs.

"You tell Keena that Ronnie held about twenty times during the game, and he got called once and you're pissed," Theismann said when told of Turner's anger over the calls. "Just tell them they're lucky there weren't twenty other calls."

Gibbs laughed when he was told some 49ers players from that game are still bitter about the calls all these years later.

"They should have called it [holding] four times," Gibbs said of the penalty on Lott. "The man was hanging on our slot back for the entire game, and they finally got one called. I can tell you that he was hanging on."

DeBartolo recalls the game as if it were yesterday.

"I can still hear the sounds, still feel the steel pounding in the stands when those Redskins started stomping their feet on the steel," the former owner said. "It was driving me crazy. Then we get this fictitious call on Ronnie Lott. I thought we had a chance to win that game."

They didn't, but the loss would ultimately serve a purpose for Walsh, who now had a ready-made motivational tool to prepare his team for the following season.

There was a valuable lesson to be learned from the defeat, and the Niners knew it intuitively as they processed the entirety of the season and how the playoffs ended sooner than they'd hoped. Walsh seized on it as he prepared for the 1984 season, and he reinforced the notion that nothing this team had done in the past—even winning a championship in 1981—could guarantee future success. Success had to be earned as a result of the preparation in the here and now, not the memory of what had once been.

"What we learned from that is that we knew what it took to get there, and that getting there once doesn't guarantee you anything," Turner said. "I felt like we were good enough to win it that year, but to have that disappointment, it made us come back the next year with a mission. Every year is a year unto itself, and the obstacles that you deal with one year won't be the same the next. All those kinds of learning experiences happened to us from 1981 to 1984, and it set an attitude that stayed here for years to come. Those were very important formative years."

Walsh would get a good sense of whether his message had gotten through during a Week 2 game against the Redskins.

Washington had made it to the Super Bowl with that white-knuckle win over the 49ers at RFK in the conference title game, but the Redskins were then humiliated two weeks later in Super Bowl XVIII. Despite being favored to beat the Raiders, Gibbs's team was destroyed, 38–9, leaving the coach, who only a year earlier had been sky-high after his Super Bowl win over the Dolphins, thoroughly embarrassed.

One particular play from that game still haunts Gibbs, and is emblematic of all that went wrong that day:

In the final seconds of the first half, with the Raiders leading, 14–3, and the Redskins on their own 12-yard line, Gibbs called a play named "Rocket Screen." The play was designed to be a high-percentage pass to the left to tailback Joe Washington, who had burned the Raiders for a 67-yard gain in the regular season.

On the Raiders sideline, Raiders assistant coach Charlie Sumner alertly replaced middle linebacker Matt Millen with seldom-used Jack Squirek. Millen was furious that he was taken off the field, but the move turned out to be brilliant. As Theismann faded back and looked to his right to try and make the Raiders think he was throwing deep to that side, he then turned to his left and floated a pass over Raiders lineman Lyle Alzado's head. Squirek anticipated the play and stepped in front of Washington to make the interception and return it 5 yards for the touchdown to make it 21–3.

"That game was a classic for me, because it showed how short the trip is back to a normal place in the world," Gibbs said, thinking back on the play. "Rather than just fall on the ball, I'd called an under screen, hoping we could get to midfield. Theismann threw a perfect strike to the Raiders' linebacker [Squirek] who scored. In the *Washington Post* the next day, I went from being a pretty sharp coach to being called a buffoon. It was a short trip back to reality. That thing really hurt."

Gibbs wouldn't feel much better after the Niners rematch, because this time the script was flipped. Unlike the conference championship game, when the Redskins got out to a dominating lead, it was the 49ers who got off to the fast start.

The 49ers built a 27–0 first-half advantage before the Redskins finally got on the board, with Montana throwing one touchdown pass and Tyler scoring two rushing touchdowns to go with two Ray Wersching field goals.

Theismann finally heated up in the second half, using Art Monk as his favorite target (the receiver finished with 10 catches for 200 yards). Riggins scored two rushing touchdowns, but the 49ers held off the furious rally in a 37–31 win to get off to a 2-0 start.

"That first half is as bad as we've played since I've been here," Gibbs told reporters afterward.

Walsh was delighted after the win, even though the Redskins' second-half rally nearly ruined all that brilliant work in the first half. As far as Walsh was concerned, his defense, which held Riggins to just 12 rushing yards on 10 attempts and thwarted a late drive, was superb.

"I'm satisfied with every aspect of our game," he said.

That satisfaction would continue through the following month, as the 49ers reeled off wins over the Saints, Eagles, Falcons, and Giants. Their 31–10 win over Bill Parcells's Giants was a simply masterful performance that saw the 49ers score three touchdowns in the first quarter. At 6-0, they were set to face the Steelers at home in a game that should have been a routine victory.

The 49ers were now the hot team. When the Steelers visited Candlestick Park, backup quarterback Mark Malone was making only his third career start after replacing the injured David Woodley, who had been traded from the Dolphins that year to compete with Malone after Terry Bradshaw had retired.

Perhaps overlooking the Steelers, the 49ers were flat for most of the afternoon yet still carried a 17–10 lead with less than five minutes to play. The Steelers then reeled off 10 unanswered points—including a touchdown after a hotly debated pass interference call in the end zone on Wright.

"I can see that play like it was yesterday," Wright told Eric Branch of the *San Francisco Chronicle*. "[John Stallworth] just ran a crossing pattern on the goal line and, shoot, I just thought I made one of the best plays I've ever made to knock down a pass. And here comes the old flag. I couldn't believe it… That was the play that sealed our fate."

Montana didn't help matters with an uncharacteristic interception that the Steelers converted into the go-ahead field goal.

Even so, the Niners had a chance to tie it after Montana put them in field goal position in the final seconds. But Wersching missed a 37-yard attempt, and the 49ers had suffered their first loss of the season.

In hindsight, though, that might have been the best thing that could have happened.

"It made us refocus and gave us our drive," fullback Earl Cooper told Branch. "We didn't get the big head."

Could there have been something else at work in the loss? Former 49ers safety Tom Holmoe wonders if it was the choice of Donny and Marie Osmond to sing the national anthem that threw the 49ers off their game. The 49ers had frequently used Huey Lewis and the News to perform the anthem, but on this day, the Mormon pop singers might have created a different vibe.

"I went to [Brigham Young University], I'm Mormon, and they sang the national anthem," Holmoe told Branch. "People were looking down the line at me. They were like 'What's up with this?' They blamed me for the loss."

Said Wilson: "Oh, yeah, if Huey or Jeffrey Osborne would have sung the national anthem, we would have won that game. Hands down. Guaranteed."

No matter the reason, the 49ers responded well to the loss. In fact, they didn't lose again for the rest of the regular season, earning the top seed in the playoffs with a 15-1 record, the best in franchise history and bettered only by the 16-0 Patriots in 2007.

Walsh had regained his bearings, and his system was now in full bloom, with the right players to operate his offense—starting with Montana, Clark, and Solomon, and now including a dynamic runner and pass catcher in Craig.

The 49ers' first playoff matchup was against the Giants, who had been regular-season fodder in a blowout win at Giants Stadium. But after Parcells's team had gutted out a wild card victory over the Rams the week before, Walsh knew he had a formidable opponent.

The 49ers certainly didn't roll over the Giants in what turned out to be a 21–10 win, and Walsh was impressed enough after the game to correctly label them "a team of the future."

Up next in the NFC Championship Game: Mike Ditka's Bears, a team that was coming into its own under the fiery coach and Hall of Fame tight end. The Bears had finished the regular season with a 10-6 record, and their defense—which was overseen by cantankerous coach Buddy Ryan and included dynamic playmakers like Mike Singletary, Richard Dent, Dan Hampton, Wilber Marshall, and Steve McMichael—had turned into one of the NFL's best defenses ever.

The Bears were good enough to beat the Redskins in the divisional round at RFK Stadium to set up a showdown against the 49ers at Candlestick for the conference championship. Could Walsh's offense, which had developed a reputation as a finesse unit, deal with the kind of speed and power the Bears presented? Walsh, who'd now revived his reputation as The Genius, would be tested like never before against a team that was shaping up as a potential champion in its own right.

But while the Bears would later blossom into arguably the most dominant single-season team in NFL history, that would have to wait, because Walsh's guile proved a more fearsome adversary than Ditka's power football approach.

Not this time for Da Coach.

As he game-planned for the Bears, Walsh felt he could actually take advantage of the Bears' hyperaggressive defense, not by trying to match their strength, but by trying to match Chicago's power with the 49ers' intellect. In a team meeting during the week, Walsh set the psychological stage by appealing to his players' resourcefulness and by actually mocking the Bears' reputation as bullies.

"I think you can knock their ass off, the more I think about it," Walsh said as he stood at the front of the meeting room. "They're setting themselves up as a football team. Any time a guy thinks he's rough and tough, four out of five of those guys get their ass kicked, 'cause most of those guys are dumb."

Walsh had perfectly calibrated his team's psyche, and his words proved correct.

After a shaky first half in which Montana threw two interceptions and San Francisco clung to a 6–0 lead, the 49ers dominated the second half to pull away. And once again, Walsh's genius showed itself with a new wrinkle on offense.

On a third-quarter drive, he told rookie guard Guy McIntyre to go into the game at fullback to replace Craig. Walsh saw that Craig was often overpowered by the physical front of the Bears' 46 defense, so he needed to give the inside running game a boost.

It came in the form of the six-foot-three, 280-pound McIntyre, a former high school tight end who originally played defensive line at Georgia but was then switched to offensive tackle. Walsh saw McIntyre as more of a guard, but the rookie was a backup that first season.

Now it was his time to do something never before done.

With the 49ers in position to add to their lead, Walsh went over to McIntyre on the sidelines and gave him the play to relay in to Montana. Walsh had used McIntyre as a fullback earlier in the drive, but McIntyre realized this could be a deciding play in the game.

"I remember Bill giving me the play to take in, and I'm like, 'What?' There's a lot of parts to the play, and I'm trying to memorize it as I'm running onto the field."

Montana saw McIntyre come on for Craig, and the quarterback stepped out of the huddle. Then McIntyre stepped on his foot.

"I'm wearing studded cleats, and I stepped on his foot, and I'm like, 'Oh, my goodness, I broke his foot.' Joe actually pushed me in my chest to get me off his foot. Him being the tough guy that he was, he sucked it up and we ran the play."

The play called for Tyler to take a handoff and run inside, with center Randy Cross clearing a path and McIntyre assigned to block All-Pro defensive tackle Dan Hampton, one of the NFL's fiercest defensive linemen. Montana called for the snap, handed off to Tyler, and McIntyre immediately headed for Hampton, knocking him backward and opening the hole for Tyler, who scored to make it 13–0.

Ditka would take note of the effectiveness of that play and would use a similar variation the following year, turning William "the Refrigerator" Perry into a household name when he was used in the backfield and actually scored a touchdown in the following year's Super Bowl.

But not before the 49ers embarrassed Ditka's Bears, 23–0.

The 49ers had made it to their second Super Bowl in a four-year span, and Walsh would face Don Shula and the Miami Dolphins at the stadium where Walsh once coached for Stanford.

The game was billed as the ultimate quarterback duel: Montana, the gifted conductor of Walsh's precision offense, versus second-year gunslinger Dan Marino, the Dolphins' 1983 first-round pick who threw 48 touchdown passes in leading Miami to a 14-2 regular-season record.

Walsh was once again a master at game planning, but also at getting into his players' heads in just the right way to have them perform at peak efficiency. A man who used sarcasm as well as anyone, Walsh's final message to his players before leaving the locker room for kickoff was some of his best work.

"I can remember Walsh lying down in the middle of the floor," cornerback Dwight Hicks recalled during an NFL Films retrospective on the Niners' 1984 season. Hicks imitated his coach, sarcastically wondering if the 49ers could do much of anything against the Dolphins. "'Miami, they have such a great offense. My God, how are we going to stop them? Their defense and the Killer Bees, how are we going to get a first down? Or even a yard?'

"Then he turned and looked at me and said, 'God, don't you want to break the wall and kick their ass right now?'"

It was classic Walsh, appealing to the 49ers' sense of pride and casting the Dolphins as this unbeatable team with the greatest quarterback in the game, a smothering defense, and a coach who had presided over the NFL's only unbeaten season in history. Walsh knew exactly what he was doing, the players knew exactly what he was doing, and the mood he set was absolutely perfect.

"I can remember Bill before the Super Bowl in 1984, and he's shadowboxing like Ali in the locker room," Lott said. "He thinks we're fighting for the world championship. I realized then he had a little Golden Gloves in him. In his early days, he wanted to be a fighter. The whole theme of his life was 'Hit people before you get hit.' You had to be quicker than the other guy. You had to move faster than him."

How confident was Walsh before that game?

"He told his sister's husband to bet the mortgage on this game,"

Craig Walsh said. "He was very relaxed, and when he lay down in the locker room before the game, it sent the message, 'I've got this.' The players picked up on that, and it really loosened up the team and took away the pregame jitters. It was one of those games where my dad knew he had the upper hand."

Walsh was at the peak of his game by that point, having perfected an offensive system that had proved virtually foolproof when executed properly. He had spent his entire adult life trying to come up with a method of moving the football and scoring points that could counteract any defense, and the combination of his coaching expertise and acquiring the right players to implement his game plans was now on full display.

In many ways, the genius of the West Coast offense is its simplicity. As his thinking evolved, Walsh relied on concepts that would enable his offense to find the weak points in a defense and to exploit those weaknesses with regularity. Much of his time was spent trying to discover where open spaces would appear, particularly in the passing game.

For example, if Walsh sent a tight end in motion, and the defense countered by shadowing the tight end with a linebacker, could Walsh then create a better opportunity for a slant pass to work because the space originally occupied by the linebacker had been vacated by putting the tight end in motion and would thus give his receiver more room?

Walsh's mind was constantly at work trying to piece together snippets of his game plan, and he had taken the concept of situational football to a new level. He would prepare for every conceivable situation during a game—third and five or less from inside the opponent's 20...second and six or more at midfield...first and goal from the 5... and on and on and on.

He had multiple plays for every situation, and his use of varied formations to disguise those plays would make it that much tougher for defensive coordinators to react to tendencies. Walsh would often have as many as ten different formations for a simple off-tackle running play or a swing pass. And while the play itself might have been a basic element of the 49ers' offense, running the play from a formation the defense had never previously seen consistently gave Walsh the upper hand.

"Bill would draw up plays for one specific defense at one place on the field, and you'd run it in practice," Montana said. "Sometimes, it would be the worst play, and then he'd call it in a game and he'd say, 'Okay, guys, here we go. In the game, this is going to be wide open.' And that's what would happen. He just had this way of doing things. I think that's why we worked so well together, because I understood what his offense was about, and I wasn't trying to do anything outside of it."

Lott was fascinated by Walsh's ability to create open spaces. Lott himself was one of pro football's great students, and understanding Walsh's offensive concepts helped his own game, as well as gave him an appreciation of the coach's genius.

"He allowed players to use their creativity by allowing them to create advantages in defenses," Lott said. "That was the essence of his game. Any time you have three people in a space and three people trying to cover them in that space, there are absolutely ways to get people open. Bill was very smart about using angles and ways of allowing people to understand that in those angles, you can find a way to get yourself open."

The versatility of the system was breathtaking, especially when you realized that Walsh could create opportunities for a wide variety of players.

"A Dwight Clark doesn't have to be fast, but Bill put him in positions to be open," Lott said. "Bill knew that having different guys at different speeds, he could get them open. Bill was ahead of his time, because if you played a zone defense, then he could flood the zone," Lott said. "If you played man to man, he could find ways to create space so your man could get open. His genius was putting pressure on the defense, forcing the defense to do something it can't do. He was like [legendary UCLA basketball coach] John Wooden. In John Wooden's offense, there were things that he did that were unstoppable. Same with Bill."

With the 49ers about to face the Dolphins, Walsh's confidence in his system was soaring. And that confidence turned into reality with a flawlessly executed game plan from the coach, who would later consider it the best game he'd ever called. It was his masterpiece moment, when all his intellectual powers had coalesced into a sweeping victory over the Dolphins and a second Super Bowl championship.

The 49ers demolished the Dolphins, 38–16, as Montana threw for 331 yards and 3 touchdowns, and also scrambled for a rushing touchdown. The 49ers built a 28–16 lead by halftime and shut out the Dolphins the rest of the way before once again hoisting Walsh atop their shoulders and carrying him off the field at Palo Alto—the same field where he'd completed his personal and professional rehabilitation.

Not only was Walsh's offensive game plan a work of art, but his genius also showed itself on defense. With Marino starting to heat up just a bit in the second quarter, Walsh turned to defensive coordinator George Seifert and suggested the 49ers go to a 4-1-6 alignment, using just one linebacker and six defensive backs to confuse Marino. It worked perfectly.

When it was over, Walsh knew he'd come as close to coaching a perfect game as ever.

"That was the best game we ever played since I joined the 49ers," he said. "It was a great performance by a truly great team." Walsh said Montana "is clearly the best quarterback in football today. And maybe the best in many years."

He confided to his son afterward: "God, we were one play away from having a perfect offensive game, and that's unheard-of."

Montana had won his second Super Bowl MVP, and he reveled in the victory.

"All we heard all week long was 'Miami's offense, how are you gonna stop them?'" Montana said afterward. "Inside each of us, we knew we had an offense, too, and nobody was thinking about how to stop us. So I think we were out to prove something."

After the game, Hicks gathered his teammates in the locker room.

"Nobody knew what kind of offense we had," he told them, "and then, how in the hell are we gonna stop Marino? Nobody knew but us."

Then he turned to Walsh. "Game ball, Bill Walsh."

The players erupted in cheers.

Walsh was on top once again.

PARCELLS

FROZEN OUT ONE YEAR, ON TOP THE NEXT

There was an unmistakable sense of confidence when the Giants opened training camp on July 15, 1985.

Parcells even carried himself differently. There was a swagger, and his self-assurance was impossible not to notice.

"Bill had started to believe in us, and when we were able to make the playoffs and win a playoff game [in 1984], that meant a lot to him," linebacker Harry Carson said. "He had a lot of 'his guys,' and there was a belief in one another."

"We definitely had a great feeling coming into the season," Lawrence Taylor said. "We weren't perfect, by any means, but we felt like we could play with anybody."

Even after losing to the eventual Super Bowl champion 49ers in the divisional round of the playoffs, the Giants felt good about themselves. As Simms had said after the game, "I still think we can play with them."

That feeling had spread to the entire team, and Parcells knew it.

"Confidence is born of demonstrated ability," the coach liked to say. Well, the Giants had demonstrated their ability with their first playoff run under Parcells, and the hunger only grew as the players and coaches considered the possibility that this could one day be a championship team.

Simms was holding out in a contract dispute, although his absence didn't last long, as Young and Simms's agent, David Fishof, hammered out a five-year, $3.8 million contract.

Two days into camp, Simms showed up, nearly jumping out of his skin with enthusiasm—both at his personal gain and at the potential of his team.

"I'm excited to be here," Simms told reporters upon his arrival. "I was nervous. I was driving my wife nuts. At twelve forty-five this afternoon, I got a call from my agent. He said I could come to camp. I said, 'Good, because I'm already packed up.'"

Young himself was quietly confident of his team's potential, mostly as a result of his careful roster-building moves, starting with Simms in 1979 and continuing with strong drafts that included running back Joe Morris, safety Terry Kinard, linebackers Carl Banks and Gary Reasons, and the greatest pick of them all—Taylor, who not only won Rookie Defensive Player of the Year but Defensive Player of the Year for the entire league in 1981.

Young and Parcells had an uneasy alliance, though, and Parcells could never truly put all his trust in Young because of the GM's attempt to replace him with Schnellenberger near the end of the 1983 season. But one thing that kept them together was their common belief in how to build a team.

"Listen, George was a good guy to balance me," Parcells said. "You can't get more conservative than he was, and I was fighting every windmill. That's the truth. But here's the one thing George and I never had a dispute about, and that was the kind of players we were looking for. Now, sometimes, we had to fight other people in the organization on that, but he would acquiesce most of the time to what I was looking for, because philosophically, we kind of knew what we were looking for. We were, 'Let's get the best athlete available most of the time,' and I was basically for doing that, because that's the way I'd been raised in the system in New England.

"Like when we got rid of Van Pelt and got Carl Banks," Parcells said. "People said, 'Well, why are you getting another linebacker?' Well, Carl Banks was one of the best players the Giants ever had. So, what we were looking for was never a problem. How to acquire it sometimes was a problem, because George didn't like to move around in the draft. We moved up five spots to get [Ohio State offensive tackle] William Roberts [in the 1984 draft], and you'd think we mortgaged the future. George was very conservative by nature. He was not a risk taker."

With time and reflection, Parcells has come to appreciate Young, who died in 1991 at age seventy-one after being diagnosed with a rare neurological disease.

"I fault myself retrospectively," he said. "I had a lack of patience. I'm like, 'Let's do something this minute.' That kind of thing. I don't have time to pontificate on this stuff. But I understand, having been to other organizations and seeing other sides, there were a lot of things I didn't understand when I was with the Giants."

But the creative tension at the time had actually helped Parcells, because it played to his competitive side; Parcells simply couldn't let go of the doubt Young once harbored in the coach. Parcells had been a hothead on the football field and basketball court at River Dell High School back in the 1960s, and he was fighting those battles inside his head once more, with Young as his primary adversary, even though their ultimate objective was to win a championship together.

Parcells might have been impatient at Young's deliberate style, but the general manager was about to infuse the Giants with more talent in 1985, thanks to the impending collapse of the United States Football League. The USFL was completing its third—and ultimately its final—season as the Giants were about to report for training camp, and most of the league's players were no longer under contract once the Philadelphia/Baltimore Stars beat the Oakland Invaders, 28–24, in the championship game at Giants Stadium.

There would never be another USFL game after that because the league, at the urging of then New Jersey Generals owner Donald Trump, had voted to switch to a fall league in 1986 to directly compete with the NFL. That move was a precursor to an eventual antitrust lawsuit against the NFL—a trial that ended with a jury finding that the NFL had been guilty of violating anti-monopoly laws. But the victory was only a symbolic one, because the USFL was awarded damages in the amount of $1. Under antitrust laws, that total was tripled, leaving the USFL with a $3 award.

While a handful of the USFL's top players still under contract would be dispersed through an NFL draft, several players were already free agents. Young had targeted three of them—center Bart Oates and punter Sean Landeta of the Stars and fullback Maurice Carthon of the Generals. The three were signed over the summer, and all would become starters in the regular season, with Landeta unseating the long-time punter Dave Jennings. Another former USFL player, guard Chris Godfrey, had already joined the Giants in 1984 and was another starter.

This was all starting to come together, and the Giants went into the regular season with as good a roster as any in Young's tenure. Even after starting tight end Zeke Mowatt suffered a season-ending knee injury in the Giants' final preseason game in Pittsburgh, rookie Mark Bavaro out of Notre Dame, a physical blocker who also had great hands, would more than make up for Mowatt's absence.

The season began in auspicious fashion for Parcells. Fresh off another brutally physical training camp like the one the year before, the Giants got off to a 3-1 start in advance of a home game against the rival Cowboys.

The run-up to the game featured some of the most remarkable trash-talking you'll ever see, with outspoken Cowboys safety Dextor Clinkscale's words providing plenty of bulletin-board material for the Giants. Clinkscale's target: Simms.

"The myth is that Phil Simms is a great quarterback, which he isn't," he told reporters on a conference call. "He has no special gifts or intangibles like Joe Montana, Dan Marino, or even Joe Theismann."

Want more? Clinkscale was dealing as Giants writers—myself included—listened with mouths agape as he ripped Simms.

"The Giants are a fake," he said. "They're just imitating potential conference winners. They have a defense to put them where they want to go. They have special teams that put them where they want to go. But they have an offense that keeps them from where they want to go."

Referencing Hurricane Gloria, the late-September storm that had ravaged the New York area, Clinkscale kept it up.

"New York may have been struck by Hurricane Gloria, but she didn't have the impact and intensity and fury of the Dallas Cowboys," he said. "My advice to the people of New York is to secure all valuables when the sun sets Sunday and the storm hits, because Thurman's Thieves will steal the evening."

Thurman's Thieves—aka the Dallas secondary led by another outspoken defender, safety Dennis Thurman—were about to get their comeuppance at Giants Stadium. Simms torched the Cowboys' defense for three touchdowns in the third quarter and wound up throwing what was then a career-high 432 yards. But he fumbled twice in the fourth quarter, and Rafael Septien kicked two field goals off the turnovers to provide the difference in a 30–29 Cowboys win.

Simms would throw for 513 yards the following week in Cincinnati, but it was another Giants loss, this time 35–30.

Up next: Gibbs's Redskins at Giants Stadium.

With the Giants' defense having underperformed the past two weeks, the heat was on the Giants' first-year defensive coordinator, and Parcells needed more from the man he promoted from linebackers coach after the 1984 season.

Yes, Bill Belichick was on the hot seat.

A football savant who had grown up in the sport with his dad, the former Navy coach and scout Steve Belichick, Bill had come up through the coaching ranks with a keen eye for talent, a spectacularly strong work ethic, and an understanding of football concepts that would eventually translate into him becoming the most accomplished coach in NFL history.

A twenty-two-year-old graduate of Wesleyan who played center and tight end for the football team, as well as captained his lacrosse team as a senior, Belichick paid his dues as a special assistant for $25 a week under Colts coach Ted Marchibroda in 1975. He joined the Lions the following year as assistant special teams coach, worked as Detroit's receivers coach in 1977, and was then a defensive assistant and assistant special teams coach for the Denver Broncos in 1978 before joining the Giants in 1979 as special teams coach and defensive assistant under Ray Perkins.

Seeing Belichick's firm grasp of defensive concepts, Perkins promoted him to linebackers and special teams coach in 1980, where he remained until 1984. Parcells had already turned over the defensive play calling to Belichick, showing an innate trust in his young assistant while allowing himself to take a more global approach to coaching the entire team.

"Bill was a very smart, very observant coach," Parcells said. "He understood the game in a very good way, and we were very much on the same page in terms of philosophy. He was ready to have an opportunity."

———————

The players respected Belichick's mind, although his personality left something to be desired.

"Guys were calling him Captain Sominex," Carson said, referring to the popular sleeping pill. "The name was somewhat appropriate, because Bill had that monotone voice that could lull you to sleep. We found ways to stay awake, and any time he would ask a question, most of the guys were alert enough to answer. He was gregarious at times, but there were other times he was an asshole. Belichick was different, but he knew his stuff."

Former Giants cornerback Perry Williams was astonished at Belichick's brilliance.

"I remember I had bruised my thigh in a game and I came in to the training room the next morning at 6 a.m., and I figured I would beat everybody there," Williams said. "I went and got a bag of ice, and I heard some noise in the meeting room. It was Belichick riding a stationary bike and watching film."

"You had a good game yesterday, Perry," Belichick told him. "I'm going to show you a few things."

For the next half hour, Belichick watched film with his cornerback.

"That was one of the greatest skull sessions ever," Williams said. "I learned more with him in those thirty minutes than I learned in my eleven years in the NFL, four years of college, and three years of high school."

Parcells needed his wunderkind coordinator to find a way to stop his defense from hemorrhaging yards and points, and it had to happen fast. With Gibbs's high-flying offense coming to town the following week, this would be a defining moment for Belichick.

The coach responded with a masterpiece game plan, as the Giants completely shut down Gibbs's offense. Theismann had 3 interceptions and was sacked 7 times, including twice by Taylor. Riggins was held to just 35 yards on 11 carries.

"Probably our best overall game all year," Parcells said afterward.

Taylor's off-field habits were continuing to be a problem even after Parcells got rid of Kelley and Van Pelt, whom he'd considered bad influences on his young star linebacker. But Taylor acknowledged he'd played better this game because he had taken some time off from partying.

"I prepared this week," he told reporters after the game. "I got some sleep. I didn't go to bars much. I decided to go back to my old self."

The Giants caught fire, winning four straight heading into a November 18 rematch against the Redskins at RFK Stadium in a Monday night showdown.

The game would have ramifications that would reverberate for both teams long after it ended.

Parcells's first tactical move of the game had nothing to do with X's and O's, but it did have a direct impact on the game. With the game not scheduled until 9 p.m. on Monday night, he opted to have the Giants fly down later in the day on Sunday.

"That's one of the times when Bill made a strategic mistake," Harry Carson said. "It's a Monday night game, so instead of coming down on Sunday afternoon, he didn't want guys sitting around, visiting with different people in the Washington area. So he decides we're going to come down on Sunday night."

The Giants were set to take the short flight from Newark Airport into Washington National Airport, but there was no plane. It took more than an hour to line up another aircraft, but by then, they couldn't land at National, which was a short drive from the team hotel in Arlington, Virginia.

"We didn't fly into National because there was a moratorium on flights coming in after midnight," Carson said. "So we flew into Dulles [International Airport]."

But there was another problem at Dulles, and the team wound up flying to Baltimore-Washington International Airport. That wasn't the end of it. Because the team buses had assembled at Dulles Airport, they had to go to BWI to pick the team up. The buses didn't arrive for another hour or so.

"We didn't get in until around 3:30 a.m.," Carson said.

Rather than let the players catch up on their sleep, Parcells kept the team to the same schedule on game day—which meant a morning wakeup call.

"We went through the day sleep deprived," Carson said. "As we're sitting in the meetings, guys were dozing off."

When the team finally did make it to RFK, the players were certainly not rested and ready.

———

After a four-game winning streak, the Giants came into the game at 7-3, while the Redskins, who were just two years removed from their most recent Super Bowl appearance, were 5-5 and struggling to stay afloat in the ultracompetitive NFC East.

With the game tied at the start of the second quarter, Gibbs called for a flea flicker from the Redskins' 46. Theismann would hand off to Riggins, who would pitch the ball back to Theismann for a deep pass. Belichick called an all-out blitz, sending linebackers Carson, Taylor, and Reasons. The flea flicker fooled none of them and they closed in on Theismann, with Taylor leaping in the air and coming down on the back of Theismann's right leg.

The impact of the hit was devastating, with a loud pop heard by the players. Theismann's right leg had snapped. Literally snapped. The force of the collision broke the tibia and fibula, and one of the bones had broken through the skin. Taylor quickly realized what had happened, nearly got sick when he saw the broken bone sticking out, and immediately waved to the Redskins' sideline to signal for help. He then put both hands on his helmet and began to cry.

Theismann had almost gone into shock—he later described it as "the endorphins kicked in"—and said he felt no pain, despite the gruesome injury.

"That was horrible, man," Taylor said of the injury. "Just awful."

"Once the leg broke and he was lying on the ground, I didn't want to look," Carson said. "Lawrence was spazzing out, because he knew right away. It's chaotic on the field with the medical people and everything that was going on, but the thing that amazed me was just like that, everybody stopped being football players and you could see the humanity in all the players.

"When you go out to play, you always say a prayer, not so much to win the game, but to make sure that everybody finishes the game and they're safe and sound," he said. "You're just praying for good health. Here was a case of a guy not being able to walk off the field from a catastrophic injury, and it could have been anybody. I was just amazed at how guys stopped being Giants and they stopped being Redskins or football players, and they worked together to make sure he didn't go into shock. Guys were talking to him and keeping his mind off of what had happened."

After several minutes, Theismann was carted off the field, never to play another football game.

Despite players and coaches from both teams appearing visibly shaken by the injury, the game pressed on. And what an unbelievable game it turned out to be.

Gibbs and Parcells matched wits like never before, and Theismann's backup, strong-armed Jay Schroeder, who passed up a career in baseball to play football, went to work on the Giants' defense. So did Redskins special teams coach Wayne Sevier, whose units executed two successful onside kicks and a fake punt that led to all three touchdowns in a 23–21 win.

"Nobody knew who Jay Schroeder was, but I did," Carson said. "He played minor-league baseball in my hometown of Florence, South Carolina, so I knew about him."

The move to Schroeder, who had better speed and mobility than the thirty-six-year-old Theismann, turned out to be a critical development in the game. And Parcells was at least partly to blame for the Giants' inability to contain him. Despite going into the fourth quarter with a 21–14 lead, the Giants gave up a Schroeder touchdown pass and a field goal in the final period.

"Schroeder took the snap, rolled to his right, rolled to his left, and we were gassed," Carson said. "We were winded from all the running we were doing, and he's trying to save his own skin and we wound up losing the game. I attribute that to Parcells because of the decision he made to fly us down late. If we had gone down in the afternoon, we'd have been settled."

Parcells admits he messed up.

"I probably shouldn't have traveled so late, but I didn't want the players just hanging around on Sunday and Monday," he said. "It was a mistake on my part."

As if there wasn't enough intensity from the game itself, there was nearly a brawl in the Giants' locker room afterward.

As left tackle Brad Benson returned to his locker after taking a shower, a handful of reporters waited to interview him. Benson, who could be surly after a game, especially a loss, noticed a local radio reporter looking at him.

"What are you looking at?" Benson sneered.

The reporter, who worked for a radio station in Washington, D.C., paused a moment and looked right at Benson.

"I'm looking at a bunch of losers," he said.

Benson's eyes widened and he lunged at the reporter. Several teammates, including Carl Banks, interceded and prevented a full-scale brawl. Even Giants president and co-owner Wellington Mara, who was sixty-nine years old at the time, helped pull his players away.

Banks was furious.

"I didn't like him calling us losers, and I went at him pretty hard," he said in reflecting back on the moment, which he still remembers in vivid detail.

Taylor was visibly shaken after the game, but he made sure to call Theismann a day or two later.

"Mr. Theismann, Mr. Taylor is on the phone," a nurse said to the quarterback as he lay in his hospital bed.

"Joe, how you doing?" Taylor asked Theismann.

"Not very well," he said.

"Why?"

"Because you broke both bones in my leg," Theismann said.

"I never do anything halfway," Taylor cracked. "Okay, gotta go to practice."

For years, neither man could watch a replay of the injury.

"LT used to own a bar on Route 3 in New Jersey, and I flew up there four or five years after the injury for an event that he had," Theismann said. "They played a tape of the injury, and neither one of us looked at it."

Taylor said he learned a valuable lesson.

"Joe, I learned that, no matter how great you are at what you do," Taylor told Theismann that night, "it can be over in an instant. So, every day, you have to practice and play like it's your last game."

It was a life-altering experience for Theismann, and not simply because the injury led to his retirement.

"It was the moment that changed my life," Theismann said. "I had enjoyed so much success, my ego had gotten so out of control. I felt like I was the be-all and end-all, and that the world revolved around me. It slammed my feet back on the ground, because it took away the one thing that I held above everything else. It stripped away my football identity, and it forced me to look at myself as a person.

"So to me, it wasn't a tragedy, it was a blessing," he said. "It came at a time in my life where I wasn't capable of making the decision to be a different person. Something had to happen, and that was it. It was the day that changed my life."

The Giants went on to finish at 10-6 in what turned out to be a three-way tie at the top of the NFC East, along with the Redskins and Cowboys. But the Cowboys and the Giants owned the tiebreakers, with Dallas winning the division, the Giants earning a wild card playoff berth, and the Redskins finishing out of the playoff mix for the first time since Gibbs's rookie season in 1981.

The Giants' first-round opponent at home: Bill Walsh's defending champion 49ers.

The Niners had made it back to the tournament with a 10-6 record the year after winning Super Bowl XIX, but this time as a wild card after finishing second to the resurgent Rams, who won the NFC West at 11-5.

In some ways, Walsh had an even better team going into the playoffs than he had the year before. The biggest reason: Jerry Rice.

Walsh first became transfixed by Rice's talent when the 49ers were on the road in the 1984 season. The coach was watching highlights of a Mississippi Valley State game during Rice's spectacular senior year.

"It was near midnight and I was beginning to doze off when I heard the sportscaster say, 'Following this break, we have some incredible highlights of Jerry Rice and the Mississippi Valley State game,'"

Walsh wrote in his book *Building a Champion*. "That caught my attention and I sat up to take a look at this 'living legend.'"

Walsh was mesmerized by Rice, even though there had been some skepticism of the receiver's flat-out speed. That speed turned out to be a 4.6 in the 40-yard dash the following year at the Scouting Combine, a flaw that prompted some teams to give him lower than a first-round grade. But Walsh knew he wanted Rice, and he executed a bold trade from number 28 to the Patriots' number 16 on draft day.

Rice, the son of a bricklayer in rural Mississippi, initially had difficulty adjusting to life in the Bay Area. Rice finished his rookie season with 49 catches for 927 yards and 3 touchdowns, but dropped several passes and invited skepticism about whether Walsh had paid too high a price to get him.

The coach remained convinced Rice could be a star.

But not on this day. And not against the Giants.

In his rematch against the coach now called The Genius, Parcells's guts ruled the day. With Parcells imposing his iron will over his team and Belichick outscheming Walsh, the Giants dominated the 49ers, 17–3, and never let Montana get into any kind of rhythm. The Giants sacked him four times, didn't allow a touchdown, and came up with one interception in Montana's second career playoff loss. Rice was limited to just 4 catches for 45 yards and fumbled once.

The Giants had won a home playoff game for the first time since 1962.

"I thought our defense did as good as it ever did," Parcells said afterward. "Those were the world champions. Somebody had to get rid of them. I'm glad we did."

Parcells had shown he could beat Walsh, with a defensive plan executed brilliantly by Belichick against a unit that Parcells had offhandedly referred to as the "West Coast offense." It was the first time anyone had referred to Walsh's system that way, even though Walsh had actually designed the system in Cincinnati.

"I didn't mean it in a derogatory way, because obviously it was a tremendously effective system," Parcells said. "Those guys would still run the damn ball. Back in the day, that's how they functioned against pressure. So if you could figure out who the bailout guy was [for Montana to release his passes], you could do some things to take it away and make it difficult on him."

Parcells and Belichick had done just that against Montana.

Finally, someone had cracked the code.

After the win, Parcells was quick to remind his players that this was just the start.

"We've got a big game next week," he said. "The stakes are going up. We have a long way to go. But it's who's standing at the end, and we're standing. It's down to eight teams now, and we're one of the eight."

Parcells did find curious one thing that had happened at the beginning of the game. Just before the 49ers' first series, the team's coaching headsets went out, and Walsh had told the referee of the problem. Under league rules, any time the headsets went out on one sideline, the other team must turn off its headsets until the problem was rectified.

After the 49ers' first drive, the headsets came back on.

Parcells filed that away in the back of his mind.

Up next: the Bears at Soldier Field.

It was an incredible regular season for Mike Ditka's team, as the Bears came close to becoming the first team since the 1972 Dolphins to go unbeaten in the regular season. In fact, it was the Dolphins who ruined the Bears' perfect season in a Week 13 game in Miami. Shula's Dolphins drubbed the Bears, 38–24, the only blemish in a 15-1 season.

Chicago's 46 defense featured one of the most relentless pass rushes in NFL history, with defensive coordinator Buddy Ryan unleashing blitz after blitz against every team he came across. On a frigid, blustery day in Chicago, with winds whipping off Lake Michigan, the Giants were overmatched from the start.

Even punter Sean Landeta, who had a splendid regular season in his first year since coming over from the USFL, had a nightmare moment early on. With the Giants backed up at their own 12-yard line on fourth and seventeen, Landeta lined up in his own end zone to punt. But as he dropped the ball onto his foot, a gust of wind moved the ball a few inches and Landeta swung and missed. The ball grazed the outside of his foot and was picked up by Shaun Gayle, who returned it five yards for a touchdown.

"It was such a fluke thing," Landeta said in recalling the play. "The ball did a one-and-a-half [revolutions] to my right, and I almost didn't swing. But I thought I should try and get a piece of it. I probably would have been better off not swinging and jumping on the ball. It would have been a lot easier for me through the years. You get nothing for that, but it's just a gust of wind, and I was the unfortunate guy to have that happen. Later in the game, I had a 63-yard punt, a 54-yard punt, and three punts inside the 20. I had an outstanding game. But I could have had the greatest day in the history of any NFL punter, and it still wouldn't have taken away from the bad luck I had on that one."

That was a signature moment from the game, but it was indicative of the Giants' overall inability to compete against the physically superior Bears. This was an ass-kicking, pure and simple, and the Giants would go on to lose, 21–0, to a team that went on to win the Super Bowl in one of the greatest single-season defensive performances in NFL history.

But out of that game emerged a resolve from Parcells and from his players. They understood they'd been physically whipped by a more dominant team. They also knew what they had to do to make sure this would never happen again.

"That game was a catalyst," said Carson, who stood before his teammates after the loss and delivered a speech that resonated with everyone. His message: Do for themselves next year what the Bears had done this year. "We were good, but we weren't as good as we thought we were. We came away from that game understanding that we needed to have home field advantage in the playoffs. Everybody should be coming to us."

"In order to roll to the Super Bowl," Lawrence Taylor said, "we had to get the home field advantage. We found out in that game how much of an advantage that was for the Chicago Bears. Their fans, with their weather, and they played their game. You got to get home field advantage."

A somber Parcells told his players after the game what they needed to do to get past this point, and he appealed to his veterans to set the tone for what lay ahead.

"You older players," he said, "you might not have the opportunity again."

A month later, when several Giants players went to the Pro Bowl the week after the Bears had demolished the Patriots, 46–10, in Super Bowl XX, Joe Morris drew even more inspiration for getting over the hump and past a team like the Bears. He had a conversation with Bears middle linebacker Mike Singletary a few days before the Pro Bowl.

"Joe, all we did was intimidate your offensive line, and they gave up," Singletary told Morris. "They were afraid to fight us. That's what got them down. We intimidated you guys. You were the only person that wanted to fight us. You and Simms and Bavaro. We could sense fear."

Morris seethed, as did the other Giants players who were in Hawaii for the annual all-star game.

"Simms, Bavaro, Burt, Benson, Harry [Carson], Lawrence [Taylor] were all at that damn Pro Bowl," Morris said. "We were sitting there when they announced those sons of bitches [from the Bears]. We looked at each other and said, 'That's where we want to be next year.'"

Morris kept that conversation in the back of his mind throughout the off-season conditioning program. So did his teammates.

"We had to be better," Parcells said. "We were good. We weren't good enough."

Parcells was once again relentless in driving his players during off-season workouts. He injected his inimitable brand of sarcasm while overseeing his players during their workouts, using those barbs as motivation for a team that understood it could be on the cusp of greatness.

Simms had made it through a sixteen-game season for a second straight time, Morris had a breakout year in 1985 with 1,336 rushing yards and an NFL-best 21 touchdowns behind an offensive line that had coalesced with the addition of Bart Oates, and Taylor was coming off a career-best 13 sacks.

Taylor was one of the few players who didn't participate in the off-season training program, and Parcells was well aware that he had a problem with his star linebacker, even though the depth of that problem—heavy drinking and a growing dependence on crack cocaine—was unknown to the public at large.

In his 1987 autobiography, *LT: Living on the Edge*, Taylor acknowledged using crack as frequently as three times a week during the 1985 season. He also admitted to having cheated on drug tests by submitting the clean urine of an undisclosed teammate instead of his own after the Giants, who had been aware of his drug use, instituted their own testing program.

Parcells, who had already gotten rid of linebackers Brian Kelley and Brad Van Pelt, in part because they were a bad influence on Taylor, had tried to intercede several times in hopes of helping LT come to terms with his problem. He and general manager Young were able to convince the troubled linebacker to enter a rehab program at Houston Methodist Hospital in February 1986.

For Parcells, dealing with Taylor was complicated. He'd consulted experts in the field of addiction and grew to understand the depth of Taylor's problem, but the coach also knew he couldn't afford to risk losing Taylor's ability to help the team. After five seasons, Taylor had established himself as the league's best pass rusher, and he was the team's most indispensable player.

"The thing I resented most was when people said the Giants looked the other way," Parcells said. "That was not true. It was never true. I tried to help him from the first day. I went to places with him, rehab places. I took him to places. I tried to help him. You know, he was a young guy, a small-town guy. A couple of players on the team [Kelley and Van Pelt] were bad influences, and I finally got rid of them. Now, he likes Kelley. They're friends to this day. Kelley had changed a lot, too. He's a grown man. But Kelley was smart. He never went over the edge. He was smart enough to know where the rope limits were. I had so many things going on with Taylor, so many highly volatile conversations, doing everything I could.

"He's like my own kid," Parcells said. "I liked him. I always liked him. He always gave me what he had, and he was loyal to me. He was very loyal to me. It just got out of control. It got out of hand. It got worse when he was finished playing, but even to this day, if I call him right now and I need to talk to him, he's calling me back in five minutes."

Parcells went out of his way to publicly defend Taylor, even when the coach knew the linebacker's drug problems were spiraling out of control. During training camp in 1987, Taylor had been seen drinking regularly at the bars in Pleasantville—nothing new for him, but still a major concern after he'd already tested positive for drugs. Having gotten wind of Taylor's continued drinking, I wrote a story for Westchester Rockland Newspapers detailing his behavior and quoting substance abuse experts warning that consuming alcohol would eventually lead Taylor back to using his drug of choice—namely cocaine.

Parcells had tried to warn me off the story, suggesting there might be legal ramifications if our newspaper published it. I ran the information by Taylor as he walked toward the cafeteria for dinner. After hearing the details, Taylor said, "I don't give a shit what you write."

The next day, after the story came out, Parcells was livid. During his daily news conference with reporters, he glared at me and said, "That was a horseshit story, and you're horseshit for writing it."

Parcells still gets pissed at suggestions that he looked the other way with Taylor.

"It's like, 'Oh, Parcells, he just let that go,'" he said. "That's not true. I didn't let that go. I was on his ass. I was trying to get some help, and I was insistent that he get help. Wellington stuck with him, too."

Taylor's drug use was an open secret among the people who knew him.

"I made no effort to hide it," he wrote in his autobiography. "I could do it, and I could stop it. I knew what I was doing, how to use."

But he acknowledged the problem began to grow out of control.

"I started giving myself excuses to use cocaine," he wrote. "Where I had been using half a gram over a month, I was using a good part of that in a single evening. Twice a month became three times a week and maybe more...I did crack too many times to count and more times than I want to remember.

"I did crack from the middle of the '85 season to the end," he said, "usually when we were at home. I'd stay out all night, get blasted on crack and then try to pick up as though nothing had happened the next day...I don't know how long I could have gone on that way. Through much of this, I thought I could still play good ball."

Taylor recounted an incident late in the 1985 season when his wife, Linda, went to an apartment where he was doing drugs. Taylor heard his wife's voice and closed the door to his room.

"I'll break the damn door down if you don't open it, Lawrence Taylor!" Linda screamed. "I'm not leaving 'til I leave with you! You're going home with me!"

Taylor said police and NFL security people often followed him, but he was never arrested.

"If I were Joe Blow, OK, there'd be the slammer or some midnight trip to Betty Ford's farm...It was almost a thrill in itself knowing that people knew what I was doing and wouldn't do a damn thing to stop me."

Taylor's stint in rehab lasted only a few days. He left the facility, although he remained in Houston and continued to speak with therapists. He would eventually test positive for cocaine—this time after the league had instituted a testing program agreed to by the NFL and the players union—and he would serve a four-game suspension to start the 1988 season.

"Bill Parcells taught me about life," Taylor says now in reflecting back on his time with the coach. "There have been only a few coaches in my life that actually have helped shape my life. Melvin Jones from [Williamsburg, Virginia] high school, Jim Tressler [North Carolina's outside linebackers coach], and then Bill Parcells. Bill and I had a relationship where, when I went out there, I wanted to do well, not just for myself. I wanted to do well for Bill Parcells, too."

It was often a love-hate relationship between the two from the start, with plenty of arguments—and hugs—along the way.

"We argued all the time, and that's how I knew we were good friends. He actually thought he ran the team, but I ran it," Taylor said with a laugh. "We got in arguments all the time, but no matter what, come Sunday at one o'clock, I'd be standing right beside him for the national anthem. Nowadays, it's fun to be around him, because I give him the shit he used to give us back in the day."

With expectations high after two straight playoff runs, the Giants came into training camp in 1986 with an air of confidence. Yes, they had been destroyed by the Bears in the playoffs, but with a victory over the defending champion 49ers and a team that had returned all its key starters, there was legitimate reason for optimism.

There was one complicating factor, however.

Morris, who had produced career highs in rushing yards and touchdowns in 1985, was looking to renegotiate his contract. He didn't report immediately to training camp, and was told by Young there would be no new deal unless he showed up. Eventually, Morris reported, but with a caveat: He would not participate in any contact drills.

Parcells was not happy and told Morris as much.

"Bill, I've trained my ass off," Morris, who was scheduled to make $130,000 in 1986, told him. "You know what kind of shape I'm in."

Morris reported, but was eventually sent home because Parcells couldn't live with his no-contact arrangement.

Morris eventually returned, but the day before the regular-season opener in Dallas, he missed the walk-through practice. Young and Morris's agent, Tom Toner, eventually hammered out a four-year, $2 million deal, and Morris suited up for the *Monday Night Football* opener.

It wasn't enough for the Giants, though, as the Cowboys, featuring former USFL star running back Herschel Walker, won, 31–28, at Texas Stadium. Walker scored 2 touchdowns, including the game winner late in the fourth quarter.

Parcells was livid after watching his defense collapse in the fourth quarter, giving up 14 points. Asked about Walker's touchdown run up the middle, Parcells told reporters at his postgame news conference, "Just a draw play, fellas. Everybody's got one."

But Parcells quickly recovered, and the Giants responded with a string of victories following the opening-night loss to the team's long-standing NFC East rivals. They reeled off five straight wins before losing a clunker in Seattle, 17–12, to fall to 5-2. But in a rematch against the Redskins less than a year after that gut-wrenching Monday night loss in which Theismann broke his leg, Parcells got the better of Gibbs in a 27–20 win at Giants Stadium.

Back-to-back 17–14 wins over the Cowboys and Eagles, now coached by former Bears defensive coordinator Buddy Ryan, put the Giants at 8-2 heading into a game in Minnesota.

Say hello to fourth and seventeen.

With the Giants' offense playing poorly against a Vikings team that had continually frustrated Simms, Parcells's team trailed, 20–19, with just 1:12 left in the fourth quarter. Faced with fourth and seventeen at midfield, there was one chance remaining, and Parcells knew he had to go for it.

Now it would come down to whether Phil Simms could deliver in a tight spot, one of the most important in his career. Parcells thought back to a conversation he'd had with his quarterback just a few days earlier, when he pulled him aside during practice.

"I think you're a great quarterback, and you got that way by being daring and fearless, so let's go," Parcells told Simms.

Here was his chance.

"It was really a basic play," Simms said. "[Phil] McConkey up the seam, Stacy [Robinson] on an in cut, Bavaro on the other seam, and Bobby on the out."

Just before breaking the huddle, Simms looked into Johnson's eyes.

"Bobby, be alert, I might have to come to you," Simms said.

Simms dropped back and saw that three of his four receivers were covered. Just as he was about to get hit, he spotted Johnson near the right sideline and delivered the pass.

"It was real quiet and the play happened in slow motion," Simms said. "I was lucky to get it over the fingertips of the cornerback."

"I just ran to the first-down marker and stopped," Johnson said. "And when I turned, the ball was there."

Johnson caught the pass and just barely stayed in bounds at the Vikings' 30. And with twelve seconds left in regulation, Raul Allegre kicked a field goal—his fifth of the game—to win it, 22–20.

The sideline erupted in joy, and Parcells raised his hands in victory.

"That game," Simms said, "is my favorite game of all time in my whole career. It was wicked. It was just so hard, but we just made so many rough plays. They hit me the whole game. They were great pass rushers. It was so hard, so emotional. And then we win it, and it was probably the most excited our locker room was that year after a game."

Parcells became even more convinced this could be a special year.

"My players know the race is on, and it started today," the coach said after the game. "But this schedule has made our team better. With this schedule, you've got to be competitive. You've got to go."

A week later, more magic and more momentum: Veteran defensive end George Martin, who had survived Parcells's sweeping roster purge after 1983 to emerge as an unqualified team leader, intercepted a John Elway pass and raced 78 yards for a touchdown in a 19–16 win over the Broncos.

And the following week, at 10-2, another statement game against a team for the ages.

It would be Parcells versus Walsh—again—this time on the *Monday Night Football* stage at Candlestick Park in another installment of what was now turning into one of the best rivalries of the decade.

The 49ers dominated the first half and took a 17–0 lead on 2 touchdown passes from Montana to Rice and a Wersching field goal. Early in the third quarter, the Giants finally caught a spark on a play that would become one of the most important in franchise history.

With the Giants at midfield, Simms dropped back and fired a 10-yard pass over the middle to second-year tight end Mark Bavaro, who turned and began to run upfield. Linebackers Mike Walter and Riki Ellison bounced off Bavaro before Lott jumped on his back at the 36. Bavaro not only didn't go down, but he dragged Lott and eventually four other defenders before finally going down at the 18.

The Giants went on to score a touchdown on Simms's 17-yard pass to Morris, and they didn't allow the 49ers another point the rest of the way. Simms hit Stacy Robinson for a 34-yard touchdown, and then Ottis Anderson, acquired earlier in the season in a trade with the St. Louis Cardinals, scored the game-winning touchdown in a 21–17 victory.

"That game right there was big," Parcells said. "We were a confident team going in, but to do that in difficult circumstances was very important."

But while his players were rightly impressed with the victory, Parcells was furious about the Giants' inability to run, and he let his offensive line have it afterward. After seeing that the Giants had rushed for only 13 yards on 19 carries, Parcells gave his offensive line a new nickname, one they grew to hate: Club 13.

"He treated us like lapdogs," Ard said. "You can't run the ball when the other team has two extra guys in the box. That's the offensive coordinator calling runs. Finally, in the second half, we crushed them because we opened it up."

Yet Bavaro's play was still the signature moment of the game, and yet another reminder of how integral he had become to the team.

"His toughness, his overall complete play as a tight end and blocker, just as a total competitor, was just outstanding," Belichick said of Bavaro. "I don't think Mark has ever gotten the recognition that any of us that coached him or played with him know that he deserves."

Belichick flashed back to the epic battles Bavaro had in training camp.

"All the time that LT and Carl [Banks] would line up against Mark in one-on-ones," Belichick said. "There were no better battles in my entire career than watching Carl and LT go against Bavaro one-on-one. I mean, it was just awesome. All three of them were so good, so competitive, and so tough."

Six days after Bavaro helped lift the Giants over the 49ers, the Giants went on the road again, this time against Gibbs's Redskins. And Parcells's tough-minded team pulled out another impressive win, beating Washington, 24–14, at RFK.

First Walsh, then Gibbs.

It wouldn't be the last time Parcells would face his rivals in consecutive weeks.

The next time, it would be for the right to advance toward the Super Bowl.

Heading into their final game, the Giants had a chance to clinch home field advantage throughout the playoffs with a win over the Packers. But they led by just a touchdown at halftime, 24–17, and Parcells was furious. Just before his team went out for the third quarter, he delivered a blistering speech, ripping his defense and reaching for a garbage can. After emptying it in the locker room, he threw it against the wall.

The Giants won the game, 55–24.

The road to Pasadena for Super Bowl XXI would now go through East Rutherford, New Jersey.

It was Walsh-Parcells in a third consecutive playoff game—this one at Giants Stadium for a second straight year.

The 49ers had completed a 10-5-1 season under Walsh, winning the NFC West for the fourth time since 1981. It was a monumental feat, since the 49ers were without Montana for much of the season because he required surgery to repair a ruptured disk after the first week. Just fifty-six days after the surgery, he was back in the lineup and led the 49ers to a 5-2 record over the final seven games to win the division.

Walsh's conviction on Rice, meanwhile, had been borne out with a spectacular season from the second-year receiver, who led the NFL with 1,570 receiving yards and 15 touchdowns. There was no doubt Walsh would try to use Rice as his most formidable weapon against the Giants. So convinced was Walsh in his game plan against the Giants that John Madden was stunned by it when they sat down during TV production meetings.

"Yesterday was the most confident I've ever seen Bill Walsh," Madden said on the CBS broadcast a few minutes before kickoff.

Parcells had a different interaction with Walsh, one that came to define their relationship over time.

During warmups, Walsh and Parcells chatted at midfield—Walsh in his red waist-length jacket, trimmed in gold, and Parcells in a blue hooded jacket—and exchanged a few pleasantries. After a minute or so, Parcells, with arms folded, brought up what happened at the beginning of last year's playoff game, when the 49ers' headsets went out.

Parcells was convinced Walsh had done it on purpose, and he called him out on it.

"Bill, you pull the same shit you pulled last year," Parcells told Walsh, "I'm going to expose you. I'm going to the league with it."

Walsh smiled. Then he winked.

"It's just a little gamesmanship," Walsh told him.

Parcells would never forget that moment, the time he essentially accused Walsh of cheating.

"It was really the start of mutual respect from both of us," Parcells said. "He knew I didn't say anything, and I knew he was fuckin' with me, and he knew I understood it."

Not long afterward, when Parcells went into the locker room, he faced an unexpected problem.

With the Giants players getting into uniform and preparing to go out on the field for warmups, one player was missing. It was Bobby Johnson, who had caught the momentous pass on fourth and seventeen at Minnesota.

Johnson had missed the entire warmup period, and Parcells suspected he knew the reason why: a drug problem.

"I remember telling Phil Simms one time, I said, 'Phil, we're going to read about Bobby in the paper. He's going to be dead,'" Parcells said.

Finally, just minutes before the players and coaches were about to go on the field for the start of the game, Parcells heard a ruckus in a corner of the locker room.

"So I'm talking to [offensive coordinator] Ron Erhardt about what we're going to do if we lose a receiver, that maybe we'll have to go with a third tight end, and I'm not sure I had one. Probably didn't. [Defensive end] Dee Hardison and [nose tackle] Jerome Sally come running back to the dressing room and get me. I go out and look, and I see there's a pile of players on top of Bobby Johnson. He walked into the dressing room and they pounced on him. They've got the son of a bitch in the pile. Burt ripped his shirt off. Someone said, 'You better play, you little motherfucker. You don't play, you ain't gonna be alive.' They're all on his ass."

Johnson made it onto the field in time for the start of the game, and Parcells could devote his full attention toward facing Walsh.

The respect the 49ers coach already had for Parcells was about to grow exponentially, because the Giants delivered the worst playoff beating of Walsh's career. Even Rice couldn't save the 49ers this time. In fact, his first-quarter fumble after catching a slant pass just across midfield and heading for what would have been a touchdown was an omen for what was about to happen.

With a relentless defense and a running attack that decimated the 49ers' defense—this after Parcells had taunted his offensive linemen and running backs after rushing for only 13 yards against San Francisco in the regular season win—the Giants dominated.

Montana was knocked out at the end of the first half, as Burt rushed up the middle and delivered a punishing hit on a pass that was intercepted and returned for a touchdown by Taylor to make it 28–3 at the half. The Giants went on to win, 49–3, to knock the 49ers out of the playoffs a second straight year.

"They played a perfect game," Walsh said afterward. "We were shattered by a great team. I believe they will go all the way."

Belichick, a hypercritical coach who rarely felt that good was good enough, was downright effusive about what had just happened.

"Our best defensive game of the year?" he asked rhetorically. "I'd say so—the aggressiveness, the intensity, the effectiveness, not letting up for even one play. And the way we kept after them for sixty minutes."

"It wasn't perfect," Parcells said, "but we played very well." The best he'd ever seen from his team? "Pretty close," he said.

P.S. Parcells never said a word to anyone about Walsh's headset shenanigans from the year before.

P.P.S. Parcells's endless chiding of his offensive linemen wound up being the perfect psychological ploy. The final total in the 49–3 demolition against the 49ers: 44 carries for 216 yards and two touchdowns.

P.P.P.S. In the six quarters after the 49ers took a 17–0 halftime lead in their regular-season matchup against the Giants at Candlestick Park, Parcells's team had outscored Walsh's team by a combined 70–3.

Now it was on to the NFC Championship Game at home—just the scenario Parcells had envisioned after that 21–0 humiliation at Soldier Field the year before. It was another matchup against Gibbs, with only the Redskins standing in the way of the Giants' first-ever Super Bowl appearance.

By now, Gibbs had become consumed with figuring out ways to minimize Taylor's effectiveness. He'd already come up with the idea of using an H back—putting a tight end in motion to try to at least get a piece of Taylor as he flew in from the outside. But even that had only mixed results, with Taylor having some of his best games against the Redskins.

Gibbs had the answers for every coach he faced—including all-time greats like Walsh, Shula, Landry, and Pittsburgh's Chuck Noll. But against the Parcells-Belichick alliance, he had come up frustratingly empty too many times. In fact, Parcells had beaten Gibbs in four of their five previous regular-season meetings, including both matchups in 1986.

"Phil Simms, LT, and Parcells were larger-than-life figures at Redskins Park," said Richard Justice, the former Redskins beat writer at the *Washington Post.* "You could walk in the door and say, 'Lawrence Taylor is in the parking lot,' and they'd go into battle mode."

Justice recalled a time when the Redskins caught wind that Parcells was thinking about moving Taylor to middle linebacker, and it drove Gibbs nuts.

"The coaches get into this whole discussion of, 'Okay, LT's going to play middle linebacker, so what are we going to do?' Joe goes, 'Shut up. That's crazy. He's not going to play middle linebacker.' Fast-forward to Wednesday, and the offense goes out onto the field. When they line up, there's a guy with a blue 56 jersey at middle linebacker. Gibbs said, 'Get him out of there. Stop that.' So the center, Jeff Bostic, turns around and says, 'What if he does play there?' Then the tight end says, 'Yeah, what if he does line up there?' That's the impact LT had on the Redskins."

With Parcells, there was an incredible amount of respect for Gibbs, who had already won one Super Bowl and gone to another. The Giants-Redskins games were some of the most physical, competitive, and emotionally exhausting games he'd coached.

"You go where the competition is," Parcells said. "They were the competition."

A few days before the game, Parcells held a press conference in a concrete, windowless room at Giants Stadium, and he was asked if having to play the Redskins a third time that season scared him.

Parcells thought a moment and then delivered one of his all-time great quotes.

"Let me tell you what I'm scared of," he deadpanned. "I'm scared of spiders, snakes, and the IRS."

Not scared of the Redskins then?, New York sports anchor Russ Salzberg asked as a follow-up.

"They're in our league," Parcells said. "It's competition. I look forward to that."

With winds whipping close to thirty-five miles an hour through the stadium on a twenty-nine-degree afternoon, Parcells knew that conditions would play an important role in the game. So he told Carson if he won the coin toss to make sure to go with the wind in the first quarter.

It was perhaps the most crucial decision of the afternoon.

The Giants defense forced three punts in the first quarter, and Steve Cox had trouble with each one. The punts went for 23, 27, and 24 yards, and the Giants capitalized in the opening quarter with an Allegre field goal and a touchdown pass from Simms to Lionel Manuel for a 10–0 lead.

Meanwhile, Giants punter Sean Landeta, who had been embarrassed by the wind the year before in a playoff loss to the Bears at Soldier Field, was magnificent on this day. He averaged 42.3 yards on six punts, and his performance proved critical in terms of field position.

"Against Washington, the winds were much worse than Chicago," Landeta said. "I was so fortunate to have a very good day. To have that kind of game was big."

Simms and Taylor look back on Landeta not only as being a difference maker in that game, but as being *the* difference maker.

"I was at a function once with Lawrence and we were talking about the '86 run," Simms said. "Lawrence said, 'You know what's unbelievable? We got to the Super Bowl and Sean Landeta was probably the biggest reason why.' People forget, but that was the greatest punting exhibition I've ever seen. It changed the game around. He was hitting bombs. He was a freak punting the football. Sean Landeta may be the best punter in NFL history, and he never even gets mentioned. He should be in the Hall of Fame. He's affected hundreds of games."

Simms led a touchdown drive in the second quarter with the wind in his face to make it 17–0, and the defense pitched a shutout the rest of the way.

The Giants were going to the Super Bowl for the first time in franchise history, with a chance to win an NFL title for the first time in thirty years.

For that to happen, though, the Giants had to beat a Denver Broncos team that had reached the Super Bowl in spectacular fashion behind star quarterback John Elway. The number 1 selection of the 1983 draft got the Broncos into the Super Bowl with an epic performance that came to define his career. It came to be known simply as "The Drive," a fifteen-play, 98-yard series Elway led to tie the Browns, 20–20, in the final seconds of regulation in the AFC Championship Game. Denver won it in overtime, a soul-crushing blow to a Browns team that has still not fully recovered from that moment.

Elway had already gotten a taste of the Giants' defense in the regular season, and it did not go well in the 19–16 loss at Giants Stadium. He didn't throw a touchdown and was intercepted twice, including the return for a touchdown by George Martin.

Parcells's plan of attack against Elway was to apply a relentless pass rush. But the coach also had a surprise for Broncos coach Dan Reeves when it came to offense. Rather than continue with his run-centric approach featuring Morris, Parcells was ready to turn his team over to Simms.

Now was the chance for Simms to cement his own legacy as one of the Giants' all-time greats.

But it wasn't an easy start. With the Giants trailing Denver, 10–9, at halftime, Parcells gathered his players in the locker room, telling them it was time to take control. He would give them the means to do just that, thanks to some daring play-calling decisions.

The first came on a fake punt near midfield on fourth and one, as backup quarterback Jeff Rutledge ran for the first down. Simms then completed the drive with a 13-yard pass to Bavaro that gave the Giants the lead.

Simms went on to put together one of the most remarkable performances in Super Bowl history, going 22 of 25 for 268 yards, 3 touchdown passes, and no interceptions in a 39–20 win. He was a runaway choice for Super Bowl MVP, and began a tradition that continues today.

"I'm going to Disney World!" he shouted to a camera as he came off the field, a post–Super Bowl commercial every Super Bowl MVP from then on would participate in.

"We knew we had to go after them offensively," Parcells said after the win. "I challenged them. Every time I challenged them this year, they've made the play."

"They changed their whole offensive attack," Broncos Pro Bowl linebacker Karl Mecklenburg said. "Pass first, run second. It surprised us. They made the big play all day when they had to."

"In my wildest dreams, I couldn't have hoped it would work out this way," Simms told reporters in the Giants' locker room. "We just had a great game plan and executed it like the coaches wanted us to. Everybody said we couldn't throw. I talked to the receivers all week and I said, 'Look, nobody's giving us any credit. Let's just come out of the gates running and I'll get the ball to you.'"

By the end, Parcells was doused with a bucket of Gatorade, a victory celebration that began earlier that year thanks to Burt and Carson, who literally showered their coach with praise. The ritual started as less than a celebratory show of affection. It started because Burt had been furious at Parcells before a regular-season game against the Redskins.

"He pissed me off so much that I said to myself, 'Okay, if we win this game, you're going to have to pay,'" Burt said. "So we're winning the game, and I went and poured Gatorade over his head. I'm like, 'Holy shit.'"

Parcells glared at Burt, but then smiled because the coach knew he'd done his job. After that, the Gatorade shower had become a tradition.

And after this latest one, the most glorious victory celebration the coach could have imagined, Parcells was carried off the field on his players' shoulders, his right fist raised to the sky.

"We buried all the ghosts today," the coach said after winning the team's first championship in three decades. "They're all gone."

Parcells's own ghosts were gone, too.

Three years after he was nearly fired, he was now a champion.

"They can never take that away from you," he said. "Never."

GIBBS

THE HUNCH THAT MADE ALL THE DIFFERENCE

Doug Williams made his way down the steps of the plane in the early-morning hours after an all-night flight from Los Angeles to Dulles Airport. The Redskins had just returned from their final preseason game against the Rams on September 6, 1987, and Williams was ready to head home to get some sleep.

But Gibbs and Beathard had to tell Williams the news: The Redskins were trading him to the Raiders.

"Doug had told me he wanted to be traded," Gibbs said. "He has talked about still wanting to start, so I told him, 'Let me look around.' The Raiders decided they wanted Doug, and I told him we're trying to get it done."

Even after Gibbs told Williams, the quarterback was surprised. But shock quickly gave way to joy. At age thirty-two and still a backup to Jay Schroeder, Williams wanted to play, and the Raiders were a perfect landing spot.

Gibbs told Williams to meet with him later that morning to go over why he was making the move.

At around 11 a.m., Williams walked into Gibbs's office at Redskins Park. Both men were smiling.

Williams sat down across from the coach.

"Douglas, I've changed my mind," said Gibbs, letting out a laugh.

Williams's smile disappeared.

"Hey, Coach, you can't change your mind," he told Gibbs.

Williams was upset that his dream of returning as an NFL starter was evaporating. A first-round draft pick of the Buccaneers—at the urging of Gibbs, who was Tampa Bay's offensive coordinator at the time—Williams knew in his heart that he still had a few good years left. And he didn't want to spend them languishing on the Redskins' bench.

"You can't do that," Williams said.

The coach's smile vanished.

"Hey, I don't work for the Raiders, and I can," Gibbs told him. "I work for the Washington Redskins, and we're not going to trade you."

Infuriated, Williams walked out of Gibbs's office.

———

Williams had been close to Gibbs for years, ever since they first met in the spring of 1978, when Gibbs had been dispatched to Monroe, Louisiana, by Bucs head coach John McKay to meet with the Grambling State University quarterback and see if Williams was worth taking in the first round of that year's draft.

"John McKay said to me, 'I want you to go to Grambling, and I want you to find out everything you can about him,'" Gibbs recalled.

Gibbs traveled to Louisiana, and even before he met with Williams to discuss football matters, the coach sat in the back of a classroom to simply watch.

"I was doing my student teaching in Monroe, Louisiana, at Carroll High School, and Joe came to the school," Williams said. "He didn't bother me. All he did was sit in the back of the class. He did more observing of me than talking about football."

They met over cheeseburgers and fries at a nearby McDonald's, and were joined by Williams's girlfriend, Janice Gross. "We talked mostly about life, about family," Williams remembered. (He eventually married Janice, who died in 1983 after undergoing surgery for a brain tumor.)

Gibbs was the only NFL coach to visit with Williams, whose draft status was a highly debated topic, since NFL teams had not embraced African American quarterbacks like they do today. After lunch, they drove to Grambling to talk X's and O's.

"He wanted to ask me about the Wing-T and everything else, and explain how it worked, get different plays on the board," Williams said. "I think a lot of it had to do with seeing if I could remember things."

Gibbs returned to Tampa after a two-day visit with Williams and reported back to McKay.

"I came back and I said, 'Coach, this guy is football smart, and I think he's gifted,'" Gibbs said. "He's a first-round quarterback."

McKay drafted Williams with the seventeenth overall pick, and Williams was the Bucs' starter through the 1982 season.

A contract stalemate led to Williams's ouster from Tampa and created acrimonious feelings, not only on the quarterback's part but from Bucs fans as well. Williams was being paid only $120,000 a year, by far the lowest salary of any NFL starter, and less than a dozen backups. Williams asked for a raise to $600,000 a year, but the Bucs wouldn't go higher than $400,000, despite McKay's recommendation that the team pay Williams a fair market contract.

Notoriously tight-fisted Bucs owner Hugh Culverhouse refused, and Williams left the team, eventually joining the USFL's Arizona team. When the league folded after the 1985 season, Gibbs reached out to see if Williams was interested in joining the Redskins, who were now in the market for a backup to Schroeder after Theismann's career-ending injury.

Williams didn't think twice about joining the Redskins.

But after a year in which he took only one snap, Williams still yearned to play, and Gibbs wanted to give him that chance when Al Davis reached out to make a deal.

After sleeping on it, Gibbs thought better of it.

"I guess you could call it a gut feeling," Gibbs said in looking back on his change of heart. "When I sat and thought about it, I've always said that one of the most important positions on any team is the backup quarterback. If you've got a good team, one injury to your [starting] quarterback could cost you a playoff game or the Super Bowl. The way I looked at it, if we had a young quarterback, we wanted a veteran behind him. If we had a veteran, we wanted a younger guy. Doug was the perfect fit."

A day or two before the Redskins opened the season against the Eagles at RFK, Gibbs pulled Williams aside. He addressed Williams by his given name. "There were only two other people who called me Douglas, and that was my mom and my oldest brother," Williams said. "And when they called me that, I knew I was in trouble and I immediately thought about what I had just done."

"Douglas, I got a feeling that somewhere along the line," Gibbs told him, "you're going to come in here and win this thing."

This thing?

The Super Bowl.

⸻

Gibbs's decision to keep Williams paid off immediately. Schroeder was injured in the 1987 season opener, and Williams came on in relief and threw two touchdown passes in a 34–24 win over Buddy Ryan's Eagles. A week later, Williams came off the bench again to throw three touchdown passes, albeit in a 21–20 loss to the Falcons.

And then: another players' strike, long anticipated because of the saber rattling by NFLPA executive director Gene Upshaw, but disconcerting nonetheless.

Unlike the 1982 work stoppage, when the entire league shut down for fifty-seven days, the owners wanted to take a more aggressive stance and threatened to continue the regular season with replacement players.

If the NFL Players Association thought the owners were bluffing, union leaders quickly found out otherwise. After canceling the Week 3 slate of games, replacement players—and any unionized players who decided to cross the picket line—would play regular-season games that would count in the standings.

Many teams weren't fully convinced the games would actually count after the strike ended, and were less motivated to come up with strong replacement teams. But the Redskins took the strike games very seriously, and Beathard dispatched his longtime assistant Charley Casserly to form the best replacement team he could find. Casserly worked the phones tirelessly and came up with as many viable players as he could. Quarterback Ed Rubbert, running backs Lionel Vital and Wayne Wilson, wide receiver Anthony Allen, punt returner Derrick Shepard, offensive linemen Darrick Brilz and Eric Coyle, tight ends

Craig McEwen and Joe Caravello were just some of the players Casserly signed.

He even found former Tennessee quarterback Tony Robinson, a one-time Heisman Trophy candidate who'd been sentenced to prison in 1986 but was out on a work furlough.

It was one of the most chaotic times in NFL history, with the regular players trying to remain united and work out in groups around the country, while the replacement players crossed the picket lines and took their jobs—at least temporarily. As the strike went on, several prominent veterans defied the union and went back to work. Among them: Joe Montana, Lawrence Taylor, and Cowboys stars Tony Dorsett, Randy White, and Danny White.

Former Redskins safety Mark Murphy, who had been released in 1985 and believed that his ouster was at least partly related to his previous union activities as a member of the NFLPA's executive committee, was again a leading voice in the union's attempt to secure a new Collective Bargaining Agreement and continue the push for unrestricted free agency.

Murphy thought the owners risked the league's credibility by using scabs, but the owners eventually broke the strike by making the games count.

In the meantime, Gibbs went about coaching the replacement team as best he could. That three-game stretch proved pivotal for what was to come the rest of the season.

"Without knowing it, we probably had an advantage there, because we were all together the whole time and there wasn't the kind of turmoil that other teams had [with players who crossed the picket lines]," Gibbs said.

The Redskins won their first two replacement games, beating the Cardinals, 28–21, at RFK and then routing the Giants, 38–12, at Giants Stadium. It was a particularly humbling game for Parcells, who was frustrated by Young's unwillingness to be more aggressive in assembling a replacement team.

Walsh had only added to Parcells's misery, when he had replacement quarterback Mark Stevens run the wishbone offense in the second half. After Stevens opened the third quarter with a 5-yard run, Parcells looked across the field at Walsh with an *Are you kidding me?*

look. Walsh looked back and shrugged his shoulders with a *Gotta do what I gotta do* expression.

With back-to-back wins in his first two strike games, and with the labor dispute about to be resolved, there would be one more replacement game for Gibbs: at Dallas on *Monday Night Football*.

The Redskins were given little chance of winning, since several Cowboys regulars—including their star running back, quarterback, and defensive tackle—had crossed the picket line. With none of the Redskins' regulars in uniform, Gibbs took on the improbable task of facing his NFC East rivals with a decidedly undermanned team.

The strike had actually ended the Thursday before the game, but because the players had voted to end the strike the day after a league-imposed deadline, there would be one more replacement game.

Gibbs faced his team before they took the field against the Cowboys, and challenged them to play the game of their lives. With one more chance to prove they could win in this league, he exhorted them to show a national television audience they could do it.

And that's exactly what they did. With Robinson replacing an injured Rubbert, the Redskins beat the Cowboys, 13–7, giving Gibbs a 3-0 record in replacement games (and 4-1 overall) and keeping his team ahead in the NFC East now that the "regular" season was about to resume.

"Somebody had crossed the line on every team, and we had no veterans do that," Gibbs said. "That takes away a lot of the turmoil. Everyone [on the replacement team] knew they were done, and very few of them were going to stay. It was a great story that we were able to get the win."

(Thirteen years later, *The Replacements*—a movie starring Keanu Reeves and Gene Hackman based loosely on the Redskins strike team that pulled off the upset in Dallas—was released. In the movie, the Washington Sentinels would beat Dallas to make the playoffs.)

Once the Redskins' regulars returned from the strike, Gibbs had them in fine form, and Washington won three of its next four games to take a commanding lead in the NFC East with a 7-2 record. But Gibbs still had nagging concerns about Schroeder, who could be very good when he was hot, but very inconsistent at other times.

Heading into the final week of the regular season against the

Vikings at the Hubert H. Humphrey Metrodome, Schroeder had thrown just one touchdown pass and two interceptions over his previous two games. And when he started off the Vikings game with two interceptions, Gibbs turned to Williams, who led the Redskins to a come-from-behind 27–24 win.

After the game, Williams showered and dressed and was asked by reporters what he thought about Gibbs's decision.

Decision? What decision?

Minutes earlier, Gibbs had said in his postgame press conference that Williams would be his starter in the playoffs.

"It was to benefit the organization," Williams said. "I understood when you make decisions, you do what's best for the team."

Williams couldn't help but think back to that day before the season, when Gibbs had shared his gut feeling about turning to him when the Redskins needed him most.

Now here was his chance.

Gibbs's first game with his newly anointed starting quarterback was about as challenging as it could get, perhaps outside of another road game against the Giants. After a first-round bye, the Redskins had to travel to Chicago to face the Bears at Soldier Field.

Even though Buddy Ryan had left the team a year earlier to become head coach of the Eagles, the heart of the Bears' Super Bowl team—the defense—was still intact. That defense, in fact, had been the source of some of Gibbs's greatest frustration in another playoff game three years earlier.

In the divisional round of the 1984 playoffs, the Bears upset the Redskins, 23–19, at RFK Stadium, with Ryan's defense absolutely manhandling Gibbs's offense. Theismann was sacked seven times, didn't throw a touchdown pass, and was intercepted once. Riggins rushed for only 50 yards on 21 carries. Ryan's 46 defense, a scheme that revolved around pressuring the quarterback, had knocked the Redskins out of the playoffs a year after Gibbs had lost the Super Bowl to the Raiders and been unceremoniously labeled "a buffoon" for his ill-fated decision to have Theismann pass from deep in his own territory.

"We had not seen that defense," Gibbs's trusted lieutenant, running backs coach Don Breaux, said of the 1984 playoff loss to Chicago. "They snuffed us, and I can remember Joe being really mad after that game. He said to the coaches, 'Hey, we're fixing to spend some time after this.' We ended up spending a tremendous amount of time on that Bear defense."

Though Vince Tobin had replaced Ryan at the controls of the Chicago defense, the Bears were still stacked with talent—from Mike Singletary, to Richard Dent, Dan Hampton, Otis Wilson, and Wilber Marshall. While the '85 Bears defense is held up as arguably the greatest single-season defense of all time, Tobin's group was statistically just as good.

But on this day, with Williams as his quarterback and unheralded rookie Timmy Smith as his top runner, Gibbs found a way. Williams threw for 207 yards, one touchdown pass, and an interception, while Smith ran for 66 yards to lead the Redskins to a 21–17 win.

Thanks to an upset win by the Vikings over the 49ers in the other NFC divisional-round game, the Redskins got to host the conference championship game at RFK.

This time, it wasn't Gibbs's offense that put the Redskins into the Super Bowl. It was his defense, an underappreciated component of his success in Washington and a tribute to longtime defensive coordinator Richie Petitbon, one of the most ingenious play-callers of his era.

"We had such a great defensive staff with Richie, [defensive line coach] Torgy [LaVern Torgeson], [defensive backs coach] Emmitt Thomas, [linebackers coach] Larry Peccatiello," Gibbs said. The defense also had great players, like defensive linemen Dexter Manley, Dave Butz, and Charles Mann, linebackers Neal Olkewicz, Mel Kaufman, and Monte Coleman, and All-Pro cornerback Darrell Green. "Those guys were outstanding, and I don't think they get enough credit. I know people talk about the offense a lot, but defense and special teams were huge for us. That defense led us to Super Bowls."

On a day when Williams was ordinary, it was Petitbon's defense that was the difference in a 17–10 win that sent the Redskins into Super Bowl XXII. The Vikings got inside the Redskins' 10-yard line twice in the fourth quarter, the first ending in a field goal to make it 10–10.

Williams then drove for the go-ahead score, finishing it off with a 7-yard touchdown pass to Gary Clark to make it 17–10 with 5:15 left in regulation.

The Vikings again drove inside the Washington 10, but were held outside the end zone until one final attempt on fourth down to send the game into overtime.

"Smoke 83 option."

Quarterback Wade Wilson called out the play in the huddle, and the Vikings lined up for a play that would put running back Darrin Nelson in a one-on-one situation against linebacker Monte Coleman at the goal line.

Gibbs dropped to his knees on the sidelines to say a prayer, unsure whether the game would go into overtime or he would go back to the Super Bowl for the third time.

Wilson dropped back and waited for Nelson to run his route toward the left, then fired a pass that hit the running back in the chest. Just as the ball made contact, Green came flying over and slammed Nelson. The ball fell incomplete.

The Redskins were going to San Diego to face Elway's Denver Broncos, who had once again beaten the Browns in the AFC Championship Game.

Now the narrative was inescapable: With Gibbs correctly trusting his gut to go with Williams over Schroeder in the playoffs, the possibility of Williams becoming the first black quarterback to win a Super Bowl was a massive story line. Thousands of reporters would descend on San Diego for a week of Super Bowl hype, and Williams would become the central focus.

Even if he was a reluctant participant.

Williams wasn't outspoken in his quest to make history, although he certainly appreciated what it meant to be the first African American quarterback to play in the Super Bowl, and of course the first with a chance to win it. And Gibbs felt the issue was never a central focus among the players and coaches.

"I didn't even realize that was taking place," said Gibbs.

Surprised? Don't be—Gibbs was famously oblivious of outside events. Once, Oliver North had visited Redskins practice, and Gibbs noticed the commotion. He was asked if he knew who North was. This was during the height of the Iran-Contra scandal that rocked Washington, D.C.

"Gibbs comes over to the writers, and he says, 'All right, now, who is this guy?'" recalls Richard Justice, the *Washington Post*'s beat writer. "He's the most famous person on the planet this week," someone told Gibbs. The coach eventually struck up a friendship with North and even invited the former Marine Corps lieutenant colonel and member of the National Security Council to give a pep talk to the team shortly before the Redskins left for the Super Bowl in San Diego.

"Doug was just our quarterback," Gibbs said of Williams. "I didn't think of him as being black. We had a great quarterback."

Williams provided thoughtful answers to a battery of questions asked by reporters about his place in history, but one question in particular became a source of controversy. Football writer Butch John of the Jackson (Mississippi) *Clarion-Ledger* framed his question this way:

"Doug, it's obvious you've been a black quarterback all your life. When did it start to matter?"

Williams couldn't quite make out the entirety of the question, but said what he thought he heard:

"What? How long have I been a black quarterback?"

Despite the fact that wasn't the actual question, a media brushfire ensued, with John accused of asking an insensitive question and putting Williams in an awkward spot.

"I've been a black quarterback since high school," he said. "I've always been black."

The story took on a life of its own, and the urban legend continues that John had asked the dumbest question in the long history of Super Bowl media events. John, who died in 2014 at age sixty-one, never lived it down, and he was heartbroken that people misinterpreted what he'd actually asked.

He did, however, clear the air with Williams years later.

"Butch called me and he told me," Williams said. "I was glad we talked, and I know he had a lot of pain later in his life from back surgery [and later the cancer that took his life]. I understood exactly where he was coming from, and we talked. In my mind, it was how long have [people] been putting an emphasis on it. I told him ever since I left Grambling. After I got to Tampa, I was a black quarterback."

By the time Williams was ready to take the field against the Broncos, he was focused not on making history, but on being the best quarterback he could be now that he had the opportunity he'd yearned for.

And if the enormity of the moment wasn't big enough, the fact that Williams faced the biggest game of his life with only a couple hours of sleep added to the drama. Williams had developed a severe pain on a tooth connected to a dental bridge, and the night before the game, he underwent a root canal.

There was no way the discomfort in his mouth, as well as lingering knee soreness that had bothered him much of the season, would prevent him from achieving his years-long goal of winning a championship.

The Broncos came into the game as three-point favorites, and the Redskins faced early trouble. Gibbs had hoped to start fast and get some early momentum, but the Broncos carried the game early, building a 10–0 lead in the first quarter on Elway's 56-yard touchdown strike to Ricky Nattiel and a 24-yard field goal from Rich Karlis.

Something was wrong with the way Gibbs was attacking the Broncos' defense, and he knew it.

"It gave us fits for that first quarter," Gibbs said.

Broncos defensive coordinator Joe Collier had used an alignment the Redskins had never seen on film, employing a version of the Bears' 46 defense.

"They hadn't shown that look all year long," said the Redskins' veteran center, Jeff Bostic. "They were not that big up front with guys like Greg Kragen, Rulon Jones, Karl Mecklenburg, Ricky Hunley. But we weren't moving it against them."

Gibbs went over to Bostic on the sidelines after a failed series and asked what was going on. Bostic explained what the Broncos were doing and why he thought they were having trouble with the alignment.

"They were running like a 46 defense, but they were running [defensive line] stunts inside with the defensive end and the nose tackle," Bostic said. "First two drives, we lost twelve yards, and we just weren't prepared for this scheme."

Bostic then witnessed what he called the greatest in-game coaching adjustment he'd ever seen, a strategic change that Gibbs came up with on the spot. Bostic watched as Gibbs stood up, folded his arms, put his right index finger to his cheek while deep in thought, and then mapped out the strategy.

"He goes, 'Okay, here's what we're going to do,'" Bostic said.

Gibbs had abandoned the blocking schemes he'd prepared all week to use, and went back to the bread-and-butter plays that had worked so well earlier in the decade, when the counter trey or counter gap had flourished with the Hogs doing the heavy lifting up front and John "Diesel" Riggins gaining the tough inside yards.

This time, it would be the almost unheard-of Timmy Smith, a fifth-round rookie out of Texas Tech, doing the running. It was another gut reaction that prompted Gibbs to go with Smith as the starter ahead of veteran George Rogers, who had struggled in the previous two playoff games.

But it was Williams, who had suffered a sprained knee late in the first quarter but returned after missing two plays, who started what would become one of the most epic turnarounds in NFL history.

"Charlie-10 hitch."

The play called for Ricky Sanders to line up to the right of the formation and simply run up the field. Williams needed to make sure to keep a safety away from the vicinity, which he did, and fired off a perfect pass to Sanders, who turned the catch into an 80-yard touchdown to get the Redskins on the board.

Williams then hit Gary Clark on a crossing route for a 27-yard touchdown to make it 14–10. Then it was Smith turning a counter trey run into a 58-yard touchdown to make it 21–10. Williams hit Sanders on a 50-yard touchdown pass for a 28–10 lead, and he found tight end Clint Didier on an eight-yard scoring pass to make it 35–10.

Eighteen plays, thirty-five points: a Super Bowl record that still stands today.

The Redskins would cruise to a 42–10 trouncing of the Broncos, Williams would be named the game's Most Valuable Player, and Gibbs would leave the field with his second Super Bowl championship and further burnish his reputation as one of the game's legendary strategists. He had the guts to go with Williams and the rookie Smith, who was told only forty-five minutes before the game that he would start so he wouldn't have time to be overcome by the enormity of the situation. And he had the genius to know when to adjust his game plan to counter what the Broncos had tried.

Gibbs had once again reached the top, had once again done a magnificent job despite unforeseen circumstances, and had made good on that gut feeling he'd shared over the summer with Williams that they could indeed do something special.

Seven months after nixing the Williams trade to the Raiders, Gibbs showed his genius once more, and his players carried him off the field in triumph.

WALSH

THE PRESSURE FROM WITHIN AND THE IMPOSSIBLE EXPECTATIONS FROM OUTSIDE

Steve Young got the assurance he needed from Bill Walsh, and gave the go-ahead for the trade.

The twenty-six-year-old quarterback had been deemed expendable once the Buccaneers had signed Heisman Trophy–winning quarterback Vinny Testaverde to a four-year contract a few weeks before the 1987 draft. With Walsh now convinced Montana's back surgery from the year before would further restrict him moving forward, Young had become the coach's Plan B.

But first, Walsh had to convince Young that there would actually be an opportunity to be a starter with the 49ers.

"I would not have come to San Francisco if Bill would have said, 'Hey, come back up Joe,'" Young said of his deliberations leading up to the trade. Young, who had signed a four-year, $40 million deal with the USFL's Los Angeles Express and later joined the Bucs when the USFL folded (he made only $4.8 million on that contract), had gone 2-12 in Tampa in 1986 to prompt the Bucs to draft Testaverde. "I wouldn't have done it. I wanted to play."

It turned out to be a great selling job on Walsh's part. Despite his promise to Young that he would have a chance to start, the coach said publicly that Young's acquisition would not change Montana's status.

"This move is not a reflection on Joe Montana," Walsh said after the deal was made official. The cost for Young: second- and fourth-round picks in the upcoming draft, which would turn out to be one of the biggest steals in NFL history. "We fully expect Joe to continue as the leader and mainstay of our team."

That was not what Walsh had told Young, although the quarterback understood the coach's comments to the media were intended for public consumption and did not reflect Walsh's lingering concerns about Montana. The fact of the matter was that Walsh thought Montana might be near the end because of the back surgery. Despite making what had been considered a miraculous return, Montana's play had suffered the second half of the season. He had just four touchdowns and seven interceptions over his last six games, and in the 49–3 playoff loss to the eventual Super Bowl champion Giants, he'd suffered a severe concussion on that crushing hit from Jim Burt.

Even the doctor who performed the surgery on Montana thought he was nuts for coming back.

"For him to go out and put his back under direct, unprotected trauma is crazy," Dr. Arthur White told the *San Francisco Chronicle* in 1986 when Montana was ready to return. "I told Joe the first day I met him that I don't recommend that people I do surgery on go back to anything that's out of control—that they should stay in control of their spines for the rest of their lives."

But Young needed only one training camp practice to realize that his chances at unseating Montana were close to zero.

"I can remember that first practice and the first time Joe ran out onto the field," Young said.

He saw Montana look every bit as good as you'd imagine from a two-time Super Bowl MVP. He moved effortlessly, completed just about every pass he attempted, and looked nothing like what he'd imagined based on his conversations with Walsh.

At one point during the practice, Young pulled Walsh aside.

"He's not hurt," Young told his coach.

"Bill gave me that shrug of the shoulders and was like, 'Yeah, well.'"

Was Young bamboozled by Walsh?

"I think he was concerned and he overplayed it with me, just to make sure that I came," Young said in looking back on the trade.

Walsh now had the best of both worlds. Secure in the knowledge that he had a legitimate Plan B in Young and the fact that Montana indeed appeared healthy after an off-season's worth of recovery time, he could proceed with the assurance that the quarterback position was the least of his problems.

Was there a chance that there'd be a full-blown controversy, given Young's presence? Of course, although the fact that Young's 1986 Buccaneers were the NFL's worst team record-wise took some of the heat off. But there was also the possibility that having a legitimate starter behind Montana could bring out more of the best in his two-time Super Bowl MVP.

In Walsh's mind, the competition was healthy, even if there was potential risk in creating what could become a combustible situation. How competitive was Montana? Consider that even now, all these years after his retirement following the 1994 season, it's as if time stands still when he looks back on that situation Walsh had created by trading for Young.

"I'd compete with whoever was behind me, no matter what," he said. "It didn't matter if it was Steve DeBerg, Steve Young, or Steve Bono. In my mind, I'm not letting anybody play. The only way to do that is to go out there and prepare and play to the level you can play to. You start letting the stuff behind you bother you, that's when you run into trouble. A lot of times the media played it up, 'Oh, [Montana] can't be happy.' I'm like, what do I care? As long as he's behind me, that's okay."

In an unexpected twist, Walsh's acquisition of Young would ultimately spur Montana to some of his greatest accomplishments in an already terrific career.

"Bill made it clear in 1987 that he was going to create quarterback diversity," Young said. "That's what created all the consternation and difficulty."

Controversy would not show itself immediately, however.

After coming out of the strike with a 4-1 record thanks in large part to three straight wins in the replacement games, the 49ers were virtually unbeatable the rest of the season. With only an upset loss at New Orleans, they went into the playoffs with a 13-2 record and the

NFC's top seed. Once again, the path to the Super Bowl went through Candlestick Park.

The Vikings had barely gotten into the playoffs after an 8-7 regular season—which included three losses in their last four games—and even after a 44–10 upset of the 12-3 Saints in the wild card round, there appeared little chance they could conquer the 49ers on the road.

Oddsmakers agreed the Vikings were vastly overmatched, as the 11-point betting line suggested.

And then it all came apart.

The 49ers were simply not ready for what the Vikings had in store, and Walsh's own overconfidence certainly contributed to one of the biggest upsets in playoff history. But what happened midway through the third quarter would be a turning point that even Walsh knew would have lasting consequences.

Not only for the team, but for himself.

With the 49ers' offense unable to generate any consistent attack, and with Montana under a relentless pass rush from a Vikings defensive line that included Chris Doleman, Keith Millard, and Henry Thomas, Walsh benched Montana for the first time in his 49ers career.

The sellout crowd at Candlestick Park was stunned.

So was Montana.

"Usually in that situation, you let the guy that got you there try to play his way out of it," Montana said in reflecting back on that game. "But Bill wanted to try something else."

Walsh felt he needed to do something.

"I told Joe we had to try to change the chemistry," Walsh said after the game. "But you can't say that was the answer."

It wasn't.

Walsh sent in Young, who scored a 5-yard rushing touchdown to make it 27–17. But with the Vikings' offense red-hot and wide receiver Anthony Carter having a career day with 10 catches for 227 yards, the Vikings prevailed, 36–24.

Walsh was disconsolate, having failed for a third straight year to win a playoff game and inviting second-guessing about whether he still had what it took to get back to the Super Bowl. After two years of having to go on the road to face—and ultimately lose to—the Giants, he had the perfect opportunity to do so with home field advantage against a clearly inferior opponent.

But it was the 49ers who were overmatched on both sides of the ball, and an off-season of soul-searching, exacerbated by an increasingly tense relationship with DeBartolo, prompted Walsh to again question his future. At fifty-six years old, he began to wonder whether it was time to leave for good.

Walsh had already begun to show signs of stress, partly from the sheer wear and tear of a job that consumed nearly all coaches but was especially pronounced in such a driven, yet hypersensitive man. In many ways, Walsh was a contradiction—a coach whose ambition and brilliance placed him above his peers and prompted others to call him a genius, yet a man who bristled when being second-guessed, often struggled to maintain his equilibrium, and also succumbed to moments of self-doubt.

It was a regular theme with Walsh throughout his life; because he always felt he had to prove himself, he'd frequently become racked with uncertainty. It was this personality trait that prompted Paul Brown to pass him over for the Bengals' head coaching job in 1976, and hints of dissatisfaction were starting to appear with the 49ers, particularly as the bar of expectation was being raised now that he had already won two championships.

Back-to-back playoff losses to the Giants, particularly the 49–3 humiliation at Giants Stadium in the 1986 postseason, haunted him, and it became a zero-sum game for Walsh: Anything except winning a Super Bowl meant failure.

It was why he seriously contemplated stepping down as head coach after the strike-shortened 1982 season, when the 49ers had failed to reach the playoffs the year after they'd won their first Super Bowl. But even after winning it all again after the 1984 season and coaching as close to a perfect game as he ever did in dismantling the Dolphins in the title game, the ultimate barometer for success was holding the Vince Lombardi Trophy aloft on Super Bowl Sunday.

Even Parcells could see it in Walsh.

"Bill Walsh was, in my opinion, a highly stressed person," Parcells said. "He appeared calm and reflective, but inside, I know it was churning him. I could tell when things weren't going well for them on offense and we were playing defense, I could sense his frustration. But that only comes with coaching against him and understanding. The first couple times we played against them, I didn't have that sense. But as the years went on, I could sense it."

Walsh himself knew it, though he tried not to let on.

"Losing, however you define it, even the *thought* of losing, can become so psychologically crippling that winning offers little solace and no cause for celebration, because you've imposed an internal accounting system on yourself that awards *zero* points for winning and minus points for losing," Walsh wrote in his book *The Score Takes Care of Itself*. "You can never get ahead on points...This can occur as your expectations and the expectations of others get higher and higher—they keep raising the bar on you, and you keep raising it on yourself."

Whatever would happen, the year after Walsh's second straight post-season loss to the Giants would therefore be climactic, and Walsh's trade for Young was clearly symbolic of his determination to get back to the top. Despite all that Montana had done for him in leading the 49ers out of the mess the franchise had been in when Walsh took over in 1979, there was no blind loyalty on the coach's part to his signature player. No, Walsh's loyalty was to winning and to using whatever means necessary to achieve that goal—even if it meant Montana might not be the one to bring them back to a championship level.

Steve Dils ran into Bill Walsh at an airport not long before the start of training camp in 1988. The former Stanford quarterback was stunned by what he saw.

"I remember thinking, 'Wow, he looks like it's the end of the season,'" said Dils. "He looked worn out. I said to myself, 'That ain't a good look.' You can just see it on his face."

Dils thought back to his time with Walsh at Stanford and remembered a completely different person.

"He had this great sense of humor," Dils said. "When he was in front of the team, or at banquets, we compared him to Johnny Carson."

Walsh's sense of humor was legendary to those who knew him. His sarcasm was often so biting, yet so subtle that it often took people several minutes after the jab was delivered to realize they'd been had.

Walsh was also a master at playing practical jokes. Like the time he and his wife, Geri, and close friends Mike and Marilyn White were vacationing together in Lake Tahoe. They went to see comedian Don Rickles perform at Harrah's, and at one point during Rickles's stand-up routine, he took out a book and looked over to where the two couples were sitting.

"I'd like to get Mike White up here on stage," Rickles said. Stunned at being noticed by Rickles, White walked onto the stage. "I have this book here, and it's titled *Everything I've Learned in Football*," Rickles said. Rickles then opened the book and flipped through the pages. They were all blank. Walsh cracked up, his prearranged gag with Rickles a resounding success.

Then there was the time Walsh pulled off a practical joke on Dolphins coach Don Shula after the two had become friends late in their careers. Shula was interested in joining the Monterey (California) Peninsula Country Club where Walsh and former Raiders coach and TV announcer John Madden were members.

Walsh, who had been retired as the 49ers coach, told Madden he wanted to make Shula think he'd have a hard time being approved for membership. So as Shula and his wife, Mary Anne, approached the two during a meet-and-greet with some other club members, Walsh and Madden pulled the Dolphins coach aside.

"Look, Don. They like Mary Anne, but you're right on the border," Walsh told Shula. "It can go either way. It may be 50-50. It may be 49-51. You're not in, because you're not really showing yourself. You're not bringing out your personality. You know we're on your side, but all the other people here, half of them are against you."

Madden did all he could not to laugh.

"That chin's out with that serious look from Don," Madden said.

Bill told Shula, "Look, take a lap around this crowd and go talk to them. Show your personality."

Shula did just that, mingling with the members to try and create a better impression, when in fact his membership was completely assured. Walsh and Madden snickered as they watched the winningest coach in NFL history make his case at the golf club.

P.S.: They never told Shula about the joke.

But now, Walsh looked like a burned-out husk of a man. His hair had already turned snowy white, and his face was now etched with more lines brought on by the inordinate pressure of his job. Of his life. Of his legacy. He had feared failure, and now he was a failure—at least in his own mind. No amount of winning in the regular season could assuage the pain of three straight playoff losses, and Walsh was lurching toward an inevitable ending.

When that ending would come, he didn't quite know, only that it was coming. Maybe sooner rather than later.

"To get to the level that a guy like Bill Walsh has gotten to, you have to be different," Dils said. "Very few people can operate at that level of intensity and discipline, and you could see how tired he looked at that point."

In truth, Walsh was exhausted—physically from the toll of working countless hours throughout the year and especially during the season, and mentally from the burden of expectation he carried after having reached the pinnacle twice before.

Walsh himself contributed to the pressure with his decision to bench Montana in the playoff loss to the Vikings, and a quarterback controversy only added to his problems. The coach was still convinced Montana had enough left to remain the starter, but that didn't quell the speculation from outside the organization that the Montana-Young arrangement wasn't healthy.

While the media-driven scrutiny was intense, Walsh skillfully avoided internal conflict by making sure his two quarterbacks could peacefully coexist. And part of that had to do with Walsh's own judgment of the psychological makeup of Montana and Young. He firmly believed that both were confident enough in their own abilities that they wouldn't engage in the kind of backbiting that tore many teams apart from within.

"Everybody [on the outside] tried to force [controversy] between us, and there are going to be things that will happen where people are going to take you out of the lineup," Montana said. "That's just the way it is. But there was never anything there between Steve and I. A lot of times, the media would play it up."

Young is convinced that part of Walsh's calculus in making the trade wasn't only because of the quarterback's physical gifts. It was because of his psychological makeup as well.

"People always talk about controversy, but one thing Bill understood fundamentally was that Joe and I were not toxic people," Young said. "We can complain and moan, but we weren't toxic. [Walsh] knew that no matter what he did that we weren't going to create toxicity, and that's the truth. We didn't. The truth is that the 49ers were the beneficiary of both of us competing with each other in a very difficult but constructive way. That's the difference. If you have toxic people in quarterback controversies, you're dead. You're just dead."

Young said he and Montana got along exceedingly well, despite the potentially treacherous circumstances of their arrangement.

"Joe and I never had a cross word, never fought, never argued," Young said. "Not even once. Never. Our conversations were collegial and we effectively tried to do the best we could in the situation. It went as well as it possibly could. That first season I got there [in 1987], Joe had been hurt a lot and I played quite a bit, but that Vikings playoff game was the first time he ever pulled Joe when he was healthy, and that was a pretty dramatic moment."

Though clearly showing signs of physical and emotional fatigue heading into the next season, Walsh was still committed to doing everything he could to not only prepare his players for the season, but to help them grow as people. He'd regularly talk to them about preparing for their time after football and making sure they could sharpen not only their football skills, but their life skills.

"Bill really cared about his players," Guy McIntyre said. "Outside of the game, he really looked at us as men with families, not just as football players. He put a lot of emotional intelligence into knowing his players. He wanted to see his players be successful not just on the field, but off the field, too. He wanted his guys to see different people in different walks of life and appreciate what we had and what we could do with having been in the NFL."

Walsh eventually created an internship program for minority

230 | BOB GLAUBER

coaches—later called the Bill Walsh Minority Coaching Fellowship—
a program that helped young coaches like Anthony Lynn, Marvin
Lewis, Herman Edwards, Hue Jackson, and Lovie Smith become NFL
head coaches.

Walsh often had guest speakers from a wide spectrum of profes-
sions address his players, and one of them was Dr. Harry Edwards,
a highly respected sociologist and civil rights activist who taught at
UC Berkeley. Edwards created the Olympic Project for Human Rights,
a movement that deeply impacted U.S. Olympic sprinters Tommie
Smith and John Carlos, who raised their fists in the black power salute
at the 1968 Olympic Games and sparked worldwide discussion about
civil rights.

Walsh eventually hired Edwards as a consultant, a role he still holds
today.

"Bill had a tremendous amount of vision and intelligence and
courage, and there was a track record of concern about his players,"
Edwards said. "He encouraged a counseling structure in the locker
room. When I asked him where my office is going to be, he said it's
going to be in the locker room. Wherever the players are—whether
it's the locker room, the cafeteria, the weight room—that's your office.
I want you to be there. We had issues like every other team in the
league. The difference was, we dealt with them more intelligently. Bill
never buried his head in the sand or tried to ignore it."

Inevitably, though, football came first, something Walsh had clearly
set out in his Standard of Performance manifesto, which he'd created
from a lifetime of experiences. Even back to his early days with the
49ers, Walsh demanded a team-first approach, and that never wavered
throughout his tenure.

"My dad never talked of color, never talked of black players or white
players," Craig Walsh said. "He talked about players."

Craig believes his father would not have tolerated a situation similar to the one in 2016, when 49ers quarterback Colin Kaepernick took
a knee during the national anthem to protest racial injustice.

"He would have asked Kaepernick, 'Are you an activist, or are you a
football player? If you're an activist, I'm going to release you. You have

to tell me right this second.' He'd tell the team that Colin had a choice to be an activist or play on this team, and it would have been done and he would have moved on."

Edwards thinks Walsh would have dealt with Kaepernick differently.

"When Tommie Smith and John Carlos came home from the Olympics and were kicked out of track and field, got death threats all over the place, Bill Walsh was a coach with the Bengals, and he gave them a tryout, even though neither one of them played college football," Edwards said. "Bill Walsh brought me into the 49ers organization, knowing how hard I organized, knowing that I was a member of the Black Panther Party, knowing I had been outspoken about the inequities in college sports. He was not afraid of these kinds of issues. He admired Muhammad Ali for his courage, conviction, and commitment. He admired Jesse Owens to have the guts to go to Munich [in the 1936 Olympics], knowing he was going to come home to segregation and death threats just by being successful."

What would have happened if Walsh had coached Kaepernick?

"Bill wouldn't have kicked him off the team, wouldn't have made a big deal of it," Edwards said. "It's a First Amendment right. It's not an assault on the flag, against soldiers, it's not an assault on the anthem. It's a statement about something that's very, very serious in our society. Bill would have taken all of that into consideration and figured out a way where we could accommodate both concerns—Kaep's interest and move from protest to progress. How do we make this thing work? It wouldn't have blown up into this situation where they made him a martyr."

***

The 49ers started off well enough the year after their playoff flop against the Vikings, and Walsh got at least some payback with a mid-season win over Minnesota to go 6-3. But back-to-back losses to the Cardinals on the road and the Raiders at home created a crisis point that ultimately convinced Walsh he couldn't go on beyond that season. Much of his angst was self-inflicted, but DeBartolo's increasing impatience was also an unmistakable factor.

The owner's frustration boiled over after a 24–23 loss to the Cardinals, as the 49ers blew a 23–0 third quarter lead and lost it with three seconds left in regulation on a Neil Lomax touchdown pass to Roy Green. DeBartolo stormed into the locker room and berated the players. And then he directed his ire at Walsh himself, the first time DeBartolo had ever blasted him in front of the team.

"That was the absolute dregs, the lowest point of that year," Randy Cross said. "Eddie considered all of us employees, including Bill. It went above and beyond. It wasn't too hard to figure out after being in that locker room that day that everybody's job was in harm's way."

Like most of the players, Cross was mortified when DeBartolo ripped Walsh.

"It was an embarrassing moment for [Walsh]," he said. "It was the first time that we'd seen that publicly. I was with Bill all ten years, and nobody ever talked like that to him."

Walsh was clearly wounded at the owner's second-guessing, and it only contributed to the inner turmoil that had already consumed him. A 9–3 home loss to the Raiders at Candlestick the following week made things even worse. A subsequent meeting with DeBartolo further inflamed the coach's distress.

"Increasingly, Eddie kept raising the bar," Walsh wrote in *The Score Takes Care of Itself*. "Soon enough, if his team didn't win that year's Super Bowl, he was distraught, enraged. Just getting to the playoffs each year was insufficient; in fact, it drove him crazy—it was unacceptable to him, perhaps because his pride was involved...He was beginning his heavy-handed approach to micromanagement, occasionally offering ideas to me...But then he began questioning my decisions, occasionally belittling them, wondering out loud to anyone who cared to listen whether there wasn't a better way than what I did—whether he, perhaps, knew more about it than I did. That was embarrassing because, among other reasons, when it came to technical football, Eddie knew about as much as the average fan, which is to say, not too much."

Walsh didn't respond to DeBartolo during that postgame tirade in Phoenix, even though he was certainly tempted. Retrospectively, he regretted not standing up to his boss.

"It was something I should not have allowed," Walsh wrote. "I let him haul me over the coals in regard to my effort or performance when he had no basis for doing it. His only basis was that he owned the team, a pretty good basis, but not enough for me to let him excoriate me without significant cause in front of the team even once. I regret that I didn't back him down... I let him set a preposterous standard and then humiliate me when I couldn't reach it."

DeBartolo could sense something had changed in Walsh after those two midseason losses, but he didn't necessarily think it was something that the coach couldn't overcome.

"Our record was not good, and it looked like we might not make the playoffs," DeBartolo said. "He had a real rough time, and he was emotional. I won't say he had a breakdown. He was just very emotional. I just sat there and I tried to say, 'Bill, c'mon, we'll be fine.' But I think that was the beginning. There was a buildup of a lot of things."

But just as Walsh had experienced several times before throughout his life, those lowest moments turned out to be a prelude to some of his greatest. Which turned out to be the case once more, but only after Walsh had decided this would be his final run as the 49ers' coach.

"Emotionally, he was just wrung out," Craig Walsh said of his father. "If I was the analyst listening to him and trying to help him, he really just wanted to be wanted. Ownership had grown accustomed to winning, and I don't think he felt that appreciated. The other part of it was in his conscience. He asked so many other guys to step away when they had time left."

In the meantime, Walsh still had work to do. There was still something left to prove.

After the loss to the Raiders, it was Gibbs versus Walsh, with the Redskins coming to Candlestick Park as the defending Super Bowl champions and Williams still riding high off his Super Bowl MVP performance. But it was Walsh's team that ruled the day in a 37–21 win, as Montana threw two touchdowns and ran for another. That was the beginning of a four-game winning streak that clinched the divisional title ahead of a season-ending matchup against the Rams.

Despite that game having no bearing on the 49ers' playoff positioning, it did end up impacting Walsh's long-standing rivalry with Parcells. Because the Giants had lost earlier in the day to the Jets, they needed the 49ers to beat the Rams to clinch a playoff spot. But the 49ers were blown out at home, 38–16, thereby knocking the Giants out of the playoffs.

Truth be told, it wasn't the worst thing in the world that the 49ers wouldn't have to see the Giants in the playoffs, after having been outscored by a combined 66–6 in back-to-back postseason losses in 1985–86.

"Let's face it," Randy Cross said. "I would be a bold-faced liar if I didn't say I was going to be disappointed not to play New York in a playoff game."

Jerry Rice had justified the faith Walsh had shown in him—with one notable exception.

Though Rice had bedazzled the NFL and become the ultimate weapon in Walsh's offense, the young receiver's playoff performances had been disturbingly muted in those back-to-back losses to the Giants, as well as the colossal upset loss at home to the Vikings. Against the Giants, he had a combined 7 catches for just 93 yards and no touchdowns, and that drop in the 1986 divisional round matchup haunted him.

In fact, it still haunts him. More than three decades later.

"I'll never forget that play," Rice said. "After all the plays I have made throughout my career, I always go back and reflect on that one. I wanted to be perfect. I know you can't be perfect, and you're going to have some situations where there will be some hiccups."

But that play also spurred Rice to never let something like it happen again.

"That gave me the incentive to work a little bit harder," he said.

It was Walsh who turned the drop into a teaching moment for Rice, and helped mold the receiver into the greatest of all time.

"I never got complacent, and that was because of Bill Walsh," Rice said. "He kept that drive going for me, and I was always hungry."

Rice flashed back to his second season, when he had 3 touchdown catches in a game for the first time in his career. Walsh asked him to come to his office the next day.

"That was my coming-out party, and I'm thinking Bill is calling me into his office to pat me on the back," Rice said.

That was not what Walsh told him.

"I want more from you," the coach said.

"I'm walking out of that meeting, and I have this stunned look on my face," Rice said. "I noticed Joe Montana was headed up to Bill's office, and I can only imagine he told Joe the same thing."

It always came back to that for Walsh. The Standard of Performance. The unceasing search for perfection, and never settling for good when great is achievable.

It was Walsh, too, who prompted Rice not to engage in over-the-top celebrations after scoring touchdowns—something that many other receivers of his era, and virtually all receivers in today's game, have done routinely.

"It was team first with Bill," Rice said. "He didn't care what religion you were, where you came from, what color you were, it had to be the team concept. We were all in it as a team. No superstars. I had done a couple of celebrations early, and I would look at myself on film and think, 'What are you doing?' It's okay to celebrate with your teammates, but I didn't want to bring attention to myself. Act like you've been there. I just felt like I didn't want to disrespect anyone. Just be a professional."

Now was another chance for Rice to live up to his potential, and a chance for Walsh to deliver some payback for perhaps the worst loss of his career.

The Vikings were coming to town once more for the divisional playoffs. This time, there would be no letdown for the coach. Or for Rice, who had just three catches for 28 yards and no TDs in the 36–24 loss the previous year.

This time, Rice had three touchdowns in a 34–9 rout of the Vikings, as Walsh made certain there would be no repeat of last year's disaster. It had all come together for the fourth-year wide receiver, who had lived up to all his potential in the playoffs after willing himself to the forefront of all NFL receivers.

Rice had all the requisite skills to become a great receiver. Plenty of football speed—even if his 4.6 forty-yard dash in 1985 convinced some scouts that he wouldn't become an elite player. He also had great hands, and plenty of power to break the initial tackle.

But what separated Rice from his peers and would eventually transform him into the greatest receiver of all time was his will. Rice was extremely hard on himself whenever he made a mistake, but he transformed that frustration into motivation. And he credits Walsh for bringing out the best in him; Walsh was a coach who was able to see the player's ability and know precisely what approach to use.

"When I first came into the league, I had some problems learning the playbook and just thinking about where I belonged on an exceptional team," Rice said. "You have a team with players like Joe Montana and Ronnie Lott, and you don't know where you're going to fit in.

"Bill just said, 'Jerry, look, you're doing it in practice, you're exceptional,'" Rice recalled. "'Just keep working hard, keep preparing, and you're going to get a chance to showcase your abilities.' He never got down on me, and that helped me a lot. That gave me extra incentive to focus in a little more. Once the game came to me, I felt comfortable. Now I could just showcase my abilities."

Walsh also knew when to lighten things up for a player like Rice, who drove himself harder than almost any other player of his era. Or any era, for that matter.

"Bill was a prankster," Rice said. "As receivers, we always tried to be real flashy, wear the tights or have the towel, our shoes taped a certain way. Bill once walked into the locker room wearing tights and a long towel. We cracked up. He was always that type of guy. He'd say certain things that were funny, but at the same time, he demanded greatness."

Rice heeded that call, running full speed on every single practice play, often to the astonishment of his teammates.

"Jerry had just a tremendous work ethic," Montana said. "He was always working hard to improve his game, and that rubbed off on others."

Rice would now be in a position to help the 49ers get back to NFL dominance. His signature performance against the Vikings put the

49ers into the NFC Championship Game for the first time since Walsh won his second Super Bowl after the 1984 season. Unlike his first two title runs, the 49ers would be on the road for the conference championship. It would be 49ers-Bears, with Mike Ditka's team one step away from a second Super Bowl appearance.

The Bears had already beaten the 49ers in the regular season, grinding out a 10–9 win at Soldier Field on October 24. And with sustained winds of nearly thirty miles an hour and a wind chill of about ten degrees below zero, the odds seemed very much against the 49ers.

But during practice the week before the game, Walsh was supremely confident in his game plan. And he mocked the weather conditions he knew his team would face, using that inimitable brand of sarcasm the players had come to adore.

"Of course, you guys know this is Bears weather, so you fair-haired fellas from California, you're not made to play in this," he told his team. "You probably don't have much of a chance."

Walsh then started shadowboxing, one of his favorite reminders to let his team know that it was important to hit their opponents first.

"If there's an evenly matched boxing match—or at least a fight that's perceived as being even—Bill said that your opponent doesn't understand that if you're a little quicker, and you're a little stronger, and you hit just a little harder, that's going to be the difference," Cross said. "You can't see it in the first three or four rounds. You probably can't even see it in the fifth, sixth, or seventh rounds. But that imperceptible difference early starts showing up in the tenth round or later. Or in the third quarter or fourth quarter in a football game. So you hit him harder and faster, and they can't react, and they can't catch back up."

Walsh said that's how they would beat the Bears.

"You're going to hit them and pound them," Walsh told the players. "And by the end of the game, you'll be far ahead of them."

The 49ers destroyed the Bears that afternoon, and Walsh's game plan was magnificent.

Facing a defense that still had its greatest players from the 1985 team, Montana picked the Bears apart, hitting Rice on touchdown passes of 61 and 27 yards in the first half and then cruising to a 28–3 win. It was the 49ers' first road playoff win in eighteen years, earning

Walsh a third trip to the Super Bowl in what only he knew would be his final game as Niners coach.

The symmetry of the Super Bowl XXIII matchup in south Florida was breathtaking. Walsh would go out against the team and the owner that had snubbed him as a head coach, the team he had conquered to win his first Super Bowl, the team that had eventually rued the day that Walsh walked out the door when Paul Brown told him he wasn't good enough to be his head coach.

Walsh versus Brown's Bengals one more time.

One last time.

Walsh kept his personal feelings about retirement a secret, so the players had no idea this would be his final game. He did, however, make at least one cryptic remark about what might happen.

As he sat in his front-row seat in first class on the team charter from San Francisco to Florida—always leaving a seat open for anyone to visit with him—Cross walked up from coach to sit beside Walsh. Cross told him he would be retiring after this game. It would be the end of a spectacular career for Cross, one of the few holdovers from the pre-Walsh era.

After Cross told Walsh he was hanging up his cleats, Walsh said something that only later made Cross realize he'd dropped a hint about the future.

"Hey, if we win this game," Walsh told Cross, "there's no telling what I'm going to do."

———

Walsh was about to face Sam Wyche, his onetime quarterback in Cincinnati and former assistant with the 49ers—one of Walsh's many assistants who would go on to strong careers of their own. The Bill Walsh coaching tree would eventually grow into the most successful in NFL history, and seventeen Super Bowl–winning teams since his first title run in 1981—nearly half of the thirty-seven champions— can trace their lineage either directly or indirectly to him.

Walsh knew he had a formidable adversary in Bengals defensive coordinator Dick LeBeau, who had done a terrific job in helping Cincinnati's defense complement the gun-slinging quarterback Boomer

Esiason's offense. The Niners coach did indeed struggle against LeBeau's defense through the early part of the game, and Walsh's offense could only manage a pair of field goals through the third quarter.

But it was a sluggish start for both teams, with the Bengals also coming up with just a field goal before the first half ended in a 3–3 tie. Wyche faced a significant problem even before the game: His fullback, Stanley Wilson, was caught doing cocaine in his hotel room the night before the game, and Wyche deactivated Wilson.

Wilson had already tested positive for cocaine twice before, and a third violation of the NFL's drug policy meant he would never play again. The fact that his relapse happened the night before the Super Bowl only magnified the controversy, and Wyche, instead of focusing his entire energy on the game plan, was now forced to deal with a distraction that threatened to undo all the work that had gone into getting the team this far.

The Bengals were clearly out of sorts early on, but they stayed in the game thanks to their defensive coordinator's superb plan. LeBeau's 3-4 scheme was highly effective against Walsh's offense through much of the game, and Walsh was stymied in dealing with a system that disguised coverages and pass rush and challenged Walsh's intellectual capacity to counter the alignment.

LeBeau's theory of defense revolved around attacking specific pass protections, often overloading one side or the other to get a sustained pass rush. LeBeau knew he had to get Montana off his game by trying to pressure him as often as possible, and the Bengals did a great job in consistently frustrating the 49ers' passing attack.

In fact, after Stanford Jennings's 93-yard kickoff return in the third quarter, the Bengals went into the final period with a 13–6 lead. Considering how dominant the 49ers' offense had been during their late-season run to the playoffs and in their postseason wins over the Vikings and Bears, this was as good as the Bengals could have hoped for.

But as he had done so often throughout his career—even in high school and college—Montana was at his best when he was needed most. He and Rice, who would have another monster receiving day with 215 yards, connected on a 14-yard touchdown a minute into the fourth quarter to tie it, 13–13. After the Bengals retook the lead, 16–13, on Jim Breech's 40-yard field goal with 3:20 left in regulation, the 49ers took over at their own 8.

As the teams waited to resume play following a commercial break, a relaxed Montana turned to offensive tackle Harris Barton and pointed to the crowd. "Hey, look, there's John Candy," Montana told Barton as a way to calm his nerves.

"Harris is always uptight, and he started mumbling stuff, something about the Super Bowl, and I'm looking at John Candy," recalled Montana.

As Montana prepared to go to work on the Bengals' defense, there was a palpable sense of impending doom on the Bengals sidelines.

"It was the world of all worlds," said then Bengals receiver Cris Collinsworth, who had previously lost to Walsh's 49ers in their first Super Bowl matchup. "I knew they were going to score. I knew they would try to eat up the clock. In some weird way, if they're gonna score, do it now. At least it gives us a chance to get the ball back."

Wyche recalls Collinsworth "coming over to me and poking me with that bony elbow he's got and says we may have left too much time on the clock," Wyche said. "I turned to him and said, 'I know.' And really, and truly, I did know, because I was on [Montana's] side before."

Wyche went over to LeBeau and took the rare step of asking him to play his defense a certain way. In all the years they'd been together in Cincinnati, Wyche was completely hands-off when it came to letting LeBeau run the defense.

Not now.

"We were wired for NFL Films, and the producers had told me there would be a camera on me, Boomer, Bill Walsh, and Joe Montana the entire game," Wyche said. "So, don't go to the crotch or anything. Well, I turn my back to the camera and I go to Dick LeBeau."

He didn't want to talk because he knew someone could hear him, so he mouthed the words *Bring five guys*, a request that LeBeau apply heavy pressure on the series rather than sit back in a prevent defense.

"I know Joe Montana. I coached him," Wyche said in recalling the drive. "I know his rules, and I know the two-minute rules. You bring five guys, he throws underneath. So we got into a prevent defense, we're bringing three and dropping five."

The defense played right into Walsh's hands, and Montana went to work.

He drove the 49ers from his own 8 to the Bengals' 35 on a series of passes to Craig, tight end John Frank, and Rice. But right before the next play, Montana felt ill.

"I almost blacked out," he said. "I was just hyperventilating. I started getting that TV screen look in my eyes."

It turned out that Montana hadn't eaten enough before the game, partly as a result of getting to the stadium so early.

"I got there around seven or eight in the morning," he said.

Nearly eleven hours before kickoff? Why so early?

Montana had been so shaken by the 49ers' late arrival for the previous Super Bowl against the Bengals that he didn't want to chance getting stuck again. Even though there was no chance of snow in south Florida like there was that Super Bowl Sunday in Pontiac, Michigan— when the 49ers' buses were delayed because of a blizzard and Vice President George Bush's motorcade—Montana still didn't want to risk having his pregame routine altered. So he and Cross took an early cab to Joe Robbie Stadium as a precaution.

When he started feeling woozy, Montana had the presence of mind to buy himself some time.

"I was just hyperventilating, so I just threw the ball out of bounds," he said of his only incompletion on the drive. "It looked like I overthrew him, but I did it on purpose."

Montana gathered himself and regained all his faculties. He completed three straight passes to Craig and Rice to get to the Bengals' 10 before the 49ers called time-out. With the Bengals looking on helplessly from the sidelines, Montana hit John Taylor on a slant in the end zone to complete one of the most dramatic comebacks in Super Bowl history and give the 49ers a 20–16 win.

"When John Taylor made that catch, I finally heard the crowd," said Rice, voted the game's MVP. "Before then, we didn't hear it. That's how focused we were."

After it was over, Walsh and Wyche made their way through a throng of players and media and embraced at midfield.

"As we're going off, Bill literally collapses," Wyche said. "I could feel the weight of him going down. I'm thinking he's going to pass out on me. So we were kind of bracing ourselves for just an instant. I'm holding him up and I say, 'Man, I love you.' Both of us said it to each other. 'I just love you.' Both of us looked at each other."

Wyche flashed back to all the memories he'd had with Walsh, from his days as a Bengals backup quarterback, to their time together with the 49ers and a Super Bowl championship over a different Bengals team, to now.

"That was the last handshake that he made as a coach," Wyche said, "and the last win he has as a coach, and the last championship game he won as a coach."

In the winners' locker room for what would be the final time, Walsh was overcome with emotion. After accepting the Vince Lombardi Trophy, he saw his son Craig, put an arm around his shoulder, and wept.

Ten years after Walsh and DeBartolo first met and formed a partnership that would lead the 49ers to unprecedented success, they sat down for a meeting in Pebble Beach, California, to talk about Walsh's future.

DeBartolo knew. So did Carmen Policy, who had been named team president after the previous season and was also in on the meeting.

At fifty-seven years old and just days after winning his third Super Bowl championship, Walsh was done.

"Bill was pretty much convinced he was going to retire or at least step away from football for a while," DeBartolo said. "We had a few laughs, we had a few drinks, it was just something that you can't sit and talk somebody into something that he really doesn't want to do. He was a little burned out, which happens. It was time for him to at least take a break."

Four days after winning the Super Bowl, Walsh announced his resignation as the 49ers' coach.

He was to become vice president of football operations and turn the coaching job over to his longtime defensive coordinator, George Seifert.

"We're pleased with the evolution of this organization and I am pleased with this decision for George Seifert," Walsh said.

Walsh would soon realize he'd made a terrible mistake.

A mistake that would haunt him for the rest of his life.

The 49ers held a press conference in nearby Monterey to introduce Seifert, who had worked alongside Walsh since his early days at Stanford. Walsh would now handle personnel issues, including trades and draft-day decisions.

Seifert becoming the 49ers' next coach was a testament to Walsh's promise that he would always do whatever he could for the people who worked under him.

"I look forward to my new career," Walsh told reporters at his retirement press conference. "It's been ten great years. It was a thirty-one-year [coaching] career, and there's a time for everybody at some point to step aside. It's an uplift to me to step aside on a most positive note. This is the way most coaches would like to leave the game."

Walsh was only the second coach in NFL history to step down after winning a Super Bowl; Vince Lombardi had done it after winning Super Bowl II with the Packers.

Walsh would soon come to regret the move.

"It was within a month that he realized he'd made a mistake," said Walsh's son Craig. "It was a strange time for him. He was emotionally wrung out. He almost wanted to be begged to stay, and that wasn't happening at the time because Carmen Policy was starting to spread his wings and was starting to become the face of the organization. Ed DeBartolo had newfound fame. Ownership had grown accustomed to winning, and I don't think he felt that appreciated.

"The other part was in his conscience," Craig said. "He had asked so many other players to step away when they had time left. He could have become a figurehead coach like so many others had been, but my dad had a big problem with that. He couldn't be that guy. Paul Brown didn't even know the plays at the Bengals. He would say, 'How about a sweep?' and my dad would say, 'Which one? We've got ten.' My dad never wanted to be that guy, because that was a cop-out. He wanted to be the guy steering the ship. He wanted to have his fingerprints all over it."

Walsh never coached another game in the NFL.

After spending six months in the 49ers' front office—and making just over $300,000, a two-thirds cut from his salary as coach—he joined NBC as the network's lead analyst for $750,000 a year, where he worked for three years.

Shortly before leaving the network, he did get the chance to meet with the man who'd ultimately been the catalyst for what turned into Walsh's Hall of Fame journey.

"When Paul Brown was dying, he reached out to my father," Craig Walsh said. "My father flew out and saw him on his deathbed in the hospital, and Paul acknowledged he'd made a mistake and that he should have hired him. He did apologize."

It was a profoundly emotional moment for both men, and certainly a sense of closure for Walsh. Brown died on August 5, 1991. He was eighty-two.

Walsh still had the itch to coach and returned to Stanford in 1992, leading the Cardinal to a 10-3 record and the Pac-10 co-championship, as well as a win over Penn State in the Blockbuster Bowl. One of his players that year was a wide receiver named David Shaw, who would go on to become the coach at Stanford, where he still is today. Shaw got to hear one of the final motivational ploys of Walsh's legendary career.

"Penn State was a really good team, but I don't know that we were as focused and motivated to beat a team like that," Shaw said. "Bill insinuated that he heard through the grapevine that Penn State was looking past us, and that they were in cahoots with the [Blockbuster Bowl] people and that we were chosen to play them because they didn't think we were very good. That really lit a fire under us, and our practices were phenomenal."

The Cardinal upset Penn State, 24–3.

Nearly fifteen years later, Shaw found out Walsh had made up the whole story about Penn State purposely asking to play Stanford.

"They're giving this sendoff here to Bill after he retired as associate athletic director," Shaw said. "He goes off to tell this story in front of a whole group of people about how he uses these tactics to be at their best. He goes on to say he had to concoct this story because he knew we needed more motivation. I'm sitting there saying, 'Oh, my God, he didn't tell us the truth.' But he knew his team so well and knew we needed something else. And we responded."

It was one final stroke of genius from Walsh, who went on to coach two more seasons at Stanford before retiring from coaching for good.

Walsh, who had served as a consultant with the 49ers in 1996, went back a third time in 1999 as the 49ers' general manager, where he remained for three years. He served as a special consultant for another three years.

Walsh was diagnosed with leukemia in 2004, and battled the disease for three years before dying on July 30, 2007. He was seventy-five.

During his illness, he'd met with hundreds of the people whose lives he'd impacted so profoundly, with many coming to see him, and with him traveling to see others. One of his frequent visitors was DeBartolo.

"Towards the end, it was very, very difficult," DeBartolo said. "The last time I saw him was at Stanford, and we spent a good two hours, just talking and reminiscing. He told me that he loved me, and obviously I felt the same way. We ended up hugging and kissing, and I told him that he made it all happen, and God bless him. I loved him."

Unbeknownst to DeBartolo, Walsh had signed a miniature 49ers helmet and gave it to his son. On it, Walsh wrote, "Dear Eddie. It's been a long time coming. Congratulations on the Hall of Fame. Love, Bill."

Nine years later, after DeBartolo had been voted into the Pro Football Hall of Fame, he received a package in his office in Tampa. He opened it, read the inscription on the helmet, and wept.

"I cried like a baby," DeBartolo said.

Though increasingly weak because of the advance of the disease, and exhausted by the frequent blood transfusions, Walsh never lost his sense of humor or his appreciation for others.

Shortly before he died, two of his best players came to his home in Woodside, California, to visit.

"Ronnie Lott and I were the last guys to see him [from the 49ers]," Montana said. "Until the day he left us, he still had that sense of humor."

After an emotional visit, Lott and Montana got up to leave.

"Wait a minute," Walsh said to Montana as he was walking out the door. "I have a question."

"What is it, Coach?"

"Do you owe me any money?"

Montana laughed and said, "I don't think so. Why, do you need a loan?"

The two men walked away for the final time.

Surrounded by his family on the day he died, Walsh was at peace.

"It's your time now," Craig Walsh told his father. "It's been a hell of a ride. Let go."

Less than a minute later, Bill Walsh was gone.

PARCELLS

WHEN NO ONE ELSE BELIEVED . . . EXCEPT HIM

As his players sat in the meeting room beneath Giants Stadium, Bill Parcells knew he needed to send just the right message to deal with what appeared to be a hopeless situation.

This was the morning after the Giants had lost at home to the Bills, 17–13, on December 15, 1990. The loss dropped the Giants' record to 11-3, but it wasn't the result that Parcells was really concerned about.

It was the fallout.

This was the third loss in their last four games after a 10-0 start, but the more significant development was that quarterback Phil Simms had suffered a foot injury in the second quarter and left the stadium on crutches. Before leaving, two reporters—*New York Times* columnist Dave Anderson and I—waited for Simms outside the X-ray room. The foot was broken, meaning in all likelihood Simms was done for the year.

The Giants' initial diagnosis, which they announced after the game, was a severe sprain, but Parcells knew Simms had broken his foot. He also knew he had to find a way to make his players believe they still had a realistic chance of making a meaningful playoff run. If they won their final two regular-season games against the Arizona Cardinals and the New England Patriots, they'd clinch at least a home playoff game. It was too late to catch the 49ers for home field advantage through the NFC playoffs, but Parcells would deal with that later.

For now, he needed to send the message that he believed Jeff

Hostetler could get the job done in Simms's absence—even though Hostetler had just two starts in the five-plus seasons he'd been with the Giants. A third-round pick in 1984 out of West Virginia, Hostetler had been mostly a third-stringer behind Simms and Jeff Rutledge, who had signed with the Redskins before the 1990 season.

"Fellas, we're not losing because of Jeff Hostetler. I can promise you that," Parcells said. "It'll be because of some of you other assholes if we lose."

The message was clear to the players: You just worry about your own jobs, and the coaches will take care of Hostetler.

"That settled everybody down," Parcells recalled. "The players say to themselves, 'Well, the coach believes in this guy.' "

The expectations from outside the locker room were far less optimistic. In fact, the general consensus was that the Giants were done. Even though they'd still make the playoffs, how could a quarterback with almost zero NFL playing time be expected to lead a team anywhere?

Hostetler himself had just about given up hope about his career, and had told his wife, Vicky, only a few days before the Bills game that he was going to retire after the season.

"I told her at the dinner table, 'We're done,' " Hostetler said. "I was a financial planner, and I was ready to start that back up in Morgantown. I just had enough of the frustration and disappointment. It was time."

He thought back to his childhood and something his father had told him.

"I grew up on a farm, and I grew up Mennonite, and my dad was a farmer and he always had things breaking down," Hostetler said. "One of the things he said was that you never give up. You just keep plugging."

Even so, Hostetler had his doubts.

"I was ready to give up," he said.

And then, suddenly, opportunity presented itself.

Before Simms's injury, Parcells knew deep down this was his best chance to win a Super Bowl since his team's remarkable run in 1986. It was a four-year wait that featured a series of setbacks, starting with the strike season of 1987, when the Giants were 0-5 by the time the replacement games were over.

"That was a team without any hope when they came back," he said. "When you're 0-5 and have got ten to play, you almost have to win all ten. That's hard to do, especially when you've had hope in your recent past and now you're 0-5."

The 1988 season was better, but still not good enough. At 10-5 with a chance to make the playoffs on the final weekend with a win over the Jets, the Giants lost, 27–21. Their only hope of making the tournament rested with the 49ers, who faced the Rams at home in a Sunday night game.

But the 49ers had nothing to play for in terms of postseason positioning; they'd already earned a bye and a home playoff game and couldn't catch the Bears for home field advantage throughout the conference playoffs. The Rams routed the 49ers, 38–16, and thus ended the Giants' playoff dreams.

As the game was going on, Simms got a call at home from sportswriter Peter King, who wrote for *Newsday* at the time and had volunteered to be a pool reporter for the New York media to get reaction about the Giants' playoff fate. King asked how Simms was doing.

"I'm just sitting here staring and watching the 49ers lay down like dogs," Simms said. The quarterback offered a few more observations about the disappointment of not making the playoffs, but it was that quote that stuck, particularly with the 49ers, who were enraged at the suggestion they purposely lost the game to avoid the possibility of facing the Giants in the postseason after losing badly to them in the 1985 and 1986 playoffs.

"I just called him and I started talking to him and the next day after I used it, I realized he wanted that to be off the record, but he never said it was off the record, so it wasn't off the record," said King, the longtime writer for *Sports Illustrated* and one of the most influential football writers ever. "I feel bad. He was so incredibly pissed off about it at the time. I liked him and he was always really good to me. I feel bad about it, but I was a reporter doing my job, really.

"I just thought it was a great friggin' quote," King said. "After the next day happened and it was like wildfire, I realized it was going to be batshit everywhere."

Simms still doesn't like talking about that quote, and has rarely addressed it publicly.

"Why am I still mad? The facts are the facts," Simms said in a 2011 interview with *Newsday*'s Neil Best. "We were just chatting." Simms added that the incident caused him to "always be on guard of everything you say to everybody at all times."

Parcells hardly cared about Simms's reaction or the public relations fallout from the quote; the coach already welcomed the fact that he and the 49ers had become bitter rivals. No, it was something much more significant that Parcells learned about his team from what happened on that final weekend of the 1988 season.

"That loss to the Jets was the turning point, because I realized then that the '86 team was no more," Parcells said. "In '87, we blamed it on the strike. We lose to the Jets to go 10-6, and we should have been 11-5. In '86, the Jets would have never driven the ball on us like they did. That would have never happened to us. That's when I knew. I told [GM] George [Young], 'We stay the same, next year, this is going to be a 7-9 team.' He agreed."

There would be significant turnover in the off-season, with veteran players like linebacker Harry Carson, defensive end George Martin, left tackle Brad Benson, and a handful of others retiring. Young had already begun to reconstitute the offensive line in 1988 by drafting Jumbo Elliott and Eric Moore, and he produced a bumper crop of contributors in 1989, including safeties Greg Jackson and Myron Guyton, tight end Howard Cross, and running back–returner David Meggett.

The Giants were a much more dependable team in 1989, going 12-4 to win the NFC East. Parcells felt very good about his chances heading into the postseason. But in a shocking end to the season, his team was beaten by the Rams in the NFC divisional playoffs, as Jim Everett threw a 30-yard touchdown pass in overtime to wide receiver Flipper Anderson, who famously ran through the end zone, then through the tunnel and into the locker room.

"Flipper Anderson, that one still haunts me," Parcells said. "It haunts me because I think we could have won it that year."

It was the 49ers who won it instead, as Seifert took the team he had inherited from Walsh and gave the 49ers back-to-back Super Bowl wins for the first time in franchise history.

And now here was Parcells in the final weeks of the 1990 season, without his top quarterback and hearing predictions of doom from just about everywhere except perhaps his own locker room. The coach himself seemed energized about the massive challenge that lay ahead.

"When you have a defense like we had, I knew we had a chance," Parcells said. "That wasn't any ham-and-egg outfit. We had some good players."

He thought back to the lessons imparted to him as a young athlete from his old basketball coach, Mickey Corcoran.

"I was trained as a coach to know there are ways to win these games," he said. "Mickey imparted this in my brain, and it never left me. Your job as a coach is to figure out how to give your team the best chance to win."

Parcells knew he had a good team, a championship-caliber team, only now he'd have to get there with an unproven quarterback who didn't always get along with the coach. In fact, their relationship was difficult from the start, because Young was sold on Hostetler more than Parcells. It was one of their few draft-day disagreements, and Hostetler felt at times that Parcells was purposely limiting his opportunities because he wasn't a "Parcells guy."

In fact, Hostetler was so desperate to contribute on game day that he volunteered for special teams duty in 1986 and even blocked a punt. He also played receiver on the scout team during practice. Parcells certainly appreciated Hostetler's willingness to do something—anything—to help his team, but that still didn't convince the coach that he could be anything more than a backup to the one quarterback—Simms—who was the Giants' best hope.

"Hostetler and I had a very tenuous relationship," Parcells said.

Hostetler was one of several players who had privately grumbled about Parcells, even though the media narrative during the coach's tenure in New York was that he was always a players' coach who was beloved by virtually his entire locker room. That just wasn't the case, though. Hostetler, Joe Morris, and cornerback Mark Collins were among a handful of players who rarely warmed to the coach and bristled at his style. Sure, guys like Taylor, Simms, Burt, Carson, and most of the other players defended Parcells, even though the coach would often bark at them. They knew he was nudging them because he wanted them to be better players, not because it was anything personal.

But not every player reacts well to that kind of style, and Hostetler, an extremely introspective and sensitive person, never warmed to Parcells's personality. And the coach himself did little to engender any warm feelings. He and Hostetler mostly just tolerated each other.

As it turned out, Hostetler might have had more backing from his teammates than anyone might have realized—including Parcells. Simms had done some of his finest work in leading the Giants to a 10-0 start, but his play had deteriorated from there. In his last three starts, he didn't have a single touchdown pass, including a 7–3 loss in San Francisco. Even Parcells had to publicly defend Simms from critics who wanted to see a change.

"Simms's production was very good for the first seven or eight games, but as the season went on, other teams started to bring more pressure on him, and that affected his play," said veteran cornerback Everson Walls, the former Cowboys star who had signed with the Giants before the 1990 season. "We had to struggle a whole lot more offensively. So when he did get hurt, I thought that, from a team standpoint, I absolutely felt our chances improved because we needed a quarterback that had running ability as well as passing ability. We needed a more well-rounded quarterback."

Hostetler was serviceable enough in the final two regular-season games, although the Giants still struggled to beat Arizona and New England to secure a first-round bye and a home playoff game. Their playoff opponent would be the Bears, who five years earlier had extinguished the Giants' playoff hopes at Soldier Field but who now had to come to Giants Stadium. This was hardly the same opponent the Giants had faced in the 1985 postseason, however. Attrition had frittered away the great Bears defense from that year, and the key players on offense this time would be quarterback Mike Tomczak and running back Neal Anderson, not Jim McMahon and Walter Payton.

If there were any questions about the readiness of either Hostetler or the Giants, they were answered on a cold, blustery day in East Rutherford, New Jersey. With the Giants playing it close to the vest on offense, Hostetler still managed to throw two touchdown passes and ran for 43 yards and another touchdown in a 31–3 rout of Ditka's Bears. The Giants' defense was breathtakingly good, as Belichick went to a four-man line instead of his traditional 3-4 alignment, and Chicago was miserable from start to finish.

There was another key injury, though. A month earlier, they'd lost Simms; now they were without rookie tailback Rodney Hampton, who suffered a broken leg while trying to recover a fumble in the first quarter.

Hampton, a first-round pick out of Georgia, had taken on a more prominent role in the final month of the season, but now he was out of the mix. His replacement: thirty-three-year-old Ottis "O. J." Anderson.

Anderson had only a bit role in the Giants' 1986 Super Bowl run, and after becoming the starter in 1989 following Morris's release, he was back to sharing time with Hampton until the injury against the Bears. Anderson did a workmanlike job filling in for Hampton, running 21 times for 80 yards and thus allowing the Giants to use the ball-control offense that provided a sound structure for Hostetler, who attempted just 17 passes.

But with the win, the stakes would go up exponentially: The Giants would have to face the 49ers in the NFC Championship Game at Candlestick Park—the two-time defending champion 49ers who were looking to become the first team in NFL history to win the Lombardi Trophy three times in a row.

"Threepeat" had become the 49ers' mantra during their second season under Seifert. And it felt like a foregone conclusion that the 49ers would get there, too. After a 14-2 regular season, the 49ers had little trouble fending off Gibbs's Redskins in the divisional round at Candlestick Park. And now they were about to face the Giants and a backup quarterback at home.

Joe Montana versus Jeff Hostetler.

Seriously, could there ever have been a bigger mismatch? Montana, a three-time Super Bowl MVP, against Hostetler, with four regular-season starts and one playoff appearance?

C'mon.

Parcells didn't flinch.

"No one is giving you a chance," Parcells said. "It was perfect."

As he met with his coaches the morning after the win over the Bears to map out the Giants' strategy, there was general agreement that the best way to beat the 49ers was to once again rely on a strong defense—particularly the pass rush against Montana—and control the ball on offense with a deliberate style that stressed the running game and put Hostetler in safe passing situations.

The key, Parcells knew, was to get to Montana, and he had an idea that would stoke the team's belief that this could be done. There would be no bye week between the conference championship and the Super Bowl, due to the league's transition to a seventeen-week season that introduced a bye week for each team. So, late in the week, he decided to bring a large plaid suitcase with him to the stadium.

"You can pack for three days, or you can pack for ten days," he told the team. Then he showed them his suitcase. "I'll tell you what I'm doing. I'm packing for ten."

The players roared their approval.

They packed for ten days—first, for a trip to San Francisco.

Then to Tampa for Super Bowl XXV.

The 49ers came into the game as eight-point favorites, but in the minds of most NFL fans, the line could have been—and perhaps even should have been—fourteen points. That was how little chance the Giants were given.

But Parcells was quietly confident in the run-up to the game that his Giants not only had a fighting chance, but they could win the damn thing. If his defense played as well as it was capable, if Anderson could provide some semblance of a running game and keep Montana off the field as much as possible, and if Hostetler didn't make any egregious mistakes, the upset was certainly within reach.

The plan worked brilliantly right from the start, and the 49ers' offense couldn't get untracked in the first half. Montana was under a heavy rush, and even when he did get his passes off, the Giants' coverage was so tight that the receivers couldn't produce the yards-after-catch they'd been used to. The Giants sent the game into halftime with the score tied, 6–6.

It was nearly as perfect a scenario as Parcells could have wanted. And then...

In the third quarter, on first down from his own 39-yard line, Montana hit John Taylor near the left sideline at the Giants' 43. Everson Walls was in on the coverage and went to bat the ball away, but he missed. Taylor caught the ball and raced down the sidelines and into the end zone for a 61-yard touchdown.

For the 49ers, it looked like one more dose of playoff magic from Montana and Taylor, who had combined for the winning touchdown pass in Super Bowl XXIII.

For Walls, it felt like another heartbreaking moment at Candlestick Park, the scene of the most memorable play in 49ers history, but also the darkest moment for the cornerback. Walls was with the Cowboys on that fateful afternoon in the 1981 NFC title game, and when Montana hit Dwight Clark in the end zone for the game-winning play, it was Walls who couldn't break up the pass.

Was another nightmare about to befall him?

"I don't know where my damn safety was," Walls said in reconstructing the play. "I whiff on the knockdown, and [Taylor] catches it. As soon as I give up my play, [CBS] had it cued up. They played that highlight of Clark's catch. What's fair is fair, I guess."

The flashback ended quickly for Walls.

"You ain't got time to think about it," he said. "When you give up a play, I don't give a damn what anybody says, everybody gives up a play. It's a team game."

But the Giants maintained their composure and kept the 49ers bottled up from there. And after Matt Bahr kicked a 46-yard field goal to make it 13–9, it was the 49ers who were struck with misfortune.

With less than ten minutes to play in regulation, Montana faded back to pass and tried to buy some time after he couldn't find an open receiver. Rolling to his left, he narrowly avoided being hit by Lawrence Taylor. But defensive end Leonard Marshall had pursued Montana from behind, and after the quarterback stepped up to dodge Taylor,

Marshall delivered a crushing blow that knocked Montana out of the game with a bruised sternum and a broken finger.

Later in the quarter, with the Giants facing a fourth and two from their own 46 and still trailing, 13–9, Parcells made a decision that would eventually pull his team closer. He called for a fake punt, one that was perfectly executed when the ball was snapped to punt protector Gary Reasons, who caught the 49ers unaware and rumbled to their 24.

"We looked at the play three times earlier in the game, and Reasons was begging for the fake," Parcells said.

It was the perfect call for the perfect moment in the game. Bahr kicked a 38-yard field goal—his fourth of the game—to make it 13–12.

The 49ers still had a chance to ice the game and advance to a third straight Super Bowl. Taking over at their own 20 with 5:47 left, a field goal or touchdown could conceivably put the game out of reach. But tailback Roger Craig, who had been such a reliable performer for so long, fumbled near midfield with 2:36 left after Giants nose tackle Erik Howard hit him. Taylor recovered at the Giants' 43.

Hostetler threw for two key completions on the ensuing drive, the first a 19-yard pass to Bavaro and the next a 13-yarder to Stephen Baker.

Bahr, a twelve-year veteran who had been released by the Browns during training camp but signed by the Giants after an early-season injury to Raul Allegre, then nailed a 42-yard field goal as time expired.

The Giants had done the unthinkable.

Hostetler had beaten Montana, 15–13.

The Giants were going to the Super Bowl.

"The players did an unbelievable job against the 49ers," Parcells said. "They knew they could do it, and we knew there was a way that it could be done."

It was on to Tampa for Super Bowl XXV, where Hostetler and the Giants would face a Buffalo Bills team that appeared every bit as unbeatable as the 49ers. While the Giants had narrowly escaped Candlestick with a 15–13 win over the heavily favored 49ers, the Bills had demolished the Raiders, 51–3, in the AFC Championship Game.

The plane ride from San Francisco to Tampa was a jubilant one, with players and coaches hugging one another and screaming in the aisle and at their seats. Parcells was as joyous as anyone, his deeply held belief in his team and his system having been vindicated with one of the most spectacular upsets in playoff history.

Hostetler was among the celebrants on the flight, although he had just barely managed to make it on board. John Madden, who was doing color commentary for the game on CBS, had interviewed Hostetler after the game, and by the time they'd finished talking, all three of the Giants' team buses had departed for the airport.

Hostetler wasn't sure what to do, and Madden was shocked the team had left without its starting quarterback.

"I felt terrible," Madden said. "I have Parcells's quarterback, who just won the game that got him to the Super Bowl, and I've got him out in the stands doing some interview, and now they're gone. Sometimes, a team will leave someone there, like the assistant equipment guy, and you'll bring him out. They don't leave without anyone."

Then an idea came to Madden.

"I told Jeff I'd take him on my bus and drive him to the airport," Madden said. "So we drove the bus right out to the plane."

"We get to the airport and some dark gate at the back end, and we go right onto the tarmac and up to the plane," Hostetler said. "I walk on and Bill's in the front seat and looks at me kind of surprised."

The coach grinned at his quarterback.

"Not bad," he said. "Not bad."

Shortly after arriving in Tampa at around 3 a.m., the Giants coaches set about game planning for the Bills, while the players caught some sleep after their dramatic win over the 49ers. The challenge was similar in its magnitude to facing the 49ers, although the Bills presented different challenges for Parcells and his staff—particularly on defense.

Jim Kelly's K-gun offense was seen as a revolutionary new system, and the Bills' pummeling of the Raiders in the AFC title game was the latest evidence. But Parcells and Belichick focused on four key players as they game-planned for the Super Bowl: Kelly, running back Thurman Thomas, and receivers Andre Reed and James Lofton.

Belichick theorized that the bigger threat lay in the passing game, and if there was one primary area of focus, that was it. But because no defense can adequately deal with every single threat an offense poses, that meant Belichick had to choose one matchup the Giants could afford to lose, if necessary.

That matchup was Thomas, one of the most versatile running backs in the league. Since he knew the Bills were equally adept at running and catching passes out of the backfield, Belichick decided that the best plan was to let Thomas get his rushing yards, but keep Kelly from exposing the Giants in the passing game.

For a defense that prided itself on shutting down the NFL's best runners, the plan was anathema to many of the players. They were stunned to hear Belichick tell them not to worry about Thomas's rushing yards.

"I thought it was a collective brain fart, like, what the hell are you talking about?" Carl Banks told Giants.com's Michael Eisen in a 2015 interview. "But he said it, we are all in an uproar, and Bill is just conceding that Thurman is just this good of a football player that we won't be able to stop him. And then he reeled us back in and kinda gave us a method to the madness."

Belichick's unique plan would require just two down linemen—Howard and Marshall—and go heavy on linebackers and defensive backs, depending on down and distances. Belichick theorized that once the Bills saw that the Giants were willing to let Thomas run, they would be tempted to keep feeding him on the ground.

Meanwhile, the plan was to overload the middle alternatively with linebackers and defensive backs, thereby limiting the effectiveness of the Bills' crossing routes, and always keeping the safeties in position to defend against the deep threat so that Kelly couldn't get his passes behind the defense.

"I think the running game was the least of our concerns in that game," Belichick said. "Thurman Thomas is a great back. We knew he was going to get some yards. But I didn't feel like we wanted to get into a game where they threw the ball forty-five times. I knew if they had some success running the ball, they would stay with it. And I always felt when we needed to stop the run, we could stop it. And the more times they ran it, it was just one less time they could get it to Reed or Lofton, or throw it to Thomas, who I thought was more dangerous as a receiver because there's more space than there was when he was a runner."

Offensively, the strategy was similar to what it had been once Hostetler took over at quarterback: Rely heavily on Anderson in the running game, put Hostetler in good play-action situations, and let him use his mobility by continuing to run bootlegs that would get him away from Buffalo's defense and one of the game's best pass rushers, Bruce Smith.

Parcells was especially concerned about Smith, who had a career-high 19 sacks during the regular season. Smith would face the Giants' starting left tackle, Jumbo Elliott, a Parcells favorite from the time he was drafted out of Michigan in the second round in 1988.

But with a Super Bowl championship at stake and Elliott about to match up against a dominant pass rusher like Smith, Parcells wanted to make sure Elliott knew what he was in for. Parcells was convinced that Belichick's defensive plan was sound, especially after watching the players take to it during their practices at a local high school in Tampa, but it was Elliott's readiness that worried him most.

Parcells came up with an idea to make sure Elliott would be prepared. He enlisted Lawrence Taylor for his plan.

"We're on the bus on the way to practice, and I say, 'Lawrence, near the end of practice, I'm going to give you a little wink, and I want you to start a fight with Jumbo,'" Parcells said.

"What? What?" Taylor told the coach when he heard the plan. "No. I'm not gonna do that."

"He's not ready," Parcells said to Taylor. "Will you just do it?"

Taylor reluctantly agreed.

"So we're getting to the end of practice, and the players are pissed at me, anyway, because they're still in pads," Parcells said. "They see Buffalo practicing in sweats, and I got my team in pads and they're pissed. So Taylor starts it up with Jumbo, who's got this bad temper. He said, 'Taylor, you son of a bitch,' and he starts chasing him. He can't catch him, though."

Parcells went over to Elliott and said loudly in front of the entire team, "Hey, Jumbo, [Taylor] is just worried about Bruce Smith winning the game for them. He's just worried about you and this fuckin' game."

Elliott looked at Parcells.

"He's not getting a sniff," Elliott told the coach.

And so ended the team's final practice of the week.

The buildup to the game was intense in its own right, but the backdrop of world events made this a uniquely different Super Bowl. Just a week earlier—on January 17, 1991—Operation Desert Storm began with a series of bombings to drive Iraqi forces out of Kuwait. Though the mission would last only six weeks and result in a defeat of Saddam Hussein's troops and their departure from Kuwait, emotions were raw as the United States began its largest military operation since Vietnam.

Players and coaches were certainly mindful of the war, and security had been tightened as a result. On game day, snipers were positioned atop Tampa Stadium, military helicopters flew overhead, the trunk of every car parked outside the stadium would be inspected, and every fan entering the stadium would be searched by handheld metal detectors. Even the Giants' and Bills' equipment was checked.

"One of my most vivid memories was waiting to be introduced in the tunnel and looking around at the American flags and realizing how big this game really was and what it meant at the time," Hostetler said.

Emotions were heightened further when music icon Whitney Houston performed one of the most unforgettable renditions of "The Star-Spangled Banner," followed by a flyover of four F-16 fighter jets from nearby MacDill Air Force Base.

The game itself would be a classic, another career-defining moment for a coach with a backup quarterback few people outside New York had even heard of until now, and a running back who had just turned thirty-four years old.

This was just the way Parcells liked it—with the odds stacked against him.

Parcells's approach in dealing with the Bills turned out to be brilliant. Just as the Giants had found a way to limit Montana's offense the week before in the NFC Championship Game, the Giants frustrated Kelly by using those 2-3-6 and 2-4-5 alignments.

The combination of Anderson's tough inside running and Hostetler's resourcefulness in the passing game, which included a handful of boot-legs to take advantage of his mobility, was a terrific counter to the Bills. The Giants might not have been scoring a lot of points; they were down 12–3 late in the second quarter, but they were keeping Kelly off the field for large chunks of time because of the ball-control style.

For Hostetler, his task became even more daunting after a punishing hit delivered in the second quarter by Bills defensive end Leon Seals. He lay on the turf for several seconds before walking off. He had suffered a concussion.

"I felt like my body was pancaked and I was only a couple inches thick," said Hostetler, who had borne the full brunt of Seals's weight when he was slammed into the ground. "I was just trying to gasp for breath and felt woozy. I don't know how I got to the sidelines, but I do remember them giving me smelling salts and taking a couple deep breaths. I remember seeing the faces of the [team] doctor and [trainer] Ronnie Barnes and this look of horror because I wasn't reacting. They just disappeared and turned away from me."

As he sat there alone trying to gather himself, Hostetler leaned back and looked up.

"I see this big helicopter gunship and you could see the guns sticking out to the sides, just hovering above the stadium," he said. "I remember thinking, 'Wow.' And then I realized the offense is up. That was an intense time, and it's a memory I've never forgotten."

Hostetler was back for the next series, and he would be sacked in his own end zone for a safety by Smith. The defensive end had indeed beaten Elliott, but Hostetler had been tripped up on the play because Anderson had drifted too close to the quarterback as he set up for his pass protection. The Bills still led, 12–3, but Hostetler kept it from being worse by holding on to the ball despite being leveled by Smith.

"Had that resulted in a touchdown, all things being equal, we win the game," former Bills general manager Bill Polian said. "We had three or four guys around him, and barring some incredible bounce, we would have recovered the ball for a touchdown. Bruce [Smith] did try to strip it, but for some reason, Hostetler hung on."

Hostetler eventually delivered on a critical scoring drive just before halftime, taking the Giants 87 yards for a touchdown. He finished it off with a 14-yard pass in the left corner of the end zone to wide receiver Stephen Baker, who stretched out to make the diving catch and get the Giants back to within two points, 12–10.

At halftime, Parcells's message was simple.

"I told them that basically I was at a Super Bowl [four] years ago, and some of you guys were with me and we were in the exact same situation as we are now," said Parcells, referencing the 10–9 halftime deficit they had faced against the Broncos in Super Bowl XXI. "The first drive of the [third] quarter was the most important of the game. We had to do something with it."

They did.

Hostetler led a 75-yard touchdown drive, as the Giants converted four third-down attempts. On one of those attempts—a third and thirteen from the Bills' 32—Hostetler found wide receiver Mark Ingram over the middle, and Ingram broke three tackles to pick up 14 yards and help set up Anderson's 1-yard touchdown run to give the Giants the lead, 17–12.

It was the continuation of a performance Anderson had expected all along.

"Parcells said we're just gonna pound them to death," Anderson said.

Buffalo retook the lead, 19–17, on Thomas's 31-yard run up the middle that caught the Giants' defense off-guard, but the Giants countered with Bahr's 21-yard field goal with 7:20 to play to put the Giants back in front, 20–19.

Just as it was the week before against the 49ers, this one would come down to the wire. And this time, the Bills would get the chance to win it at the end.

Taking over at their own 10 with 2:16 left, Kelly and Thomas went to work. On third and one from the 19, Thomas took a handoff on a draw play and raced up the middle. So open was the Giants' defense at that moment it looked as if Thomas would run for the winning touchdown right then and there. All he had to do was get past Walls, and the Bills would be headed to victory.

It was yet another momentous play for Walls, whose name was already etched in playoff infamy with The Catch in the 1981 playoffs, and he had narrowly escaped a similar fate when he allowed the touch-down pass to Taylor in the previous week's NFC Championship Game. The fact that Walls had been considered one of the league's poorest tacklers made this an even more unlikely matchup against Thomas.

Parcells knew about Walls's weakness when the cornerback called him to lobby for the Giants to sign him before the 1990 season, and the coach made a point of letting Walls know his performance had to get better during the regular season. After a 20–0 win over the Lions improved the Giants' record to 10-0, Belichick called Walls into his office.

"The man said you need to do better," Belichick told Walls. "The man," of course, was Parcells, who had noticed on film that Walls's technique, particularly his tackling, was getting sloppy.

"I mean, we shut down Barry Sanders in that game, and I'm like, why is he getting on me?" Walls said. "But I'll tell you what. That's good coaching right there."

Walls raced toward Thomas, took the perfect angle, and made the tackle after a 22-yard gain, likely preventing a touchdown.

"Probably one of the biggest tackles that I've ever been a part of was by a guy who had a reputation of not being a great tackler, and that was Everson Walls," Belichick said. "That was a huge, huge play that if you would have said Everson Walls tackled Thurman Thomas, I don't know which one of those you would have bet on."

Moments later, with the Bills down to their final play, Scott Norwood lined up for a 47-yard field goal to win it.

As Parcells looked on from the sidelines, unsure of whether he would win or lose in the next few seconds, one thought kept flashing through his mind.

"I said to myself, 'You know, it's going to be a shame if we lose this game, because we really did outplay them,'" Parcells said. "'We played it our way, and it's going to be a shame if we don't win it.'"

With Norwood beyond his comfort zone on a grass field, the kick sailed wide right.

The Giants had done the improbable. Parcells had won it.

With a backup quarterback, a thirty-four-year-old running back, and a defensive game plan for the ages, the coach had pulled off his second Super Bowl championship. At the intersection of guts and genius once more, the coach was carried off the field, his right fist defiantly punching the sky.

The next morning, as he sat in the lobby of the team hotel and chatted with a handful of beat reporters, he summed up his feelings the best way he could explain.

"Winning the Super Bowl," he said, "is better than sex."

All these years later, that feeling still holds true.

"Winning the Super Bowl really is better than sex. It just is," he said. "It's better than Christmas morning. It's better than anything."

On the way to his postgame press conference following the Super Bowl win, Parcells passed by a podium where Jumbo Elliott was being interviewed by a handful of reporters.

"Hey, Jumbo!" Parcells yelled. Elliott looked up.

"You're an ass kicker, Jumbo! You know that? You're an ass kicker!"

Elliott smiled, and Parcells moved on to Hostetler's podium. The coach didn't say anything. He just lifted a fist in the air, pumping it several times. Hostetler acknowledged the gesture, and raised his own hand, offering a smile of immense satisfaction.

The coach then walked over to his own lectern, still basking in the glow of his exhilarating win, and took several questions, offering praise for his players and his coaches, and reviewing some of the salient moments of the game. Near the end of the press briefing, he was asked about his contractual situation, and whether he had any more clarity about whether he would sign a new contract now that his current deal had just a year remaining and the Giants weren't in the habit of having a coach working on the final year of his contract.

The smile left Parcells's face, and he glared at the reporter (that would be me). He declined to answer the question.

Speculation had swirled through much of the season about Parcells's future, and the fact that he hadn't agreed to an extension by now only fueled the uncertainty. Parcells already knew that he would be losing

Belichick, who had agreed to become the Browns' coach. And Tom Coughlin, his hard-working receivers coach who got the most out of his marginally talented players, would be leaving to take the Boston College job.

Parcells's reluctance to negotiate a new deal had become a source of concern for Young, although the general manager had seen Parcells drag his feet before, and the coach had even flirted with the idea of becoming the Falcons' coach after the 1986 Super Bowl win—a source of mild consternation for Young.

Complicating any potential negotiations was the sale of 50 percent of the team. Tim Mara; his sister, Maura Mara Concannon; and their mother, Helen Mara Nugent, had decided to sell their share of the team to Preston Robert Tisch, the billionaire president of Loews. A month after the Super Bowl, the deal closed, with Tisch spending $70 million for his stake in the team.

The loss of Tim Mara was significant for Parcells, who had grown close to the co-owner during their time together. Tim had called Parcells "the best coach in Giants history" when the team was awarded the Lombardi Trophy by Pete Rozelle after the win over the Bills, and no longer having him with the team made Parcells uncomfortable.

"He was an ally. Very much so," Parcells said of Mara.

Parcells had previously negotiated his contract over dinner near Mara's home in Jupiter, Florida, after the Giants had won Super Bowl XXI.

"All right, we'll talk a new contract, but I want to have this done by the time the salads come," Mara told Parcells.

He asked the coach a series of questions.

"Do you think you should make as much as Don Shula?"

"No," Parcells said.

"Do you think you should make as much as Tom Landry?"

"No."

"Do you think you should make as much as [Rams coach] John Robinson?"

"More."

"Well, how much does he make?" Mara asked.

"He makes around $800,000 a year," Parcells said.

"Is four years okay?"

"Yeah."

"Is $3.6 million okay?"

"Yeah, but I want $500,000 up front."

Parcells agreed to take $400,000 up front, and the deal was done.

"It took about eight minutes," Parcells said in looking back on that negotiation.

But here he was, more than two months after winning Super Bowl XXV, and still no deal.

March dragged into April. Nothing.

Unbeknownst to all but a few of Parcells's closest associates, he'd not been feeling well. Parcells had frequently been subject to burnout during the season, in part because of what he acknowledged was his high-intensity, high-stress personality. But this seemed different. Even after he'd had a chance to rest up after a grueling season, he still felt something wasn't right.

"I knew something was wrong with me," he said, "but I didn't know what it was. I kept taking these tests to find out, and finally, I did find out."

Parcells, now forty-nine, had a blockage in his heart. Doctors tried an angioplasty, but it didn't work. Over the next several months, he would undergo another angioplasty, then an atherectomy—"like a Roto-Rooter," Parcells said—and finally heart bypass surgery.

Fearing that his condition would deteriorate like it did for his father, who had died after suffering postsurgery complications from heart bypass surgery, Parcells decided to step down as the Giants' coach on May 15, 1991. He was replaced immediately by Ray Handley, the Giants' former running backs coach who had previously been named offensive coordinator during the off-season.

"I feel like it's time," Parcells said at a news conference.

Why now?

"This is the '90s," he said. "I was in the '80s. It's going away from me. My interests are going in a new direction. I've given everything I could for ten years. This job for me now was going to be just to maintain."

Parcells denied friction with Young was the cause of his decision to step down.

"Contrary to published reports that surfaced over the years, a coach couldn't have had a better general manager to work for and with," Parcells said.

Within weeks, Parcells would sign a contract with NBC to do color commentary on the network's NFL broadcasts, fueling further speculation that he'd simply wanted to leave all along. But thirteen months later, still not feeling quite right, he underwent heart bypass surgery.

Wellington Mara was convinced there were no ulterior motives from Parcells.

"I think he was ready to just hang 'em up," Mara said a year after Parcells had stepped away.

Young was not as convinced. He believed Parcells simply quit.

The Giants were not the same without Parcells, and the two years under Handley were fraught with controversy and losing. Handley had chosen Hostetler to start over Simms—at one point floating a plan where both quarterbacks would share time, something Simms refused to consider—and the Giants went 8-8 in 1991 before going 6-10 in 1992. Handley, who was famously antagonistic toward the media (he once walked out of a press conference after being asked about a back injury to Hostetler), was simply overmatched in following Parcells, and the Giants wound up hiring Dan Reeves in 1993.

Parcells, meanwhile, got the itch to coach again and became the Patriots' head coach in 1993, the first of three coaching jobs for a man who admits to being addicted to competition, often to the exclusion of his personal relationships.

Parcells divorced his wife, Judy, in 2002 after forty years of marriage and several years of estrangement.

"I know [horse trainer] D. Wayne Lukas and [former baseball manager] Tony La Russa, and I've said to them we shouldn't be married," Parcells said. "None of us. Why? Because we're married to something else. That's what we were married to—something else. La Russa has been married thirty years, but ten months a year, he was gone. Lukas, he's had four wives and he's eighty-two years old, but he's up on the horses every morning."

Parcells could never stay away from football for very long. After leading the Patriots to the Super Bowl following the 1996 season, he became embroiled in a contract dispute with team owner Robert Kraft, then went to the Jets in a move that sparked a challenge from Kraft. After NFL Commissioner Paul Tagliabue held a hearing on the matter, he ordered the Jets to surrender four draft picks to the Patriots— including a first rounder in 1999—to secure Parcells's services.

But before the deal became finalized, the Giants held serious internal discussions about making a run at Parcells. The team had fired Reeves after the 1996 season, and Young had settled on Jim Fassel, who had been Handley's offensive coordinator and also worked with Broncos quarterback John Elway.

Wellington Mara, who had remained in touch with Parcells and had a good relationship with the coach, wanted him back with the Giants once it became clear Parcells was leaving the Patriots.

"My father really wanted Bill back at that point, but George [Young] was dead set against it, and I think he had influenced Bob Tisch, to the point where Bob wasn't for it either," said Wellington's son, John Mara, now the Giants' president and co-owner.

The situation came to a head in mid-January. With the Patriots still in the playoffs and the Giants uncertain when Parcells would become available, and with the likelihood that draft-choice compensation would likely be involved in hiring him back, Young issued an ultimatum.

"I can remember sitting in my office with my father there and George coming in and saying, 'What's it going to be? It's either him or me,'" John Mara said.

Young said he wanted to give Fassel—whose name he pronounced "Faze-el"—an answer.

"I've got 'Faze-el' in a hotel room," Young said, according to Mara. "He's waiting for an answer from us."

Wellington Mara reluctantly agreed to have Fassel become the coach.

"My father relented, because you needed to have an agreement of both owners," John Mara said. "With that, George left the room, and I have jokingly said that's the fastest he ever ran down the hallway."

Meanwhile, Tisch had called the Maras and said he would agree to pursuing Parcells.

"It was too late," John Mara said. "George already offered the job to 'Faze-el.'"

Fassel ended up doing solid work for the Giants; he was named the

NFL's Coach of the Year in 1997 after the team won the NFC East, and he led the Giants to the Super Bowl in 2000, losing to the Ravens. He was fired after the 2003 season, and the Giants then hired Parcells disciple Coughlin, who went on to win two Super Bowl championships before stepping down after the 2015 season.

Parcells did a splendid job with the Jets, resurrecting the team from the ashes of the Rich Kotite era and leading them to the AFC Championship Game in 1998. After stepping down following the 1999 season to become general manager, he appointed Belichick as his successor. But Belichick refused to take the job and eventually went to the Patriots, where he has appeared in eight Super Bowls, winning five.

Parcells left the Jets after only one season as GM and coached four years in Dallas under Jerry Jones, retiring for good as a coach after the 2006 season, although eventually he ran the Dolphins' football operation from 2008 to 2010.

But even in his seventies, Parcells still can't stay away from competition; for the last several years, he has owned thoroughbred racehorses and spends his summers in Saratoga Springs, New York, while living in Jupiter, Florida, in the winter.

"My life revolves around horses now," he said. "The reason I picked this business is because guys like me and Joe Gibbs, who's another poster boy for needing competition with NASCAR, we need action. He's got action down there with NASCAR every Sunday, and I've got action when they put my horse in the starting gate.

"People say it's a bad business," he said. "But I don't want to go to Cancun. I don't want to go on some cruise somewhere. I don't want to look at tall buildings someplace. Put my horse in the gate, my name on it, and let's go."

He remains a mentor to many of the people who have worked for him, and speaks regularly to coaches Sean Payton of the Saints, Mike Zimmer of the Vikings, and Todd Bowles of the Jets, as well as dozens of his players who remain in touch.

It's a pay-it-forward mentality he learned from Mickey Corcoran back in the day in Oradell, New Jersey.

"That's what Mickey taught me," Parcells said. "Your job is to pass this on. If you can help another coach, you do that. You always do it."

GIBBS

RAISING A THIRD TROPHY

They called it simply the body bag game.

Eagles coach Buddy Ryan taunted Gibbs in the run-up to a November 12, 1990, matchup, suggesting it would be so punishing that the Redskins players would "have to be carted off in body bags."

It infuriated the normally mild-mannered Gibbs, who was as competitive a coach as there ever was, but who never resorted to making incendiary comments about opposing teams.

"That's one thing that really set me off," Gibbs said. "There are times in life where you get so wound up, and that was one of them."

It wasn't just the pregame words, either.

One after the other, Redskins players were indeed carted off the field with injuries.

Starting quarterback Jeff Rutledge, who was playing in place of the injured Mark Rypien, suffered a broken thumb.

Rutledge's replacement, Stan Humphries, left with a twisted knee.

Running back Gerald Riggs suffered a sprained foot.

Wide receiver Joe Johnson suffered a concussion so severe that he had to be taken off on a stretcher.

In all, nine Redskins players had suffered injuries. By game's end, rookie running back and kick returner Brian Mitchell was the team's quarterback.

"They killed almost everybody we had," Gibbs said.

Near the end of the game, Eagles linebacker William Frizzell turned to the Washington bench and quipped, "You need any more body bags?"

The Redskins lost, 28–14.

"I don't think I've ever been involved in a game where so many players went down," Gibbs said afterward. "It seemed like every play."

It was one of the low moments of Gibbs's run with the Redskins. And it wasn't just the fact that his team had fallen to 5-4 and the coach was uncertain whether he'd soon be out of the playoff hunt in a division that already included the Giants, who were 9-0 by then, and the Eagles, who were also 5-4 but had a talented enough team to make a late-season run to the tournament.

Gibbs had rarely been so upset by a game and by an opposing coach's behavior. He understood losing was a part of the deal, and he'd suffered some crushing ones at various times. But to have a coach speak of his team—or any team—by using the term *body bags*, and to then see all the injuries pile up and hear one of Ryan's players ask if they needed any more bags . . . well, that was simply over the line.

"Joe had been embarrassed on national TV, and it really bothered him," former Redskins public relations director Charlie Dayton said.

His players saw Gibbs's anger.

They were just as pissed.

"I remember Joe Johnson getting knocked out on a punt return. I mean, when [the trainers] got out there, he was snoring," said former Redskins guard Mark Schlereth. "And the Eagles were celebrating. We all celebrate big hits, you celebrate football and toughness. But when the other team is celebrating like that, you feel like they're celebrating an injury.

"Those things are things you don't take lightly," Schlereth said. "There was a sense of frontier justice in the league back then, and you took matters into your own hands legally. But you tried not to go out there and hurt people. Things like that irritated Joe. That's a lack of respect for the game."

"Joe never swore, but he came close when we played the Eagles," said former Redskins safety Todd Bowles. "When they beat us in the body bag game, that made Joe's butthole hurt. He'd turn red, but he would never, ever swear. That was the most intense I've ever seen him as far as wanting to get back at someone. He'd say, 'It burns my butt to see them over there celebrating, and we're not going to take it. I'd go out there and play myself, but I'd probably get my butt kicked.'"

Gibbs's unwillingness to swear was legendary among his players. Some of them even tried to make him swear, but the coach would never go there.

"We called him Bunsie," Butz said. "He once said in a team meeting, 'We're going to knock them on their buns.' I'm like, what are they, bakers or something?"

Gibbs would soon get his shot at payback against Ryan.

The Redskins and Eagles both went on late-season runs to finish 10-6 and earn wild card playoff berths behind the divisional champion Giants, who went 13-3. It would be Redskins-Eagles once more at Philadelphia's Veterans Stadium in the first round.

"Going into that playoff game, that may have been as intense as I've ever seen Joe," Dayton said. "That body bag game was on his mind. He was just so focused."

The Eagles had practiced for part of the week in Tampa, partly due to inclement weather in Philadelphia, but also because Tampa was where Super Bowl XXV was to be played, and Ryan wanted his players to become accustomed to the area. That infuriated Gibbs, and he shared his disgust for Ryan's bravado with his players during the week.

"The coach that Joe liked the least was Buddy Ryan," former Redskins center Jeff Bostic said. "We all knew it."

Gibbs would avenge the body bag game the best way he knew how: on game day. The Redskins beat the Eagles, 20–6, to advance to the divisional round against the 49ers.

After falling behind 6–0 on two Roger Ruzek field goals, the Redskins' offense got in gear behind quarterback Mark Rypien, who had replaced Williams as Gibbs's starter in 1989 and had returned from a knee injury late in the 1990 season to help get Washington into the playoffs. Rypien heated up in the second quarter, finding Art Monk for a 16-yard touchdown to give the Redskins a lead they would never relinquish.

Rypien led two field goal drives to make it 13–6, and then finished off a 20–6 win with a third-quarter touchdown pass to Gary Clark.

"It was a butt kicking, and it was fun to beat them in the playoffs," former Redskins linebacker Andre Collins said. "We had so much confidence lining up against Philadelphia's offense. We knew what they were going to run every time they lined up. There was a frustration on their part because they couldn't do anything."

Gibbs was delighted afterward.

"We want to win the right way and lose the right way," he said, a clear shot at Ryan.

Ryan, who never won a playoff game in Philadelphia, was fired four days later.

Gibbs wound up losing the following week to the 49ers in San Francisco, and his team never really stood a chance against the two-time defending Super Bowl champions. Rypien threw three interceptions, and Montana was firmly in control of a team that won its seventh straight playoff game.

In spite of that loss, Gibbs felt good enough about his team moving forward next year with Rypien as his starter. And with the Redskins having gotten back to the playoffs following a two-year absence after winning Super Bowl XXII, the coach felt justifiably optimistic heading into the 1991 season.

Rypien was another of Gibbs's quarterbacks who might not have had Hall of Fame talent but benefited greatly from the coach's schemes and intuitive feel for what was needed at the position. Rypien was born in Calgary, Alberta, in 1962, and his family moved to Spokane, Washington, in 1965. Rypien was a terrific three-sport athlete at Shadle Park High School, leading his team to a state basketball championship as a senior. All three of his varsity numbers in football, basketball, and baseball were eventually retired by the school.

He had a nominal career at Washington State, throwing 28 touchdown passes and 27 interceptions over his final two seasons, but drew enough interest from GM Bobby Beathard to make him the Redskins' sixth-round pick in 1986. He spent his first two years on injured reserve, but Gibbs thought highly enough of Rypien to make him the backup to Williams in 1988. Rypien's development also hastened the trade of Schroeder, who was dealt to the Raiders a year after Gibbs had nixed the Williams trade.

Rypien saw some action in 1988 because of Williams's injury-related absences and declining play, and was named the starter heading into the 1989 season. He did not have an easy time of it, though, and came under intense scrutiny after the team's 4-4 start.

"I don't think any quarterbacks in the league are dynamic enough to suit the crowd," Gibbs told reporters before a game against the Raiders and Schroeder. "I think Ryp's probably in the same boat."

After he was booed by Redskins fans following a home win over the Cardinals, Rypien tried to take the criticism in stride.

"I've heard the State Department is looking for me, because they think I'm the only guy that can overthrow Noriega," Rypien cracked, referencing the former Panamanian dictator Manuel Noriega.

But by the end of the 1990 season, when Rypien had returned from a knee injury to win five of his last seven starts and beat the Eagles in the playoffs, Gibbs felt he had a trustworthy field general. Rypien could throw one of the best deep balls of any quarterback in the league, and he was now beginning to improve on his intermediate throws, although some of those passes would invariably wobble and cause Gibbs consternation.

The Hogs were still going strong, with Jim Lachey now at left tackle and Joe Jacoby at right, Jeff Bostic still at center, and guards Raleigh McKenzie and Mark Schlereth. Rypien was clearly good enough, as far as Gibbs was concerned.

"Joe had a great system where he allowed us as players to make the best of what we had," Rypien said. "He always went out and got the type of player he wanted. He liked smart guys, and he threw a lot at us. He'd challenge us game plan wise to an extreme. It was almost like, there's no way these guys were going to get this, but sure enough, we had a group of guys that understood."

The Redskins were clearly the class of the NFC East in 1991, and they tore through their early-season schedule with the kind of proficiency rarely seen even on Gibbs's best teams. They streaked to an 11-0 record, with Rypien enjoying by far his most productive season. His lead runner was former Browns tailback Earnest Byner, who had been known more for his costly fumble in the 1986 AFC Championship Game to set up Elway's famous late-game touchdown drive. Gerald

Riggs, the former Falcons first-round pick, was also in the backfield, and Ricky Ervins was a solid changeup back. Art Monk, Ricky Sanders, and Gary Clark comprised a dangerous three-pronged receiver set. And that offensive line kept Rypien clean the entire season.

Rypien would drop back 421 times that season and was sacked only seven times. That's an insanely low number, and one that allowed him to operate Gibbs's offense at peak efficiency.

The defense, meanwhile, was as good as at any time in the Gibbs era. Charles Mann had come into his own as a terrific all-around defensive end. Darrell Green was the best cornerback of his generation, a player who could take any great receiver out of a game with one-on-one coverage. Linebackers Wilber Marshall, the former Bears star for whom Gibbs had surrendered two first-round picks; veterans Kurt Gouveia and Monte Coleman, and rookie Andre Collins were the best collective group in the league.

This was as good as Gibbs had felt about his team in a long, long time. Maybe ever.

"I remember we're off to an 8-0 start, and Joe was in a coaches meeting and he's like, 'This season is unbelievable,'" said Bostic, who was told of Gibbs's comments by offensive line coach Jim Hanifan. "Everybody's accepted their roles, everything is just smooth sailing."

Hanifan said Gibbs was delighted the 5 o'clock club was no more.

"Joe wanted that 5 o'clock club shut down," Bostic said. "So Hanifan's tugging on a cigarette telling us this and he goes, 'Joe, I hate to burst your bubble, but the 5 o'clock club is alive and well. I was with them last night.'"

That's right. Hanifan, a welcome guest at the 5 o'clock club, told Gibbs the players were still throwing back beers at the facility.

"We were right below his office," Bostic said.

Gibbs was willing to overlook it, though, because things really were proceeding as smoothly as they had in years. The Redskins finished off a 14-2 season, matching Gibbs's 1983 team, and went into the playoffs as the clear favorites to win a third title for the eleventh-year coach.

With home field advantage in the NFC playoffs locked up, the Redskins put on a show for the RFK faithful, beating the Falcons, 24–7, in the divisional round and then crushing the Lions, 41–10, in the NFC

Championship Game. Rypien had two touchdown passes, Riggs ran for two more, and Green finished off the rout with a fourth-quarter interception return for a touchdown.

One more win in Super Bowl XXVI, and Gibbs would add to his legacy as one of the all-time great coaches by becoming the first in NFL history to win three Super Bowl titles with three different quarterbacks. The fact that none of those quarterbacks was a dominant individual performer only underscored that astonishing achievement.

The only other coach to win multiple Super Bowls with different quarterbacks: Parcells, who won with Simms and then Hostetler.

Like Parcells, Gibbs would face the Bills in his latest Super Bowl appearance. With Buffalo coming off that heartbreaking 20–19 loss to the Giants, they had again dominated the AFC the following year. They ripped through the regular season with a 13-3 record—in all likelihood, they would have matched Gibbs's 14-2 record, but Marv Levy rested his key starters, including Jim Kelly, in the final regular-season game.

Buffalo crushed the Chiefs, 37–14, in the divisional round and then put on a masterful defensive performance in holding off Elway's Broncos, 10–7, in the AFC Championship Game. With a chance for redemption in the Super Bowl, there was plenty of sentiment that the Bills stood a decent chance of beating the Redskins, despite Washington going into the game as a seven-point favorite.

Gibbs himself wasn't as confident as the oddsmakers...at least not until he caught wind of what Bills defensive line coach Chuck Dickerson had said about the Redskins' offensive line. During a television interview a few days before the game, Dickerson took aim at the Hogs with a series of insults. He said Lachey "wears his jersey real well. Tapes down his sleeves to make his guns look big. Really big...a ballerina in a 310-pound body." Dickerson called Jacoby "my type of guy—Neanderthal." He referred to Bostic as "ugly, like the rest of 'em."

Dickerson had provided a motivational tool for Gibbs—on a silver platter.

"He essentially poked fun at the Hogs, every guy," Schlereth said. "He was kind of being funny, but I'll never forget the night before the Super Bowl. We're sequestered at a hotel outside Minneapolis, and Joe Gibbs is reading this article. He was absolutely livid. [Dickerson] was trying to be funny, but Joe was beside himself that anybody would question the integrity and the ability of the Hogs. He addressed that article. It wasn't fabricated. He felt like [Dickerson] had completely disrespected what was the backbone and the heart of that organization during his three world championship game appearances."

Super Bowl XXVI was over even before it began.

The Redskins dominated the Bills from start to finish, building a 37–10 lead in the fourth quarter on the way to a 37–24 win and Gibbs's third Super Bowl title. Rypien was the game's Most Valuable Player, Monk and Clark each had more than 100 yards receiving, Riggs had two rushing touchdowns, and the Hogs didn't allow a single sack against Dickerson's defensive line, which included All-Pro Bruce Smith.

The Redskins' defense intercepted Kelly four times, and Thurman Thomas, who famously misplaced his helmet at the start of the game and had to miss the first two plays, finished with just 13 rushing yards.

"I feel humble," Gibbs said afterward. "The Lord's blessed me with a great situation. The players have really responded."

Addressing a smattering of speculation that he might walk away after the game, Gibbs said he was not leaving.

"I have no thoughts about stepping away from this," he said.

If he didn't then, he would soon.

GIBBS

SOMETHING HAD TO GIVE

Dick Vermeil could tell Joe Gibbs was at the end just by the look on his face. It was the same look Vermeil had when he realized he needed to step away from the Eagles ten years earlier.

"I remember broadcasting a Redskins game [in 1992] and I visited with Joe on a Saturday after practice," said Vermeil, who had worked at CBS and then ABC as a football analyst. "We went to his office, and I could see that he was emotionally and physically exhausted. I remember saying, 'Joe, I've been there, done that. The game can do that to you.'"

Vermeil shared his own experiences with Gibbs and tried to offer some perspective for what the Redskins coach was going through. Though not as tightly wound and emotional as Vermeil, Gibbs was nevertheless a workaholic who didn't know any other way to coach than to do it at a breakneck pace.

That meant sleeping at the office three, sometimes four nights a week, something he'd done since he first started with the Redskins in 1981.

"As a coaching staff, we tried to do everything together as far as preparation, and we went through every aspect of the offense," Gibbs said. "When you do that, it takes a lot of time, and I felt like at the time, the best way to do it wasn't to go home for a couple hours and come back. It made more sense to stay at the office, get the work done, and then go home later in the week."

Gibbs was so focused on football that he had essentially sealed off the rest of the world for most of the week, and that meant sacrificing family time he could never get back. He adored his wife, Pat, and two children, J.D. and Coy, but simply didn't have the time—or make the time—to see them during the season.

It started to eat at him.

"The thing I'll always second-guess in life is what I missed with J.D., Coy, and Pat, because I was away from home for a lot of the time," he said. "I had a burning desire to coach, and that's what I thought my passion was for—my abilities to get into coaching. I wasn't a good enough player, so I coached, and that meant so much."

Looking back now, he regrets not figuring out a way to balance football and family.

"I do think I could have done it differently," he said. "I could have arranged some things and done it differently."

The year after winning a third Super Bowl, the feelings of disconnectedness from his family only increased. And while he didn't show any outward change in demeanor to his players and coaches, he was struggling with how football had consumed his family life.

Washington Post beat writer Richard Justice, who had engendered Gibbs's trust and would frequently meet with Gibbs for off-the-record conversations, had a particularly striking interaction with the coach, a moment when Gibbs revealed just how conflicted he had become.

"Joe says, 'One night, I went to kiss my son Coy good night, and I looked, and I kissed this thing that was six foot something, 240 pounds, about to play linebacker, and I just started to cry,'" Justice recalled. "'I missed the whole thing.'"

Coy was about to head off to Stanford to play football, and wound up playing his final three seasons for none other than Bill Walsh, who had returned to coach the Cardinal.

The players had no inkling that 1992 would be Gibbs's final season.

"Not a clue," guard Mark Schlereth said. "I don't know anybody in that organization knew he was going to walk away."

To Schlereth, Gibbs was the same coach as when the guard first got to the Redskins as a tenth-round pick in 1989. The same coach who once asked Schlereth to come to his office for what the guard feared would be some bad news.

"The worst thing a coach can do is say, 'Swing by my office,'" said Schlereth, who battled an assortment of injuries during his career and underwent more than two dozen surgeries. "I'm thinking, 'Am I going to get traded? Are they going with someone else?' So I show up, rap on the door, and he has me sit down."

"Mark, I just wanted to let you know how much I appreciate you battling all season long and playing hurt and doing all the things you do," Gibbs told him. "I just want you to know I pray for your health and wellness. I pray for you by name."

Schlereth was elated—and relieved—to have earned such high praise.

"When you have someone like that who invests in your life and has that kind of relationship with his players, that kind of love for you as a player, you'd step out in front of traffic for the man."

Through much of the season, particularly later in the year, Gibbs didn't feel well. He was fatigued, developed headaches, and simply didn't have the same energy as in past years. Part of it was his diet, which was mostly awful.

"Joe was a little guy with a little voice, but he would eat a one-pound bag of M&M's," Justice said. "I'm like, 'Joe, you have to stop that.'"

"I wound up a diabetic and didn't know it," Gibbs said.

Gibbs had previously become involved in NASCAR, since he'd had a decades-long interest in car racing going back to his days in southern California, and created his own NASCAR team in 1991, or around the same time he'd won his third Super Bowl title.

Gibbs didn't let on that he was thinking about retirement in the immediate aftermath of the season, choosing instead to spend time with his family to make certain he was sure that walking away was the right thing to do.

Despite his inner conflict, Gibbs presided over a solid, albeit uneven regular season—in part because Rypien had struggled after a nearly flawless 1991 season that ended with a Super Bowl MVP award. The quarterback had just 13 touchdown passes and 17 interceptions in the regular season and was sacked 23 times, compared to just seven the year before.

Still the Redskins managed a 9-7 record and squeezed in as a wild card playoff team. Without the benefit of a home playoff game, they beat the Vikings in Minnesota in the opening round, 24–7, but fizzled the following week in a 20–13 loss to Seifert's 49ers at Candlestick Park.

Gibbs knew it was important that he take some time to make sure any decision he made would be the right one. During a four-day family trip to Vail, Colorado, Gibbs knew in his heart the right move was to walk away from coaching.

Gibbs drove to Jack Kent Cooke's home to tell him what he'd decided, and the owner was deeply disappointed. Cooke tried to talk him out of it, and asked Gibbs to take at least the weekend to see if he might change his mind. By the following Monday, Gibbs was still set on retirement, and again drove to Cooke's house to let the owner know the decision was final.

On March 6, 1993, Gibbs held a press conference to announce he was stepping down, and that longtime defensive coordinator Richie Petitbon would take over as head coach.

"Every year, we get away and talk about it," Gibbs said of discussing his situation with his family. "We always reach the same conclusion. This year, it was different. The boys didn't encourage me one way or another, but they understood when I told them what I was thinking. I think Pat's happier than anyone. This isn't an easy lifestyle for a coach's wife. The coach is the guy who stands up and hears everyone tell him how great he is. The wife is the one waiting at home alone while the coach is spending every night at the office."

Cooke said he was "devastated. I looked at him and said, 'Are you sure what you're saying?'"

It was a relatively easy transition for Gibbs, who could still pursue competitive sports while spending more time with his family. With both Coy and J.D. by his side running the car racing company, it was a natural fit.

"The good thing about racing that has really helped me is that by working in racing with both boys, I've been able to spend a lot of time with them," Gibbs said. "That's been a real rewarding thing for me."

But there has been heartache, too. J. D. Gibbs has been undergoing "treatment for symptoms impacting areas of brain function," as was announced by Joe Gibbs Racing in 2015. J. D. Gibbs played football at the College of William & Mary and raced in the Xfinity, Truck, and K&N Pro Series, and was tested after he showed symptoms affecting his speech and processing skills.

Joe Gibbs's faith has played an important role in dealing with his son's illness.

"We've been going through something here, and that's where [having faith in God] helps," Gibbs said.

Even after turning to racing as a second career upon retiring after the 1992 season, there would be one more—and final—NFL act for Gibbs, who had already been selected as a first-ballot Hall of Famer in 1996. He was convinced by Redskins owner Daniel Snyder, who purchased the team after Cooke died, to coach again in 2004. He coached another four seasons, reaching the playoffs twice before retiring again after the 2007 season.

He still lives near Charlotte and continues to run Joe Gibbs Racing.

"That time meant so much to me," Gibbs said. "I remember we had a reunion of our 1991 team when a lot of our players came back, and I thought I was going to be the only one that had great memories. But it turns out that meant so much to everybody. All the teams meant so much, all the players over the years. It was a very special time."

Former Redskins guard Russ Grimm, an original member of the Hogs, said Gibbs left an indelible mark on everyone who knew him.

"You're talking about a great individual," Grimm said. "You're not remembered by what you did here, it's what you leave behind. Joe Gibbs left a lot behind to be proud of."

Perhaps Theismann said it best about Gibbs's legacy.

"I certainly appreciate Joe Gibbs the football coach for all the things he did for me and for the city of Washington and for the Washington Redskins," Theismann said. "But I will always appreciate the man Joe Gibbs and the friendship we had in the time we spent together."

An incredible time indeed, the most successful era in Redskins history.

They hadn't won a Super Bowl before Gibbs got there.

They haven't won another since he left.

THREE UNLIKELY COACHES, THREE HALL OF FAME CAREERS, AND A LASTING IMPACT

When I first discussed the idea for *Guts and Genius* with Gibbs, he offered a revealing response that explained a lot about how he was wired as a football coach.

This was just after Gibbs had finished the 2017 NASCAR racing season and he was finally able to wind down a bit after a seemingly interminable schedule of races that goes from February through late November. (Yes, he's nearly as consumed with NASCAR as he was in coaching the Redskins—although he doesn't sleep at the office.)

When I told him I wanted to look at the three coaches who collectively dominated the period from 1981 to 1991 in the NFL—Gibbs, Walsh, and Parcells—and how each man had won multiple Super Bowls with different styles yet equally brilliant implementation of their systems, he paused for a moment to think about what it meant to compete in an era with his two Hall of Fame contemporaries.

"That was one of the greatest times of my life," Gibbs said. "The experiences we had, the battles we had. This meant so much to me. If it hadn't been for Walsh and Parcells, I'd have four more Super Bowl rings."

He might be right.

In fact, you might be able to make the same argument that Walsh might have won more than three titles and Parcells more than two rings. That's how formidable these coaches were against one another, and how their own brand of guts and genius not only contributed to their own championships, but also prevented the others from winning even more.

Gibbs, for instance, beat Walsh in their only playoff meeting (after the 1983 season), but he was 0-2 against Walsh successor George Seifert in playoff meetings. Gibbs also had trouble beating Parcells, who was a combined 11-4 against Gibbs from 1984 to 1990, including that 17–0 thrashing in the 1986 NFC Championship Game.

Parcells was also a thorn for Walsh, whose 49ers lost back-to-back playoff games in 1985 and 86 by a combined 66–6.

And while Gibbs and Walsh are considered the more cerebral coaches of the three, it was the coach known more for his old-school, physical style who got the better of them in the playoffs. Parcells had a combined 3-1 playoff record against Gibbs and Walsh, and 4-1 when you add Seifert's 1990 Niners to the mix.

Any way you want to look at them, though, these three coaches produced some of the greatest football the NFL has ever seen, and their collective domination of the decade was one of the most unique eras in pro sports history.

"It's a watered-down league that has dramatically changed from the days that these wizards coached," said Jon Gruden, a former 49ers assistant under Seifert who went on to win a Super Bowl with the Buccaneers, then enjoyed a nine-year run as ESPN's *Monday Night Football* analyst before returning to the sidelines in Oakland. "It's a different world of football now. Heck, we could all sit there and remember the players that played on those Redskins, Giants, and 49ers teams. I associated every team with the head coach. I remember the NFC East [of the '80s] like it was yesterday. That was as good a division of football as there ever was.

"And Bill Walsh? If you had a chance to get on a raft and float down a river and just talk football," Gruden said, "he'd be the first one you'd pick."

Gruden remembers Walsh visiting him in Tampa in 2005, and it was as if a rock star had come to watch the Bucs practice.

"We took him out to dinner that night," Gruden said. "I think Bill wanted my job. That's why I felt a little pressure to get him the hell out of there. I can still see [Bucs defensive coaches] Rod Marinelli and Monte Kiffin just listening to every word Bill was saying. He talked about the fourth-quarter pass rush and how it was so important. Everybody thinks about that Cowboys-49ers game [in the 1981 play-offs] when Dwight Clark made The Catch. Everyone thinks that won that Super Bowl. Bullshit. It was the fourth-quarter pass rush. If it wasn't for the fourth-quarter sack [of Danny White], there is no Super Bowl. There is no dynasty."

Gruden said Walsh "had a great charisma and superior intelligence. Combine that with his passion for the game, and he was unbelievable. He was a pain in the ass, now. If your [offensive line] split was two feet outside the numbers, he was not a nice guy. He would make a lot of corrections through the assistant coaches, and he came unglued quick. But he knew what he wanted."

They created a lasting impact on the NFL in different ways.

Walsh was the founder of the most successful coaching tree in NFL history, a testament to his promise to help others after he'd been snubbed by Paul Brown in Cincinnati. Brown could never have known his decision to go with Tiger Johnson instead of Walsh as the Bengals' coach in 1976 would eventually give rise to such a magnificent collection of coaches—with Walsh as the starting point and so many other great leaders to follow.

Cris Collinsworth constantly wonders about what might have been. The former Bengals receiver lost twice to Walsh's 49ers in his two Super Bowl appearances, and there is lasting disappointment.

"Every day of my life, I think about it," said Collinsworth, now an award-winning commentator for NBC Sports. "You look back at the history of the Bengals, and that's one of those moments when Bill Walsh walked out of the building."

Instead, it was the 49ers and a multitude of other coaches who benefited from Walsh's genius. Among his coaching descendants to win championships: Mike Shanahan (two), Mike Holmgren, Jon Gruden, Tony Dungy, Brian Billick, and the most recent Super Bowl winner, Philadelphia's Doug Pederson—a "third-generation" Walsh adherent who worked under Andy Reid, a former Holmgren assistant.

"Bill Walsh was ahead of his time in so many ways," said Shanahan, the 49ers offensive coordinator from 1992 to 1994 before taking the Broncos head coaching job in 1995. "He had every meeting filmed, so when I got hired as offensive coordinator, I could go back over several years and look at every game plan presentation he had made. He was always out front."

Walsh's influence extended to the Broncos after Shanahan took over from Dan Reeves and went on to win Super Bowls after the 1997 and 1998 seasons. It was in Denver that Shanahan got to work with Elway, the quarterback Walsh had once recruited to Stanford shortly before he became the 49ers' head coach. After losing three Super Bowls in the 1980s to the Giants, Redskins, and 49ers, Elway finally broke through with Shanahan.

"The common denominator with Walsh, Gibbs, and Parcells was their toughness and their ability to inspire players and adapt what they did for what was best for their football teams," said Elway, who won Super Bowl 50 as the Broncos general manager after the 2015 season. "They had different personalities, but they never let the personal side get in the way of what was best for their football teams. That's not easy to do."

Parcells won two championships with the Giants, but he was an invaluable influence on Belichick and Coughlin, who combined for seven more Super Bowl championships, including Belichick's five with the Patriots. Parcells protégé Sean Payton delivered the first Super Bowl championship in Saints history. That's 10 championships since 1986.

"I wouldn't have won two Super Bowls if it weren't for working with Bill," said Coughlin, who beat Parcells disciple Bill Belichick in both Super Bowls. "The way he motivated. The way we practiced. The physical aspect of the way we played. We just put the pads on, twice a day, in training camp. It was hard work. The players, Simms, LT, Carl Banks, all of the great people that knew how to practice, knew what Bill wanted, the way Bill broke everything down into the most minute detail of what you had to do to win. The experience of being around that, there's nothing like that in your career."

Parcells's opponents held him in high regard, especially the ones whose dreams were crushed by the former Giants coach.

"The one thing about Bill is that he believed there's always a way to win a football game. It's up to you to find out how," said former Bills GM Bill Polian, who lost to Parcells in Super Bowl XXV. "There are many, many people—far too many people—in the game who either haven't been exposed to that or don't believe it. People are married to systems. The system is the system and it's never going to change. They don't adjust. Bill always adjusted to the circumstances."

It left Polian with a disappointment that still haunts him. "There is no more devastating event in your life, other than a death in the family or a serious, life-threatening illness, than losing the Super Bowl. None," Polian said. "It never goes away. It stays forever. You come to grips with it, but you're never going to change the result. That's particularly true in terms of a game you felt you should have won."

Belichick, a winner of five Super Bowls with the Patriots, gives Parcells tremendous credit for helping him throughout his career.

"I coached with Bill for sixteen years and learned so many things," Belichick said. "In the early years, 1981 to 1983, I learned a lot about the 3-4 defense, technique, play calling, game planning, adjustments, and handling players. In the later years, Bill would talk to me about big-picture things like team building, discipline, and staffing. He was great about taking time to make me aware of things that, as an assistant coach, were not on my radar until he educated me on them."

Belichick credited Parcells's vision with helping the Giants build their first two Super Bowl championship teams.

"Bill did a great job on the biggest, most important things," Belichick said. "He had good vision on building and improving his team and what the most important steps were, whether it was the spring, training camp, early in the regular season, and playoffs. He was brilliant at identifying our team's strengths and weaknesses, and he would have an overall plan for how to handle them."

The fact that Parcells was a combined 4-1 in the playoffs against teams built by Walsh and Gibbs was a further testament to his brilliance.

"We were able for the most part to do the major things better than the Redskins and 49ers in those highly competitive [playoff] games," Belichick said. "Bill had a unique way of instilling confidence in the team, and we always felt like we had an edge in those games."

Oddly enough, the Gibbs coaching tree, while having produced a handful of head coaches, hasn't been nearly as productive as those of Walsh and Parcells. I think you can make a strong case that Gibbs may have been the greatest coaching tactician in NFL history—winning three Super Bowls with three quarterbacks nowhere near Hall of Fame caliber is something no other coach has come close to achieving—but he didn't leave behind a legacy of great coaches.

"Many times with head coaches, it depends on the situation—the owners, the front office, the support you get, the general manager, the people picking talent," said Gibbs, whose former assistants Joe Bugel (Cardinals, Raiders), Dan Henning (Falcons, Chargers), and Richie Petitbon (Redskins) all had losing records as head coaches. "It was obvious what I thought of my coaches. They were so talented and so good. The Redskins let me go after one of the best coaching staffs in the league. It just takes a lot, and I was fortunate to be in a good situation."

John Madden thinks it's the NFL's loss that other coaches haven't heeded the lessons Gibbs imparted during his Hall of Fame run.

"More coaches ought to look at some of the things he did in the passing game and adopt just a few of those concepts," he said. "Joe was going to block everyone. Nowadays, there's so many plays where you send five men out, and when you do that, all you have left is five blockers. That gets the quarterback killed a lot of times. Joe was just the opposite. If you brought an extra guy, he'd leave an extra blocker. He could block anything you could bring, and his quarterbacks didn't get killed. Every time I see these teams spread out and throw the ball quickly, I'm like, 'They ought to look at Joe Gibbs.'"

Each man coached in his own way, whether it was through tactical advantage, organizational structure, or motivational brilliance, but all three arrived at the same destination multiple times: the top. They were revered by their players and respected by their opponents, and the Walsh-Gibbs-Parcells era was one of the most memorable in NFL history, and in many ways it defined greatness in pro sports.

"I look back at that time and think what an incredibly fortuitous time it was to cover that era of football," Peter King said. "Parcells used to talk about how playing in that division and that conference would get those teams battle tested for whenever they had to go against whoever was going to be in the Super Bowl that year. It was just a really incredible time, and those three coaches had some amazing teams."

They shaped the league when they coached, and helped shape future generations of coaches and players, a process that continues today, particularly with the Walsh-Parcells effect.

"The longer I think about it, the more I've seen the enormity of what Bill Walsh was able to do in football and how he looked at players," Steve Young said. "Fundamentally, he saw them as partners. Yeah, he had a sharp knife at the end of careers, and that's when everyone got really mad at that. You give all of yourself and he gets rid of you a year early. But we were partners with him, and that was unusual. Bill was the first coach in history to have that as a basic mentality."

Young calls Walsh "a Swiss army knife of human beings. He had a unique thing to say about everybody, but it was contextual to you and your needs and who you were. He treated people uniquely at all times. He thought of football holistically: how we traveled, how we practiced, how much water do we give them, what kind of meals, how are they sleeping."

Like Walsh, many of Parcells's players and coaches chafed under his autocratic rule, yet they came to appreciate that demanding style and understood why he influenced his teams so profoundly. The former coach remains deeply attached to the game, offering advice to many of his former assistant coaches and still providing life lessons to his ex-players.

"The thing about Coach Parcells, when you're working for him, it's always a lot harder," said Vikings coach Mike Zimmer, a Parcells assistant with the Cowboys. "He was always trying to get me [to coach] better, and he was always poking a stick at me. He liked me, so I felt sorry for some of the other guys."

Yet Zimmer always welcomes the weekly telephone calls from his old boss.

"[Vikings GM] Rick Spielman and I will be sitting in our office

Monday morning at 6 a.m., we're watching tape, the phone rings, and here's Parcells," said Zimmer, who compiled a notebook of things Parcells has told him over the years. "He's like, 'Here's the rule on this,' 'You should have done this,' 'Here's this rule.' He taught me the most about the game of football, not just offense and defense, but about managing the game and what it takes to be a head coach."

Parcells's personal touch includes his players.

Not long after Jeff Rutledge nearly died in a 2003 car accident, the Giants' former backup quarterback got a call from his old coach.

"We talked for a while, and the thing I remember most is at the end of the conversation, he said, 'I love you, Rut,'" Rutledge said, his voice shaking at the memory of the call. "It's a side of Bill that a lot of people don't see, but to hear him say that, I teared up and told him, 'You don't know what that means for you to call me and say that.'"

Parcells had a years-long falling out with former Giants nose tackle Jim Burt after he was released and played for the 49ers. But they eventually reconciled, and it was Burt who got the call from Parcells not long ago when the coach needed help with shoulder surgery.

"He stayed at my house the night before, and I took him to the hospital," Burt said. When the surgery was over, Burt drove Parcells from Manhattan to the coach's home in Saratoga, New York. Burt couldn't help but have a little fun at Parcells's expense as they spoke to the coach's doctor and a hospital attendant shortly before leaving the hospital.

"I said, 'Doc, he ain't gonna last much longer. When I get him out on the New York State Thruway, I'm gonna throw him off a fuckin' cliff.' He looked at me and was like, 'Are you serious?'"

On Father's Day, Parcells receives nearly a dozen calls from former players, including former Jets running back Curtis Martin. "Every year on Father's Day, Curtis calls without fail," Parcells said.

For Parcells, there is an unbreakable bond with almost everyone he coached. He explained it this way when former Giants running back Lee Rouson's wife, Lisa, went up to the coach at a recent Super Bowl XXI reunion. She was fascinated that the players seemed so close to one another at the event, even though twenty-five years had passed since that championship season.

"Coach, will you answer me a question?" she said, looking around the room. "What is this?"

"That's a very good question," Parcells told her. "I know exactly what this is. This is a blood kinship that exists among these players, and as you can see, it's color-blind. They don't care what's what. Everybody is equal in this group. Those are their guys, and they're always going to be their guys, and it's going to last the rest of their lives. That's what this is. They've done a lot together, and once they're in there, they don't forget."

Gibbs, too, felt that deep connection that transcended the years. While unsure that his players appreciated just how special their time together was, the coach discovered that their bond was unshakable.

Walsh once shared a similar sentiment with Dr. Harry Edwards to explain his deep connection to football and how he viewed the essence of the sport. This was in training camp in 1986, and Edwards stood alongside Walsh as the players practiced.

"Look at this," Walsh told Edwards, scanning the field. "Joe Montana, white kid from the coal belt in Pennsylvania. Roger Craig, a kid from Nebraska. Look at that offensive line. Bubba Paris, Guy McIntyre, Randy Cross, Jesse Sapolu. This is why God gave us this violent, high-risk game—to demonstrate what we can do together. It demonstrates what we as a diverse society can accomplish together, the potential of this society and this nation to see what the San Francisco 49ers accomplished on the field."

Three unlikely coaches who lived by the courage of their convictions and persevered during their moments of doubt and uncertainty to create some of the most lasting memories in NFL history. Three men who helped transform pro football and produce some of the greatest teams ever. Three men whose unmistakable legacies left a lasting impact on today's game.

Bill Walsh. Joe Gibbs. Bill Parcells.

"Those guys," John Madden said, "they're the truth."

ACKNOWLEDGMENTS

Bill Walsh, Joe Gibbs, and Bill Parcells are three of the most compelling coaches in sports history, and the interconnectedness of their careers made for some of the greatest football the NFL has ever known. The '80s were halcyon days in pro football, and I was lucky enough to cover many of the iconic games that defined the decade.

I was also fortunate to interact regularly with all three coaches. That said, bringing their stories to life so many years later required the assistance of so many people along the way. Thanks so much to Parcells and Gibbs for sharing so many recollections about their careers and their lives, their accomplishments and struggles over the years. They were generous with their time and insight, and I am forever appreciative.

Former Eagles, Rams, and Chiefs coach Dick Vermeil provided incredible understanding of what made Walsh tick, and his suggestion to speak with Walsh's close friend Mike White opened the door to the kind of insight only he could provide. Earning Mike's trust was an honor, and his willingness to communicate that to others close to Walsh was critical in providing a window into a complicated coach's soul. Mike and Marilyn White opened their home to Walsh when he was at his lowest moment, and their willingness to share their life and times is deeply appreciated.

I can't sufficiently thank Bill's son Craig, for sharing his stories about a person who grew to become one of the most important coaches in NFL history—from Craig's days as a Bengals ball boy and watching his father interact with Paul Brown, to how Bill struggled to believe in his own brilliance and was then ultimately consumed by the pressure of living up to an impossible standard. Could not have done this without you, Craig.

Thanks so much to Bill's widow, Geri, who hasn't spoken much— at least publicly—about her husband over the years, but whose stories about watching Bill grow into a champion despite some setbacks were disarming, funny, and revealing.

There are so many players, coaches, and friends connected to all three Hall of Famers to thank.

Niners legends Joe Montana, Jerry Rice, Ronnie Lott, Steve Young, Randy Cross, Keena Turner, Roger Craig, Guy McIntyre—no wonder Walsh cherished you all so much. Your recollections and emotions about him reflected how meaningful he was to your careers and your lives.

Ed DeBartolo Jr.'s decision to hire Walsh in 1979 was a major turning point in NFL history, and his willingness to share his memories of their time together was critically important.

Walsh couldn't have had a more trusted and loyal assistant than general manager John McVay, one of the classiest and most dignified people I've ever met. Thanks again for all your help, and glad to see the McVay bloodlines continue in today's NFL. Sean is rightly proud of his grandfather.

Ernie Accorsi, your encyclopedic mind and sports knowledge are unparalleled, and your knowledge and relationships with all three coaches provided unique perspective.

Gibbs was a great coach, but also a great man who impacted so many lives. Joe Theismann knows this better than anyone, and his willingness to share his experiences at such a special time in Redskins history was sincerely appreciated. That also goes for Doug Williams and Mark Rypien, the other two quarterbacks who rose to Super Bowl greatness along with their coach. Thanks also to the charter members of the Hogs—especially Jeff Bostic, Joe Jacoby, Mark May, and Russ Grimm. You guys were incredible as players, and your storytelling is every bit as good as your blocking. Dave Butz, Mark Murphy, and Todd Bowles were outstanding. And thanks to Andre Caldwell, not only for his insights into Gibbs, but for his willingness to make contact with so many other players around the league to talk about these great coaches.

John Madden knew Walsh and Gibbs long before they rose to Hall of Fame heights, and his stories about both were spectacularly colorful, funny, and insightful. It was like listening to a private broadcast from one of football's all-time greats, and it will never be forgotten.

Tony Dungy is one of the most insightful people in football, and his history with Walsh and a coaching tree that continues to grow were a major resource from which to draw.

Parcells always liked to talk about "my guys" during his run with the Giants, and there were so many of them who shared what it was like playing and coaching for a man who was nearly fired after a year but who persevered and won two rings and a bust in Canton. Phil Simms, Lawrence Taylor, Harry Carson, Carl Banks, Jeff Hostetler, Bill Belichick, Tom Coughlin, Jim Burt, Joe Morris, Perry Williams, Everson Walls, Jeff Rutledge—thank you.

Special thanks to Valerie Panou, who stuck with this through the entire process and was incredibly patient and helpful.

Many thanks to Chris Helein, who knew when the time was right to speak to Gibbs, who remains one of the busiest people on the planet.

To Sean Desmond, your belief in an idea was what started this project, and your help along the way has been immeasurable. Cannot begin to thank you enough. Thanks to Gary Myers for making this connection, and for his guidance throughout the process.

Rachel Kambury, who knew there were so many details in putting this together? Thanks for making it go like clockwork.

Thanks to Carolyn Kurek and your staff for your careful—and patient—editing.

Thanks to every editor I've ever had, especially the ones over the years at *Newsday* who make journalism such an enjoyable, challenging, and rewarding business: Hank Winnicki, Michael Rose, Norm Cohen, Dave Whitehorn, Jeff Weinberg, Greg Gutes, and the rest of an incredibly talented staff. Dick Sandler, Bob Herzog, Jon Pessah, Jim Toedtman, Steve Ruinsky, Bill Eichenberger, thank you.

To Neil Best, Tom Rock, Judy Battista, and Kimberley Martin—better friends a journalist couldn't have. You make this crazy business a lot more enjoyable. Steve Serby, we compete, but we respect. Thanks to Vinny DiTrani for sharing his wealth of knowledge over the years, and to Dave Anderson for being the best role model a sportswriter could ever want. Yvette Michael, you knew this day was coming a long time ago.

Brian Plushanski and my soccer buddies—you rock. You, too, Brian Lehrer.

My parents—Lois and Marvin—what a ride it's been. Thanks for everything throughout all the years, and for teaching me what's most important in life. My deepest love and gratitude. Love you, Sandy and Jackie. Jogie and Marliese, no one could have been blessed with better in-laws.

My brothers—Tom, Rich, Bill, and Mick—I love you guys. Always. David, Cheryl, Chuck, Jayne, Leah, Lori, and Donnie—much love.

Andi and Emily, what can I say? You are incredible people, and being your father is the greatest blessing of my life. Talented, loving, and caring. You make the world a better place, and not just for your family.

Jutta, you wrote me a note way too many years ago saying this day would come. You were right, and I couldn't have done any of this without you. I love you with all my heart, with all my soul, and with all my might.

INDEX

Accorsi, Ernie, 18, 30, 165
Air Coryell offense, 35, 76, 78, 81
Allegre, Raul, 198, 205
Allen, George, 38, 79, 135
"alley-oop" pass, 71
Anderson, Flipper, 250
Anderson, George "Sparky," 40–41
Anderson, Ken, 112, 114–115, 116
Anderson, Neal, 252
Anderson, Ottis "O. J.," 199, 253, 259, 262
Ard, Billy "Biff," 152, 155–156, 200
Army, 50–52
Attner, Paul, 134
Audick, Dan, 104
Ayers, John, 104

Bahr, Matt, 255
Bailey, Stacey, 157–158
Baker, Stephen, 262
Baltimore Colts, 30
Banks, Carl, 155, 157, 158, 188
Bartkowski, Steve, 157, 158
Barton, Harris, 240
Bavaro, Mark, 182, 198, 200
Beathard, Bobby
  background, 38–40, 42, 43, 75, 81, 83–84
Beathard, Christine, 42
Belichick, Bill
  background, 183

on Bavaro, 200
  characteristics, 184
  move to Browns, 265
  Parcells and, 159, 160, 286, 287, 288
  Patriots and, 70, 269, 287
  Perkins and, 183
  1985 season, 186, 190–191
  Super Bowl XXV, 257–259, 263
Benjamin, Guy, 25
Benson, Brad, 188, 250
Billick, Brian, 63–64, 67–69, 285
Bill Walsh Minority Coaching Fellowship, 229–230
Blount, Mel, 101
body bag game, 270–271, 272
Bostic, Jeff
  Chuck Dickerson on, 276
  5 o'clock club, 121, 275
  on Gibbs, 272
  on Riggins, 122, 130
  1981 season, 82, 85, 86, 87
  1991 season, 275
  Super Bowl XXII, 218–219
Bowles, Todd, 271
Brandt, Gil, 104–105, 109
Breaux, Don, 77, 215
Breunig, Bob, 97
Brown, Charlie, 128, 138, 167, 168
Brown, Mike, 18

Brown, Paul
  with Bengals, 1–2, 16–22, 97, 111–112
  with Browns, 16
  death, 243
  "Tiger" Johnson and, 285
  Walsh and, 1–2, 113, 225
Brunner, Scott, 142–143
Bryant, Bear, 44–45
Buffalo Bills, 256, 276, 277
Bugel, Joe, 76–77, 137, 138, 288
Bunz, Dan, 95, 115–116
Burt, Jim, 152–153, 202–203, 290
Butz, Dave
  5 o'clock club, 121, 275
  Gibbs and, 3, 4, 272
  Simms and, 144
  training during strike, 126–127
Byner, Earnest, 274

Cahill, Tom, 47, 50, 52
Cale, Bobby, 56
Carano, Glenn, 105
Carr, Jimmy, 28
Carson, Harry
  on Belichick, 184
  "Crunch Bunch" and, 154
  1986 NFC Championship Game, 205
  on Parcells, 179
  retirement, 250
  1984 season, 159, 161
  1985 season, 185–187, 192
  on team members, 145
Carter, Anthony, 224
Carter, Virgil, 18, 19–20
Carthon, Maurice, 181–182
Casserly, Charley, 80, 211–212
The Catch, 108–110, 111
Cefalo, Jimmy, 136
Chicago Bears, 173–175, 191–192, 193,
  214–215, 237, 252–253
Cincinnati Bengals
  Brown and, 1–2, 16–21, 22, 97,
    111–112
  Johnson named head coach, 1–2, 285
  Super Bowl XVI, 111, 114–117
  Super Bowl XXIII, 238–242
  Walsh and, 16–21, 97

Cindrich, Ralph, 82
Clark, Dwight, 60, 90, 99, 107–108,
  109–110, 116, 172
Clark, Gary, 219, 272, 275, 277
Cleveland Browns, 16, 265
Clinkscale, Dextor, 182
Coleman, Monte, 275
Collier, John, 218
Collins, Andre, 273, 275
Collins, Mark, 251–252
Collinsworth, Cris, 115, 240, 285
Concannon, Maura Mara, 265
Cook, Greg, 18, 61
Cooke, Jack Kent, 3, 40–42, 75–76,
  83–85, 281
Cooke, John, 84
Cooney, Frank, 64–65, 92, 95
Cooper, Earl, 102, 115, 172
Corcoran, Mickey, 46–48, 50, 251,
  269
Coryell, Don, 24, 33, 34–36, 37–38, 81
Cosbie, Doug, 104, 106
Cosmo, George, 114
Coughlin, Tom, 265, 269, 286
counter trey play, 87
Cowlings, Al, 32
Craig, Roger, 166–167
  background, 291
  drafted by Walsh, 165
  1984 NFC Championship Game,
    174
  1984 season, 172–173
  1990 season, 256
  Super Bowl XXIII, 241
Cross, Howard, 250
Cross, Randy
  background, 291
  on DeBartolo, 232
  1984 NFC Championship Game, 174
  1981 season, 108
  1982 season, 164
  1988 season, 234
  on Walsh, 28–29, 58–59, 98–99,
    113, 237, 238
Crutchfield, Dwayne, 160
Culverhouse, Hugh, 210
Curtis, Isaac, 115

Dallas Cowboys, 96–97, 99, 104–111, 128, 132–135, 183, 189, 197, 213, 269
Davis, Al, 14, 149
Davis, Johnny, 99, 102
Dayton, Charlie, 271, 272
Dean, Fred, 93, 94, 165–166
DeBartolo, Ed, Jr.
  choice of Walsh as head coach, 9, 10–11
  Dwight Clark and, 116
  on 1983 NFC Championship Game, 169
  1981 season, 108–109
  Walsh and, 30, 100, 225, 231–233, 242, 245
DeBerg, Steve, 27, 63
Demoff, Marvin, 165
Denver Broncos, 199, 205–207, 218–220, 286
Dickerson, Chuck, 276
Dickerson, Eric, 159–160
Didier, Clint, 219
Dils, Steve, 25, 26, 226–227
Ditka, Mike, 173–175, 191
DiTrani, Vinny, 149–150, 157, 158
Doleman, Chris, 224
Dorsett, Tony, 96, 99, 106, 212
Dowhower, Rod, 165
Dungy, Tony, 65–66, 285

Easley, Kenny, 91, 102
Edwards, Harry, 230–231
Edwards, Herman, 230
Elliott, Jumbo, 250, 259–261, 264
Elliott, Lenvil, 60, 106, 107
Elway, John, 165, 199, 205–206, 218, 286
Erhardt, Ron, 54, 159
Ervins, Ricky, 275
Esiason, Boomer, 238–239
Everett, Jim, 250

Fassel, Jim, 268–269
Finding the Winning Edge (Walsh, Billick, and Peterson), 67–69
Fishof, David, 179

"40 Gut" and "50 Gut," 137
Fouts, Dan, 23–24, 42–43
Fraley, Robert, 148
Frank, John, 241
Frizzell, William, 270–271
Fuller, Steve, 60

Galbreath, Tony, 154
Garrett, Alvin, 129–130, 136
Garvey, Ed, 118–119, 124–125
Gayle, Shaun, 192–193
Gibbs, J. D., 281–282
Gibbs, Joe
  background, 35
  with Buccaneers, 37
  characteristics, 217, 272
  with Chargers, 24, 37–38, 76, 78
  coaching descendants of, 288
  with Florida State, 36
  Hall of Fame, 282, 283
  Madden and, 33–34, 36
  NASCAR and, 280, 281, 283
  religion and, 123–124
  with San Diego State, 35–36
  Super Bowl titles, 6, 7, 277, 283–284, 288
  on wife, 139
Gibbs, Joe and Redskins
  Air Coryell offense, 76, 78, 81
  bond with players, 291
  coaching staff, 76–77, 215–216, 288
  coaching style, 80, 86, 122–123, 134
  on Cooke, 85
  disconnection from family, 278–279
  Doug Williams and, 208–211
  5 o'clock club, 122, 275
  hired as head coach, 75–76
  NFC Championship Games, 132–135, 203–205, 275–276
  off-season training, 119–120, 126–127
  playoff record, 284
  retirement, 281
  return to, under Snyder, 282
  Riggins and, 77–78, 130–131, 132
  running game offensive, 87–88
  on Rypien, 274
  1981 season, 3, 81–84, 86, 87–88, 89

Gibbs, Joe and Redskins (*cont.*)
    1982 season, 126–127, 128–130
    1983 season, 167–168
    1984 season, 170–171, 214–215
    1985 season, 183, 184, 185–193
    1986 season, 197, 200
    1987 season, 210–211, 212–214, 215
    1988 season, 233
    1990 season, 270–272, 272–273, 274
    1991 season, 274–275, 275–276
    1992 season, 280–281
    1987 strike and replacement team,
      211–213
    on Super Bowl, 134–135
    Super Bowl XVII, 135–141
    Super Bowl XVIII, 170
    Super Bowl XXII, 216–220
    Super Bowl XXVI, 276–277
    Theismann and, 78–79, 81,
      86–87
Gibson, Bob, 4
Godfrey, Chris, 182
Gouveia, Kurt, 275
Grant, Darryl, 81, 134
Green, Darrell, 275, 276
Green, Dennis, 66
Green Bay Packers, 26–27, 200
Gregg, Forrest, 112, 116
Grimm, Russ, 81, 121, 126, 282
Gruden, Jon, 284–285
Guyton, Myron, 250

Hampton, Dan, 174
Hampton, Rodney, 253
Handley, Ray, 266, 267
Hanifan, Jim, 275
Harrison, Dennis, 144
Harty, John, 91
Henderson, Thomas "Hollywood,"
    71–72
Henning, Dan, 76, 288
Hicks, Dwight, 91, 115, 175, 178
Hofer, Paul, 32, 99, 102
Hogeboom, Gary, 133, 134
Holmgren, Mike, 27, 285
Holmoe, Tom, 172
Holtz, Lou, 23

Hostetler, Jeff, 156, 247–248, 251–254,
    257, 260–262, 264
Houston Oilers, 143
Humphries, Stan, 270

Ingram, Mark, 262

Jackson, Greg, 250
Jackson, Hue, 230
Jacoby, Joe, 81–82, 88–89, 121, 137,
    239–240, 274, 275, 276
Jennings, Dave, 182
Jennings, Stanford, 239
John, Butch, 217–218
Johnson, Bill "Tiger," 1–2, 21–22, 112,
    113, 285
Johnson, Bobby, 159, 198, 202
Johnson, Charles, 27
Johnson, Joe, 270, 271
Johnson, Pete, 115, 116
Jones, Ed "Too Tall," 97
Jones, Jerry, 269
Jones, Melvin, 82
Jurgensen, Sonny, 78
Justice, Richard, 279, 280

Kaepernick, Colin, 230–231
Karlis, Rich, 218
Kelley, Brian, 154, 194
Kelly, Jim, 257, 258, 260, 261, 262, 276
Kemp, Jack, 160
Kennedy, Allan, 81
Kilmer, Billy, 78
Kinard, Terry, 160
King, Peter, 289
Knight, Bobby, 51–52
Kotar, Doug, 147
Kraft, Robert, 267, 268

Lachey, Jim, 274
Lambert, Jack, 101
LaMonte, Bob, 15
Landeta, Sean, 181, 182, 192–193, 205
Landry, Tom, 45, 96, 99, 104, 105
Lansford, Mike, 160
Lawrence, Amos, 114
leather balls awards, 122–123

LeBeau, Dick, 238–239, 240
Ledbetter, Bob, 146
Levy, Mark, 276
Lewis, Marvin, 230
LoCasale, Al, 38
Lofton, James, 257
Lombardi, Vince, 45, 120, 243
Lott, Ronnie
  drafted, 91, 94
  last visit with Walsh, 245–246
  1981 season, 104, 106
  1983 season, 168, 169
  1986 season, 199
  Super Bowl XVI, 116
  on Walsh's coaching style, 175, 177
LT: Living on the Edge (Lawrence Taylor),
  194
Lynch, Dick, 158
Lynch, Jim, 18
Lynn, Anthony, 230

Madden, John
  Beathard and, 39–40
  coaching style, 68
  Gibbs and, 33–34, 36, 288, 291
  Hostetler and Super Bowl XXV, 257
  on Parcells, 291
  as Raiders head coach, 97–98
  Redskins' 5 o'clock club and, 122
  Walsh and, 14, 15–16, 201, 227–228,
  291
Malone, Mark, 171
Manley, Dexter, 139–140
Mann, Charles, 275
Manuel, Lionel, 205
Mara, John, 5, 147, 268
Mara, Tim, 45, 147, 265
Mara, Wellington, 4–5, 147, 267, 268
Marino, Dan, 175
Marshall, Lawrence, 255–256
Marshall, Leonard, 151
Marshall, Wilbur, 275
Martin, Curtis, 290
Martin, George, 155, 159, 160, 199, 250
Martin, Harvey, 97
Matthews, Billie, 63–64
May, Mark, 81, 82–83, 89, 120, 121

McConkey, Phil, 198
McCulley, Pete, 10, 27, 28
McIntyre, Guy, 174, 229, 291
McKay, John, 35, 209, 210
McKenzie, Raleigh, 274
McNeal, Don, 138
McVay, John
  The Fumble, 31
  Rocklin summer camp, 95
  1981 season, 105
  Walsh and, 29–30, 31, 57, 91, 113, 164
  weak defense and, 90–91
Mecklenburg, Karl, 207
Meggett, David, 250
Meyer, Ken, 10
Miami Dolphins, 135–139, 175, 178, 192
Millard, Keith, 224
Millen, Matt, 170
Miller, Ira, 92
Milot, Rich, 132
Minnesota Vikings, 131–132, 198, 214,
  215–216, 224, 231, 235, 236–237
Mitchell, Brian, 270
Modell, Art, 16
Monk, Art, 171, 272, 275, 277
Montana, Joe
  background, 100, 291
  Cowboys and, 104
  drafted, 25, 26–27
  late-game magic of, 59–61
  NFC Championship Games,
  173–174, 237
  on Rice, 236
  1980 season, 90
  1981 season, 94, 96, 99–101, 104,
  106–108, 109, 110
  1983 season, 167
  1984 season, 157, 161, 171, 172
  1985 season, 190
  1986 season, 201, 202, 222
  1987 season, 212, 221–223, 224
  1988 season, 233
  1990 season, 253–256
  Simms on, 62
  Steve Young and, 228–229
  Super Bowl XVI, 115, 117
  Super Bowl XVIII, 175, 178

Montana, Joe (*cont.*)
  Super Bowl XXIII, 239–241
  use of scripted plays, 99
  on Walsh, 114, 177
  Walsh and, 245–246
  on winning, 99–100
Moore, Eric, 250
Morris, Joe, 151, 159, 193, 197, 199,
  251–252
Moseley, Mark, 89, 126, 134, 136, 140,
  168
Mowatt, Zeke, 182
Murphy, Mark, 79, 119, 124, 126–127,
  140, 212

Nattiel, Ricky, 218
New England Patriots, 54–55, 70, 193,
  267, 269, 287
New Orleans Saints, 58–61, 286
New York Giants. *See also* Parcells, Bill
  and Giants
  after Parcells, 266, 267
  "Crunch Bunch," 154
  need for discipline, 145
  offensive line nickname, 199
  off-season training, 151, 155–157
  1985 roster, 181–182
  sale of, 265
  1981 season, 103–104
  1988 season, 234
  Super Bowl XXXIV, 269
  Young with, 4–5, 25, 44
New York Jets, 23, 268, 269
Noll, Chuck, 45, 65–66
Norton, Chico, 71, 114
Norwood, Scott, 263
Nugent, Helen Mara, 265

Oakland Raiders, 97–98, 170,
  208
Oates, Bart, 181, 182, 193
O'Connor, Fred, 10
off-season training, 83, 119–120,
  126–127, 151, 155–157, 193
"Oklahoma drill," 156
Owens, James, 26
Owens, R. C., 71

"Pace Party," 156
Parcells, Bill (Duane Charles)
  background, 46–49
  characteristics, 49, 52, 54, 56,
    158–159, 290
  as coach at colleges, 49–53, 54
  coaching descendants of, 269, 286,
    289–290
  on Corcoran, 48
  with Cowboys, 269
  Hall of Fame, 283
  health, 266
  Jets and, 268, 269
  Knight and, 51–52
  with Patriots, 54–55, 267
  personal tragedies, 5, 146–147, 267
  Super Bowl titles, 6, 7, 276, 283–284
  Taylor and, 56, 103–104
  Vince Lombardi Trophy, 6
  on Walsh, 225–226
Parcells, Bill and Giants
  on Belichick, 184
  bond with players, 290–291
  Brunner as starter, 142–143
  Burt and, 153
  coaching style, 55, 289
  "Crunch Bunch," 154
  early coaching difficulties, 144–147
  Giants offer to Schnellenberger and,
    148–149
  Hostetler and, 251
  Mara and, 265–266
  named coach, 45–46
  1986 NFC Championship Game,
    203–205
  nickname, 190
  off-season training, 193
  Parker hired, 150–152
  playoff record, 284, 287–288
  resignation of, 266–267
  1983 season, 4–5, 143, 144, 148
  1984 season, 154–161, 171, 172
  1985 season, 179, 182–189, 190–193
  1986 season, 197–200, 201–203,
    248–249
  1987 season, 212–213, 249
  1988 season, 249, 250

1989 season, 250
1990 season, 247, 251–256
Simms and, 142
Super Bowl XXI, 206–207
Super Bowl XXV, 256–264, 287
Taylor and, 194–195, 196
on Young, 180–181
Parcells, Charles, 146–147
Pardee, Jack, 38, 79
Paris, Bubba, 291
Parker, Johnny, 150–152
pass-centric offense, 35, 76, 78, 81
Patton, Ricky, 102
Payton, Sean, 286
Pearson, Drew, 110
Peccatiello, Larry, 76
Pederson, Doug, 285
Perkins, Ray, 44, 45, 55, 103, 145, 183
Peters, Tony, 136
Peterson, James, 67–69
Petitbon, Richie, 76, 167, 215, 288
Philadelphia Eagles, 3, 73–74, 197, 211, 270–273
Pittsburgh Steelers, 45, 171–172
playoffs
    1981, 103–104, 105–111
    1984, 159–161, 214–215
    1985, 189
    1986, 201–203
    1987, 215, 224, 227
    1988, 234, 235, 236–237
    1990, 272–273
    1991, 275–276, 281
    1992, 281
    Gibbs's record, 284
    Parcells's record, 284, 287–288
    Walsh's record, 284
Plunkett, Jim, 10
Polian, Bill, 261, 287
Prothro, Tommy, 23, 24
Pryor, Dean, 49–50

Radakovich, Dan, 28
Ralston, John, 24
Reasons, Gary, 155, 158, 256
Reed, Andre, 257
Reeves, Dan, 267, 268

Reid, Andy, 285
Reynolds, John "Hacksaw," 92–93, 116
Rice, Homer, 112
Rice, Jerry, 189–190, 199, 201, 234–238, 239, 241
Rickles, Don, 227
Riggins, John "Diesel"
    5 o'clock club, 121, 122
    Gibbs and, 77–78, 80
    1982 NFC Championship Game, 134
    1981 season, 87, 89, 130
    1982 season, 128, 129, 131–132, 133
    1983 season, 167, 168
    1984 season, 171, 214
    1985 season, 184
    Super Bowl XVII, 137, 138, 140–141
    Super Bowl XXII, 219
Riggs, Gerald, 270, 274, 275, 276
Riley, Dan, 120
Ring, Billy, 91, 106
Robinson, Stacy, 198, 199, 213
Ross, Dan, 116
Rozier, Mike, 166
Rubbert, Ed, 211
Rutledge, Jeff, 156, 248, 270, 290
Ruzek, Roger, 272
Ryan, Buddy, 192, 197, 270, 272, 273
Rypien, Mark, 270, 272, 273–274, 275, 276, 277, 280

salaries, 71, 118–119, 125
Sanders, Ricky, 219, 275
San Diego Chargers, 23–24, 37–38, 76, 78
San Diego State, 33–35
San Francisco 49ers, 9–10, 26–32, 164, 242–243. See also Walsh, Bill and 49ers
San Jose Apaches, 14, 15–16
Sapolu, Jesse, 291
Saunders, Al, 36–37
Sayre, Gary, 81
Schlereth, Mark, 271, 274, 276–277, 279–280
Schnellenberger, Howard, 5, 147–148
Schroeder, Jay, 187, 211, 213–214

The Score Takes Care of Itself (Bill Walsh), 19, 57, 98, 226, 232
Seattle Seahawks, 91
Seifert, George, 178, 242–243, 253–256, 284
Septien, Rafael, 106, 183
Sevier, William, 187
Shackleton, Sir Ernest, 69–70
Shanahan, Mike, 285, 286
Shapiro, Len, 41
Shaw, David, 243
Sheridan, John, 117
Shula, Don, 38, 135, 175, 192, 227
Simmons, Warren "Rennie," 77
Simms, Phil
    Brunner as starter and, 142–144
    on change in Parcells from 1983–84, 155
    injuries, 103, 142, 144, 247, 252
    on Landeta, 205
    on Montana, 62
    at Morehead State, 25, 61–62
    1986 NFC Championship Game, 205
    1983 season, 142–144
    1984 season, 156, 159, 161
    1985 season, 179–180, 183, 193
    1986 season, 198, 199
    1987 season, 249–250
    Super Bowl XXI, 205, 207
    training program, 151–152
    trash-talked by Clinkscale, 182
Simpson, O. J., 10, 27, 31, 32
Singletary, Mike, 193
Singleton, Ron, 70–71
Smith, Bruce, 277
Smith, Lovie, 230
Smith, Timmy, 215, 219, 220
Snyder, Daniel, 282
Solomon, Freddie, 60, 99, 106, 107–108, 115, 161, 167, 172
Spielman, Rick, 289–290
Springs, Rod, 128
Sprint Option pass, 107–108
Squirek, Jack, 170
St. Louis Cardinals, 232
St. Louis Rams, 74

Standard of Performance, 29, 69, 71–72, 100, 230, 235
Stanford, 24–25
Starke, George, 82
Starr, Bart, 26–27
Staubach, Roger, 96, 105
Stevens, Mark, 212
Streater, Steve, 56
strikes, 124–127, 211–213
Stuckey, Jim, 114
Studley, Chuck, 105
Sumner, Charlie, 170
Super Bowls
    coaching descendants of Parcells, 286–287
    coaching descendants of Walsh, 285
    Coughlin and, 269
    Gibbs and, 6, 7, 134–135, 277, 283–284, 288
    Grant and, 135
    Landry and, 135, 286
    Parcells and, 6, 7
    Shula and, 135
    Walsh and, 6, 7, 283–284
    VII, 135
    XV, 3
    XVI, 111, 113–117
    XVII, 135–141
    XVIII, 170, 175–176, 177–178
    XIX, 189
    XX, 193
    XXI, 206–207
    XXII, 216–220
    XXIII, 238–242, 251
    XXV, 256–264, 287
    XXVI, 276–277
    XXXI, 267
Swerk, Vinny "the Turk," 152

Tagliabue, Paul, 268
Tampa Bay Buccaneers, 37, 126, 209–210, 221
Taylor, Charlie, 84
Taylor, John, 241, 255
Taylor, Lawrence
    awards, 180
    characteristics, 55–56, 193–196

"Crunch Bunch" and, 154
importance of, 203–204
Jumbo Elliott and, 259
Parcells and, 56, 103–104
1984 season, 159, 160
1985 season, 179, 184, 185, 186,
    188–189, 192, 193
1987 season, 212
Testaverde, Vinny, 221
Theismann, Joe
    background, 78, 135
    5 o'clock club, 121–122
    Gibbs and, 78–79, 282
    1982 NFC Championship Game, 133
    off-season training during strike,
        126, 127–128
    with Redskins before Gibbs, 78
    1981 season, 81, 86, 87, 89
    1982 season, 125–126, 128, 129, 132
    1983 season, 167, 168–169
    1984 season, 170, 214–215
    1985 season, 184, 186–187, 188–189
    1986 season, 197
    Super Bowl XVII, 135–137, 138, 140
Thomas, Henry, 224
Thomas, Joe, 10
Thomas, Lynn, 91
Thomas, Thurman, 257, 258, 262, 277
Tisch, Preston Robert, 265
Tomczak, Mike, 252
Toronto Argonauts, 78
Trump, Donald, 148, 181
Trumpy, Bob, 22
Turner, Keena, 67, 92, 93–94, 168, 169
Tyler, Wendell, 165, 166–167, 171, 174

United States Football League (USFL),
    148, 181–182
Upshaw, Gene, 124, 211

Van Pelt, Brad, 154
Vermeil, Dick
    characteristics, 73–74
    Eagles and, 3, 73–74
    on Gibbs, 278
    with Rams, 74
    at Stanford, 24

Super Bowl XV, 3
on Walsh, 2, 67, 72

Walker, Fulton, 136
Walker, Herschel, 197
Walker, Rick "Doc," 79–80, 134
Walls, Everson, 97, 106, 252, 255,
    262–263
Walsh, Bill
    background, 12–14
    with Bengals, 16–21, 112–113
    books by, 19, 57, 67–69
    career after head coach of 49ers,
        243–245
    characteristics, 2, 11, 57, 70–71, 72,
        162, 163, 225–226, 227–228, 285
    Davis and, 14–15
    death, 245–246
    family, 2, 13
    Hall of Fame, 283
    leadership style, 13–14
    as mentor, 285–286
    Mike White and, 162–163
    offensive coordinator for Chargers,
        23–24
    Paul Brown and, 113
    with San Jose Apaches, 14, 15
    with Stanford, 24
    Super Bowl titles, 6, 7, 283–284
    with Whites after failure to become
        Bengals head coach, 1–2, 23
Walsh, Bill and 49ers
    beginning with, 26–32, 29
    bond with players, 291
    chosen as head coach, 9, 10–11
    coaching style, 58–61, 63, 64–72,
        97, 98–99, 101–102, 113–114, 164,
        166, 169, 175–177, 289
    DeBartolo and, 225, 231–233
    Dils and, 25
    end of losing streak, 74
    game attendance and, 94
    internship program, 229–230
    1984 NFC Championship Game,
        173–175, 236–238
    playoff record, 284
    pregame rituals, 114

Walsh, Bill and 49ers (*cont.*)
    quarterbacks and, 61–62
    resignation as coach, 242, 243
    on Reynolds, 93
    Rice and, 189–190
    as running backs coach, 14–15
    as scout, 60
    1979 season, 57–58
    1980 season, 90
    1981 season, 90, 91–92, 94–95,
        101–111
    1982 season, 162–163
    1983 season, 165–169
    1984 season, 160–161, 169–172
    1985 season, 189, 190
    1986 season, 199, 201, 202–203
    1987 season, 221–227, 228
    1988 season, 231–234, 235, 236–237
    Standard of Performance, 29, 69,
        71–72, 100, 230, 235
    Steve Young and, 221–223, 226
    Super Bowl XVI, 111, 113–117
    Super Bowl XIX, 189
    Super Bowl XVIII, 175–176,
        177–178
    Super Bowl XXIII, 238–242, 251
    Wyche and, 25–27
Walsh, Craig, 2
    on father and Brown, 21
    on father and race, 230–231
    on father and Super Bowl XVIII, 176
    on father during 1988 season, 233
    on father's leadership style, 13–14
    on father's relationship with his
        father, 12–13
    on father's resignation from
        49ers, 243
Walsh, Elizabeth, 2
Walsh, Geri, 2, 13, 14–15, 17, 101, 227
Walsh, Steve, 2
Warren, Don, 89, 134
Washington, Joe, 87, 89, 170
Washington Redskins. *See also* Gibbs,
    Joe and Redskins
    Beathard and search for coach, 40,
        42, 43
    Cooke and, 41–42, 75–76
    culture of, under Allen and Pardee, 79
    5 o'clock club, 120–122, 275
    Pardee as head coach, 38, 79
    Super Bowls without Gibbs, 282
    Theismann with, before Gibbs, 78
Waters, Charlie, 97
Waymer, Dave, 60
Wersching, Ray, 60, 116, 171, 172
"West Coast offense," 17–18, 19,
    190–191
White, Arthur, 222
White, Danny, 96, 99, 106, 212
White, Marilyn, 2, 23, 227
White, Mike, 1, 24, 27–28, 162–163,
    227
White, Randy, 105, 106, 212
Williams, Doug, 37, 208–211,
    214–220
Williams, Edward Bennett, 38, 41
Williams, Perry, 157–158, 184
Williams, Reggie, 115
Williamson, Carlton, 91
Wilson, Brenard, 53–54
Wilson, Mike, 116, 167
Wilson, Stanley, 239
Woodley, David, 135, 136, 171
Wright, Eric, 91, 94, 110–111, 115, 116,
    168, 171
Wyche, Sam, 20, 25–27, 238–242

Young, Charlie, 106, 115
Young, George, 30, 103
    death, 181
    Fassel and, 268
    with Giants, 4–5, 25
    Hostetler and, 251
    Parcells and, 45–46, 150, 180–181,
        265, 266–267
    Perkins and, 44
    Schnellenberger and, 147–148
    on 1985 season, 180
    Simms and, 143
Young, Steve, 219, 221–223, 224, 226,
    228–229, 289

Zampese, Ernie, 43
Zimmer, Mike, 289–290

ABOUT THE AUTHOR

Bob Glauber has covered the NFL since 1985, and was a witness to many memorable games coached by Bill Walsh, Joe Gibbs, and Bill Parcells. He is the NFL columnist for New York's *Newsday*, and worked before that at Gannett Westchester Rockland Newspapers. A Hall of Fame selector and Associated Press Awards voter, Glauber is president of the Pro Football Writers of America.

Glauber was named New York State Sportswriter of the Year in 2011 and 2015 by the National Sports Media Association. He has won numerous first-place writing awards, including the Associated Press Sports Editors, the New York State APSE, the Pro Football Writers of America, the Bob Waters Award, and the Barney Kremenko Sports Journalism Award. He was an NFL analyst/insider for ESPN's *Cold Pizza/First Take* morning show as well as NBC Sports Network's *Sportstalk*.

Glauber grew up in White Plains, New York, and has a degree in English from Manhattanville College. He is married to Jutta and has two children, Andrea and Emily.